PROJECT EAGLE

The Top-Secret OSS Operation That Sent Polish Spies behind Enemy Lines in World War II

JOHN S. MICGIEL

STACKPOLE
BOOKS
Essex, Connecticut
Blue Ridge Summit, Pennsylvania

STACKPOLE BOOKS

An imprint of Globe Pequot, the trade division of
The Rowman & Littlefield Publishing Group, Inc.
4501 Forbes Blvd., Ste. 200
Lanham, MD 20706
www.rowman.com

Distributed by NATIONAL BOOK NETWORK

British Library Cataloguing in Publication Information Available

Library of Congress Cataloging-in-Publication Data

Names: Micgiel, John S., author.
Title: Project Eagle : the top-secret OSS operation that sent Polish spies
  behind enemy lines in World War II / John S. Micgiel.
Other titles: Top-secret OSS operation that sent Polish spies behind German
  lines in World War II
Description: Essex, Connecticut : Stackpole Books, [2024] | The
  English-language Project Eagle is not a translation of the Polish-language
  book.— Library of Congress. | Includes bibliographical references and index.
Identifiers: LCCN 2023044491 (print) | LCCN 2023044492 (ebook) | ISBN
  9780811775410 (cloth) | ISBN 9780811775427 (ebook)
Subjects: LCSH: World War, 1939-1945—Secret service—United States. |
  Project Eagle (U.S.) | United States. Office of Strategic Services. |
  Espionage, Polish—History—20th century. | World War, 1939-1945—Secret
  service—Poland—Biography.
Classification: LCC D810.S7 M53 2024 (print) | LCC D810.S7 (ebook) |
  DDC 940.54/8673--dc23/eng/20231103
LC record available at https://lccn.loc.gov/2023044491
LC ebook record available at https://lccn.loc.gov/2023044492

∞™ The paper used in this publication meets the minimum requirements of
American National Standard for Information Sciences—Permanence of Paper
for Printed Library Materials, ANSI/NISO Z39.48-1992.

To my parents, Stanisław and Maria Sawinska Micgiel,
who experienced much of what this book conveys as forced laborers and
finally as proud immigrants to the United States

CONTENTS

PREFACE

Several months after the dissolution of the Office of Strategic Services (OSS), Admiral William D. Leahy[1] wrote a memorandum dated July 1946 in which he convened a historical panel whose main goal was to collect all documents related to the history, administration, and activities of the OSS during World War II. Most of these source materials were arranged thematically and chronologically and in 1946 became part of the OSS archives. In September 1947 these records were transferred to the Central Intelligence Agency (CIA) archives and classified as top secret.

In November 1988, during research on my doctoral dissertation in the National Archives in Washington, DC, the late archivist John Taylor suggested that I consult the records of the Office of Strategic Services and especially materials concerning OSS activities in London during World War II.

In the 1980s, the director of the CIA, William Casey,[2] transferred some nine million pages of OSS documents from the care of the CIA to the National Archives and Records Administration (NARA) in Washington. The process of reviewing and declassifying these materials was slow and unfinished. The status of some materials, including those of the London Branch's Special Operations and Secret Information activities, were changed from "Secret" to "Confidential" in 1977. A few years later, in 1984, the materials were entirely declassified and made public in a collection titled *OSS/London: Special Operations Branch and Secret Intelligence Branch War Diaries.*[3] In 1985 these materials were microfilmed by University Publications of America and were purchased by, among other institutions, the Columbia University Library.

Thanks to the availability of this collection of OSS documents, and especially the Interrogation Reports that included the accounts of agents' activities following their debriefing from their missions, after nearly thirty

years I returned to the subject of US intelligence-gathering operations in
Europe during the Second World War and in cooperation with the Polish
government in London. While familiarizing myself with this collection, I
also found in volume 2 of the *War Report of the O.S.S. (Office of Strategic
Services)*, edited by the official historian of the OSS, Kermit Roosevelt,[4]
brief information about Project Eagle. The account concerned a single
agent, Leon Adrian, who, as things turned out, was one of thirty-two Poles
who were members of what was to most readers a mysterious intelligence-
gathering project.

This snippet of information drove me to learn more about the enter-
prise, and I returned to research it in the now largely accessible records of
the OSS located at NARA in College Park, Maryland. During my research
there, I consulted the following materials in Record Group 226: Personnel Files, Entry 224; the SSU/Strategic Services Unit, Entry 16; microfilm
M153A and others; OSS Withdrawn Files (withdrawn and returned to
NARA by the CIA), Entry 210; and the History Office, Entry 99.

My intention in writing this book is to acquaint the reader through
the reports and other OSS documents with the intelligence activities of a
unit of Polish volunteers, trained by American, British, and Polish specialists in Scotland and England and parachuted into Nazi Germany late in the
war. An analysis of the reports that were written immediately following
the debriefing of the agents a few days after their recovery by Allied troops
offers a look into the situation in Germany just before the end of hostilities.
These documents provide insights into a not well-known period of days or
weeks before the entry of Allied forces into hostile territory and the situation of the civilian population and forced laborers there. In other words,
these reports comprise a valuable resource for historians and sociologists
researching Germany during the last two months of World War II.

My research focused mainly on documents relating to OSS activities
at its London Branch and now housed at NARA and in a few universities'
microfilm collections, but I also consulted the archival records of the Polish
Institute of National Remembrance in Warsaw concerning returning soldiers of the Polish Armed Forces in the West following the war. All archival
documents cited in this volume are clearly indicated in italics.

It should be noted that the members of Project Eagle had previously
served against their will in the Wehrmacht before their service in the Polish
Army and the OSS. I found Professor Ryszard Kaczmarek's monograph on
Poles in the Wehrmacht, *Polacy w Wehrmachcie*,[5] of particular importance in
understanding issues relating to the so-called *Wasserpolaken*.

The OSS documented its work with a photographic unit that produced short films, including one featuring Colonel Joseph Dasher, chief of
the Polish Section at OSS London, and the Polish directors of the Special
Training School that instructed the Polish agents.[6]

My work on this book lasted several years, during which I received
good advice not only from my fellow historians but also from archivists. I
would like to thank archivist Eryc van Slander of NARA in College Park
for helping me penetrate the OSS records there and for his assistance in
obtaining documents connected with Project Eagle. Until the 1980s the
reports and other materials of the Project Eagle missions were classified.
The full texts of the reports by the sixteen missions of Project Eagle are
provided in chapter 3.[7]

In the reports, information such as names, places of birth, and so forth
that were excised are indicated by brackets. Because the reports were written quickly after recovery of the agents, not much attention was paid to
syntax, spelling, and other niceties. Thanks to successive declassification of
materials in the 1980s and 2000s, I have been able to supplement data in the
reports' footnotes, providing real names and other information for Project
Eagle members with current archival file references.

It is worth noting that members of Project Eagle worked under pseudonyms in the OSS for their own safety, as did other Polish soldiers who
formerly served in the Wehrmacht. Thanks to the recent availability of a
large number of OSS files housed at NARA in College Park, I was able to
identify the real names of most but not all of the agents and to provide them
herein. Unfortunately, a fire at the National Personnel Records Center in
St. Louis, Missouri, on July 12, 1973, destroyed, among other documents,
many of the personnel records of US Army military personnel between
1912 and 1959; hence a more complete record of employment for Project
Eagle members is not possible.

The CIA returned a huge collection of OSS documents to NARA
in 1997 known as "OSS Entries 210–220 Sources and Methods Files
(Previously Withdrawn Material)," including interrogation reports from
Project Eagle. An index of this collection can be found online at https://
www.archives.gov/files/iwg/declassified-records/rg-226-oss/entry-210.
pdf. Unfortunately, the texts of the reports in Entry 2010 were even more
excised by the CIA than the reports microfilmed in 1985.

I also found two additional collections of brief reports by Project
Eagle members. The first group consisted of excerpts of agent reports that
became part of the citations for American awards forwarded by the OSS

to General Dwight D. Eisenhower's headquarters in summer 1945, now also to be found at NARA, College Park.[8] The second group consists of similar excerpts comprising parts of citations for Polish awards housed at the Archive of the Polish Institute and General Sikorski Museum in London, and cited by Dr. Waldemar Grabowski.[9]

My thanks go to Anna Stefanicka, secretary general of the Pilsudski Institute in London, for her help in obtaining information on Polish Army officers in London; Dr. Andrzej Suchcitz, longtime director of the Archive of the Polish Institute and Sikorski Museum in London (PISM), for assistance in obtaining data on Polish orders and medals for members of Project Eagle; my dear friend of many years and former director of Textual Reference Services at the Columbia University Library in New York City, Bob Scott, for improving digital scans of archival materials and copy-reading the text; and Piero di Porzio, formerly of Columbia's Language Resource Center, for enhancing graphics.

I would also like to thank Professor Andrzej Paczkowski for his insightful comments and suggestions; Professor Waldemar Grabowski, an expert on Polish émigré archives in England, for his valuable suggestions concerning my manuscript; and Professor Volker Berghahn of Columbia University for our many thoughtful discussions about my work and for putting me in touch with the late Jonathan Gould, author of a book on German OSS agents.

Thanks to people of goodwill, my search for information on the post-war lives of Project Eagle agents brought me into contact with some of their family members. Zbigniew Redlich of Warsaw; Dr. Rafał Niedziela of Szczecin; Irene Tomaszewski of Toronto, Canada; Maureen Mroczek Morris, Honorary Consul of the Republic of Poland in San Francisco; and Dr. Teofil Lachowicz of the Polish Army Veterans Association in New York each provided valuable assistance in tracking down possible contacts.

I was fortunate in finding and being able to correspond with Mark and Kim Dasher, son and daughter-in-law of Colonel Joseph Dasher, who played such a decisive role in organizing and implementing Project Eagle and its penetration of Nazi Germany. I was also lucky in establishing email, telephone, social media, or personal contact with family members in Australia, Great Britain, the United States of America, and, surprisingly for me, Poland. Special appreciation is due Krzysztof Marek Barwikowski, nephew of Zygmunt Barwikowski/René de Gaston; Elżbieta and Piotr Gatnar and Andrea and Roger Gatnar, niece-in-law, nephew, daughter-in-law, and son, respectively, of Władysław Gatnar/Turzecki; Raymond, Stephen, and Diane Hahn, the children of Thaddeus Hahn/Tadeusz Rawski;

Andrzej Koniczek, grandson-in-law of Gerard Haroński/Nowicki; Shane Donelly, grandson of Wacław Kujawski/Chojnicki; Maria Paprzycka, wife, and Małgorzata and Witold Jachowski, daughter and son-in-law, of Zbigniew Paprzycki/Strzeliński; Vanda Townsend, granddaughter of Jozef Bambynek/Gawor; Janet and Stephen Smith, daughter and son-in-law of Jan Czogała/Czogowski; Edward and Richard Tydda, sons of Zygmunt Tydda/Orłowicz; and Aleksandra Piskorska Szymańska, granddaughter of Edmund Zeitz (Zeic)/Barski.

This volume would not have arisen without my wife, Barbara Halbert Micgiel; her support, help in finding archival materials, patience, and indulgence during many discussions helped result in its publication.

1

POLISH MILITARY INTELLIGENCE AND ITS PARTNERS, 1918–1945

THE POLISH INTELLIGENCE SERVICES

In the tumultuous aftermath of the rebirth of the Polish state following World War I in November 1918, the Polish Army, following the French model, established its intelligence-gathering arm as Division Two (colloquially known in Polish as the *Dwójka* and in English as the Second Bureau), the General Staff Information Department. It sought, not surprisingly, to cooperate with its counterparts in France, Great Britain, Romania, the Baltic States, and even with Japan and Turkey.

Its aim was to prevent larger neighbors, Germany and the Soviet Union, from achieving their plans for territorial expansion at Poland's expense. That meant creating professional intelligence and counterintelligence services whose goal would be to ensure the security of the new Poland. Their most important partners in Europe were the guarantors of the Versailles order, France and Great Britain. The United States at that time was not interested in the problems of Poland—or Europe—and pursued an isolationist policy that helped enable the rise of totalitarian Germany and the Soviet Union. In the late 1930s, as another, more terrible European war drew closer, so did the cooperation among the security services of Poland, France, and Great Britain.

Polish intelligence gathering had begun in August 1914, that is, even before the reestablishment of a Polish state that had been partitioned by Austria, Prussia, and Russia in the late eighteenth century. The Polish Military Organization was created by Józef Pilsudski to collect intelligence and work on behalf of an independent Polish state. Its primary enemy was the Russian Empire. Many of its members joined the Polish Army after November 1918 when independence was achieved and participated in defending reborn Poland against the Bolsheviks in 1919–1920. A key element in helping to forge a military victory against a much larger enemy was the work of code breakers who penetrated Russian codes and cyphers during the hostilities. The importance of being able to read signal intelligence would increase over time, and the Poles' ability to innovate in radio communications and breaking cyphers would provide them and their allies with a crucial edge during the next war.

For the next two decades the Second Bureau spied on its neighbor to the east, establishing a string of centers to report on a wide variety of military and civilian targets. The reorganized Second Bureau's Eastern Office established several dozen units scattered throughout European Russia, Ukraine, the Baltic States, and the Caucasian republics, partially based on the activities of the now-defunct Polish Military Organization. Subject to increasingly intense Soviet harassment, beginning around 1928 the Poles were forced to shutter two centers in Moscow, and then units in Leningrad, Kiiv, and Minsk. The Eastern Office possessed four radio stations that quite successfully listened in on Russian radio traffic. Until 1937 they were able to read three hundred messages daily.

The Second Bureau was also responsible for counterintelligence operations, and as time went on the activity of Soviet spies and diversionists increased, as did the countermeasures employed by the Poles. Both the Soviets and the Germans used their co-nationals in that effort, just as the Poles employed non-Russians in their spying activities in the East and West.[1]

The Treaty of Riga, signed on March 18, 1921, enabled the General Staff to reorganize the Second Bureau on a peacetime basis, according to several orders enacted over the summer of 1921. Further changes were authorized until the September 1939 campaign and reflected military and political considerations. Chief among these changes was a revamped Western Office to keep tabs on a revanchist Germany that refused to accept the outcome of the Great War. The Second Bureau headquarters was in the Saxon Palace on Saxon Square in downtown Warsaw.[2] Its employees in 1921 numbered sixty-four officers, twelve noncommissioned officers, one warrant officer, and twenty administrative staff. In 1928, the General Staff was renamed the Main Staff (*Sztab Główny*). As time went on, among all of Poland's neighbors increasing attention was paid to the Soviet Union and Germany, both of which were honing their military and security services.

Few Western scholars have paid much attention to the efforts of Polish military intelligence in the interwar period, but Polish accounts, even those written during Communist times, support the view that military intelligence, and especially radio intelligence and code-breaking, provided valuable information to Polish authorities, even if the combined assets of Germany and the Soviet Union and the geopolitical situation in the late 1930s made a successful outcome of war in 1939 impossible for Poland.

Only relatively recently has the work of Polish code breakers in deciphering German codes and building from scratch cypher machines known as Enigma been acknowledged in Western scholarly literature. The delivery of such advanced technology to French and British counterparts in late July 1939 led to improvements that allowed the Allies to decipher and read most of the radio messages sent by the German military throughout the war. This was accomplished by the Second Bureau's staff of around 260 officers, and a more or less equal number of civilians.[3] The actual mathematical computations were the work of just three gifted mathematician/cryptologists: Marian Rejewski, Jerzy Różycki, and Henryk Zygalski. Together they cracked the secrets of the typewriter-sized Enigma machine in 1932 and over the next seven years innovated and adapted their device to decrypt German cyphers, even as the Germans modified their equipment and encryption procedures.[4]

The various bureaus, departments, and field offices of the Second Bureau were tasked with determining the offensive capabilities of neighbors who were determined not only to destroy the Polish state, but also to exterminate whole groups of Polish citizens based on class, religious affiliation, and ethnicity. The Second Bureau's personnel on the eve of the Second World War consisted of between 100 and 250 officers, around 500 civilians, and a few dozen people assigned to field duties.

A long and fairly comprehensive list of what Polish military intelligence was collecting and analyzing throughout the twenty-one years of independence has been pieced together by a determined archivist from fragmentary archival records that were unearthed in Poland and elsewhere during the Cold War, or returned to Poland one way or another.

In 1927, the Second Bureau outlined the tasks assigned to military attachés, including collecting information on Germany and the USSR, ensuring transit in the event of war, ensuring the development Polish military exports, providing the Polish General Staff with data on the military policies and armed forces of the host country, and obtaining mobilization and organizational plans in the event of war.

Besides the activities of the military attachés abroad, intelligence centers of the Eastern and Western Offices of the Second Bureau collected data abroad, chiefly via consulates and trade offices. Their task was to provide a broad analysis of military, economic, social, and political issues in their specific area of coverage, about Germany or the USSR, using any available sources of information.

The contents of the various sections of the Second Bureau's regional and central offices reflected the priorities assigned at various times to different sections of the bureau. For example, those units that concentrated on the USSR no doubt compiled data on the general characteristics of life in the USSR; analyses of information collected; reports and analyses concerning Soviet military intelligence (the GRU) and its activities, as well as the various domestic security services; material on Soviet politics and Communist leaders; reports on the international activities of Soviet organizations; communications with Polish diplomatic representatives focusing on Soviet international contacts; and Soviet documents that had been somehow acquired.

The documentation on Germany included reports from military attachés and branch offices focusing on Germany, the Free City of Danzig, and Czechoslovakia; reports on German forces, their armament, training, and organization; the activities of German paramilitary organizations; information on the National Socialist Party; changes that ensued after Hitler's rise to power; and reports on border incidents.[5]

Some of the employees of the Second Bureau managed to escape from occupied Poland and eventually found their way to France and later to Great Britain. They joined what became known as the Polish Army in the West and continued their efforts on behalf of their country and the Allied cause. Unfortunately for many of their colleagues and their civilian associates, the Second Bureau failed to destroy its archives, which were located in a fort in Warsaw that was captured by the Germans.[6] The Second Bureau's records in its branches in Bydgoszcz and Krakow were also captured by the Germans, as were whatever intelligence materials remained in Polish embassies in European capitals that were occupied by German forces. The records of Polish units and institutions in the East were seized by the Red Army and deposited in Soviet archives.

That lapse led to the imprisonment and death of many agents and informants who were tortured and liquidated by occupation forces, even after the conclusion of hostilities when the new Polish Communist authorities and the Soviets acquired the files and used the data to identify and chase down those in opposition to the new system.

Two decades of independence nevertheless resulted in a proficient and motivated service with great experience in operating spy networks throughout Europe and beyond.

POLISH INTELLIGENCE COOPERATION WITH
THE OSS DURING WORLD WAR II

The Poles were among the first of the six Allied governments exiled to London during the Second World War who sought cooperation with the newly established American intelligence agency. The Polish intelligence services had much more experience than did the Americans and already during the interwar years had cooperated with the British and French intelligence services. The German, Slovak, and Soviet invasions of Poland in September 1939 forced the Polish state authorities to flee Warsaw; as a consequence, until the capitulation of France in June 1940, Angers was the seat of the Polish government, which immediately set about reorganizing its intelligence activities from there and Paris and reestablished contact with already-existing spy networks and set up new ones.

During this period, for understandable reasons, Polish agents were quite dependent on their French colleagues, who insisted that all information gathered by the Poles was to be forwarded to the British Secret Intelligence Service (SIS) only through French channels. Despite these difficulties, British SIS and Polish intelligence established a close and friendly relationship that continued through and beyond the end of the war.

When France fell in June 1940, the Polish authorities and their intelligence services were evacuated to London, leaving behind some agents who were to create a new, effective network of communications channels. The situation of the Polish government-in-exile, whose prime minister was General Wladyslaw Sikorski, was somewhat exceptional compared to other Allied governments based in London at that time, chiefly because it was permitted to develop and lead its own, independent spy service, radio communications, and agent training. The Poles were also permitted to use their own cyphers and were not subject to British censorship until June 1944, when extraordinary security measures were introduced prior to the invasion of Normandy.

Because their communication channels were independent, as were their operatives in the field, Polish intelligence was more independent from the SIS than other intelligence services operating from London. SIS supplied the Poles with funds, equipment, and logistical support, and in return the Poles agreed to share all intelligence information they gathered. Despite having five intelligence agencies that reported to various government departments, as was the case with American intelligence services until the establishment of the Office of the Coordinator of Intelligence in 1941, and later the OSS in 1942, many misunderstandings with the British were cleared up by the end of 1940.

Over the course of the war, the Polish intelligence services expanded and their reports were sent directly to the various departments of British SIS for further distribution to the War Office, the Ministry of Economic Warfare, the Foreign Office, and other British ministries. In a report prepared for Prime Minister Winston Churchill, the British SIS chief liaison officer to Polish intelligence, Wilfred Dunderdale,[7] stated that between September 3, 1939, and May 8, 1945, his department forwarded 45,770 reports, of which 22,047 (48 percent) were prepared and forwarded by the Poles.[8] Another report written by the Intelligence Department of the Polish General Staff asserted that from August 23, 1940, until December 1, 1944, 71,714 reports had been forwarded to the British General Staff.[9] Just in 1944 Polish intelligence sent their British colleagues 37,894 reports, which were evaluated by the British General Staff as follows: (1) 25 percent—very valuable, (2) 60 percent—high value, (3) 12 percent—valuable, (4) 2 percent—little value, (5) 1 percent—no value. In mid-1943, Dunderdale received reports forwarded by thirty Polish spy networks active in various occupied or neutral European countries. During the same period, only thirteen French spy networks reported their findings to Dunderdale.[10]

Simultaneously, the Poles sent the American General Staff 12,068 reports, which were chiefly intelligence concerning the identification and dislocation of Axis forces, military transports, air and naval forces, industry, bombing reports, and so on, as well as 1,808 maritime and naval base reports for the US Navy.[11]

Cooperation between the Polish Second Bureau and the Office of the Coordinator of Information had begun a few weeks after Colonel Donovan was appointed coordinator on July 11, 1941. Major Jan Żychoń, head of the Intelligence Department of the Second Bureau of the Polish General Staff, visited the United States and had a meeting with Colonel Donovan. On August 10, 1941, both officers signed a confidential agreement on intelligence cooperation between their services. The memorandum set out three simple areas that would define the collaboration between the Polish and US secret services for the rest of the war:

1. Mutual exchange of documents, data, etc., related to European countries.
2. Mutual exchange of information on other countries.

3. Supplying the United States Secret Services with data on German
    activities in both Americas, as well as miscellaneous information
    referring to the Western Hemisphere and secured in Europe.[12]

In October 1941, the Poles began to send the Americans various
materials regarding northern Africa, the USSR, and Portugal on the identification and location of Axis forces, military transports, the navy, military
industry, air forces, the results of bombing raids, losses, and enemy morale.
The Poles also informed Washington of German activity in North and
South America, and provided tidbits of information on the USA gleaned
in Europe. The OSS sent questionnaires and the Poles did their best to
provide information on western, eastern, and southern Europe, and on
military, economic, and political intelligence on mostly naval matters concerning Japan. It was largely a one-sided affair, with the Poles expecting
future political support from the United States. That would prove to be
a grave assumption. Five days after Japan bombed Pearl Harbor and the
United States entered the war, the Poles proposed deeper cooperation with
the Americans, who quickly asked for information on the USSR. The
Poles promptly responded.[13]

The Intelligence Department of the Second Bureau of the Polish General Staff prepared an evaluation of its work for 1944 and found that with
respect to reports sent to Washington,

> *[i]nformation received from Polish intelligence is highly valued by M.I.S.*
> [Military Intelligence Service] *Washington. All messages concerning O. de
> B* [Order of Battle] *are decidedly useful and interesting. Polish intelligence is
> providing entirely new and highly valuable news. Generally, Polish reports are
> splendid with respect to their broad-range and first-class importance. Polish intel-
> ligence is ranked first as a source of information received by the American Staff.*[14]

For the Americans, Polish intelligence was probably their most important partner with respect to the quality and quantity of reports received.[15]
Out of 9,241 reports of various kinds that were prepared by Polish intelligence between July 1, 1942, and June 30, 1943, 4,289 were sent to the
Americans, 4,133 to the British, 637 to the Soviets, and 182 to the French.
In appreciation for such fruitful cooperation, US General Hayes A. Kroner[16] told General Władysław Sikorski that "[t]he Polish Army has the best
intelligence in the world. Its value for us is beyond compare. Regretfully
there is little we can offer in return."[17] As things turned out, in 1945, loyalty
was not among them.

The majority of Polish intelligence documents produced during World War II were destroyed by order of the British, and it is not possible to provide an accurate total number. On the basis of materials of the Polish General Staff's Intelligence Department, an incomplete summary of the Polish reports sent by the Polish General Staff's G-2 to US Military Intelligence is provided in appendix 1.[18]

The Polish military intelligence services were well organized and professional. Despite the September 1939 debacle and the fall of France in June 1940, Polish intelligence was able to rebuild and expand its spy networks. This did not happen during the first few months of the war, as in the fall of 1939 General Sikorski adopted a personnel policy aimed at isolating those Polish officers who had fled to Romania and who, in Sikorski's opinion, were responsible for the September defeat. This meant that the new officer corps was made up mainly of opponents of the prewar supporters of Marshal Józef Piłsudski, officers who were less experienced in intelligence work, knew less about the German Army, had fewer contacts and agents in the Third Reich, and who in their majority did not know the German language. This negatively affected the work of the Polish General Staff's G-2 and weakened its cooperation with French and British intelligence.[19]

Cognizant of its weaknesses, in spring 1940 Polish intelligence reorganized and rebuilt its contacts with its prewar agents active in spying on the *Kriegsmarine,* the German Navy. Polish and British cryptographers again began to work jointly on deciphering updated German Enigma codes and in June 1940 provided essential information on the deployment of over one hundred German divisions before the German invasions of Norway, Denmark, Holland, Belgium, and Luxembourg.[20] However, Polish-French intelligence cooperation can be described as one-sided. French intelligence received very valuable information concerning the Wehrmacht from Polish agents, but the French were unwilling to share information on their own armed forces with their Polish colleagues.[21]

Contacts between the Allied intelligence services did not change even after France capitulated and the Polish government and intelligence services moved to London. This was because of the foreign policy of General Sikorski's government, which sought to participate as much as possible in the Allied war effort against the Axis, with an eye toward obtaining postwar advantages.[22] Intelligence work was to play a chief role in these plans. And when France fell in June 1940, and British intelligence lost most of its contacts in Europe, the British approached the Second Bureau of the Polish General Staff with a request to help rebuild their spy networks on the continent. This is also the background of the Polish-British intelligence cooperation agreement of July 29, 1940. Whether the Polish authorities were able to utilize this advantage is a different matter. And it was a considerable advantage, both in terms of the number of intelligence reports provided and their quality. This is clearly attested by the American and British quality assessments that showed the Polish reports to be of high value and useful for the Allied military effort throughout the Second World War.[23]

The British Secret Intelligence Service was tasked with liaising between the Polish and French intelligence services. This was no easy task. The man who coordinated cooperation between the British and Polish services was Commander Wilfred Dunderdale. The Polish wartime intelligence services (loosely termed Polish intelligence herein) included not only the Second Bureau of the Polish General Staff (PGS), but also the Sixth Bureau PGS, which received reports from the intelligence units of the Union of Armed Struggle (*Związek Walki Zbrojnej*), later the Home Army (*Armia Krajowa*); the Department of Special Affairs of the Ministry of Military Affairs (which became known as the Ministry of National Defense on November 30, 1942); and the Ministry of Internal Affairs, which was involved in diversion and sabotage through its so-called Continental Action, described briefly below.

The organization and supply of military resistance in Poland and ensuring regular communication between the government-in-exile and the underground army in Poland dominated the activities of the government-in-exile from the outset. The establishment of a specialized service participating in the contacts between the government-in-exile and the intelligence headquarters in occupied Poland was to meet the requirements of secrecy. The setting up of this service was a consequence of the British idea of supporting underground movements in Europe (and of strategic planning by the British Joint Chiefs of Staff Committee). Shortly after the Polish General Staff arrived in London, the so-called Home Department was transformed into the Sixth Bureau of the PGS, and by mid-1944 its headquarters employed 961 persons including 29 staff officers, 267 other officers, 259 NCOs and privates, and 4 civilian officials.[24]

Notwithstanding formal orders of the supreme military authorities requiring that intelligence reports be transmitted to British SIS through the Second Bureau, many reports from Home Army intelligence found their way to the Special Operations Executive (SOE) and were part of the reason for mounting tensions between British SIS and SOE. And SIS clients not only assessed those reports but also passed on guidelines, requests, and instructions to be carried out. In consequence, Home Army intelligence worked primarily in accord with British guidelines regardless of whether or not they were received via the Second or Sixth Bureau. It is estimated that some 70 percent of the total of Home Army intelligence effort was expended on meeting the needs of the Allies—British, American, French, and Russian—even after Polish-Soviet diplomatic relations were broken off on April 25, 1943, due to the Katyn massacre.[25]

Altogether between 1941 and 1944, including the period of the Warsaw Uprising, 346 parachutists (316 soldiers including 34 intelligence operatives, 1 female soldier,[26] 28 political couriers, 1 Hungarian, and 5 British persons) were parachuted into or landed in Poland from bases in Great Britain and Italy, and 609 tons of arms and other equipment were also dropped. The parachutists delivered 34,823,163 dollars in banknotes and gold, 1,775 pounds sterling in gold, 19,89,500 German marks, 40,569,800 in Polish occupational currency, and 10,000 Spanish pesetas. Between 1941 and 1945 there were 868 flights, of which 585 succeeded, that is, the parachutists or cargo were delivered. Seventy planes with 62 crew and 11 parachutists were lost, as were 1,500 containers and 1,763,200 dollars. Ten percent of the equipment was destroyed.[27]

Political rivalries within the Polish government-in-exile were visible already in France, and attempts to secure control over courier communications with Poland introduced a measure of chaos into a developing situation. When France fell, numerous Polish groups there organized clandestine organizations that functioned without coordination or external support. In autumn 1940, the Polish government created an organization to supervise the new resistance movement. Called the "Continental Action," it was led by the former secretary of the Polish Embassy in Paris, Jan Librach,[28] and subordinated to the Ministry of Internal Affairs. The project was to operate in occupied countries with large concentrations of Polish immigrants (France, Belgium, the Netherlands, Denmark) and in neutral states where small cells or surveillance posts were established for information for political purposes and to provide communication between London and Poland.[29]

The Polish intelligence services had numerous advantages over other western Allied services operating on the continent, among which its most important was a well-developed radio network covering almost all of Europe. Until mid-1941, Polish intelligence units in France sent the British reports on, among other things, German submarines stationed in Bordeaux, Brest, and Le Havre. At the same time, Home Army intelligence was reporting to London on German preparations to invade the Soviet Union. These reports were of great strategic importance. According to Sir John Colville,[30] Prime Minister Winston Churchill's wartime confidential secretary, Polish intelligence was the best secret service among those of the

Allies, stating "the Poles were possibly the best players in this intelligence game." Similarly, Victor Cavendish-Bentinck,[31] chairman of the Joint Intelligence Committee during the war, was of the same opinion.

Because SIS at that time did not have its own agents in Germany and was only beginning to rebuild its intelligence networks on the continent, British cooperation with the Second Bureau of the Polish General Staff grew, especially after the German attack on the USSR. The main transportation routes between Germany and the Eastern Front crossed through Poland, and Polish intelligence was able to monitor and hamper the transport of the German Army and its equipment, report on the morale and mood of German soldiers, and intercept and read their correspondence. The Allied bombardment of German factories and research centers forced the Germans to transfer many facilities largely beyond the reach of Allied bombers into the General Government (the German zone of occupation in prewar Poland that had not been annexed by the Reich), and the Baltic became the main training area for German U-boats. Baltic shipyards became the main production facilities for these boats, and Polish intelligence activity with its disparate sources of information became even more valuable to the British.[32]

At the end of 1940, resistance headquarters in German-occupied Poland started to create a unified, centrally controlled intelligence network in accord with recommendations from headquarters in London. An offensive intelligence network named "Lombard" was subsequently established in August 1942 to obtain information on the enemy's forces, its equipment, and dislocation, as well as on the armaments industry in the Reich. Apart from systemic information on the location of German armies in the General Government and near the Eastern Front, the greatest successes of Lombard were the discovery of the secret experimental testing site in Peenemunde, the acquisition of information and material about the tests of the new V-1 and V-2 weapons, the penetration of the Focke-Wulf aircraft manufacturing plants, information on a new type of Panther tank (Pz.Kpfw. V Panther), and the capture of plans of new types of submarines (*Taschenuboot*) from the Hamburg shipyard.

Alongside the Lombard network, the Offensive Intelligence Bureau of the Polish armed resistance also had a central intelligence network known as *Stragan* and *Marcjanna*, created at the beginning of 1941. The complicated Home Army (*Armia Krajowa*, or AK) intelligence organization was systematically expanded and became the best service of its kind in Europe.[33]

As noted previously, cooperation between the Second Bureau of the PGS and US intelligence began in mid-1942, with the assistance of the British. Thanks to this mutual support, the Poles established outposts throughout North and South America controlled from New York City by a center known by its acronym "Estezet" (the phonetical initials of the United States in Polish).[34] The Second Bureau also established intelligence outposts in Scandinavia, the Baltic states, Czechoslovakia, Germany, Switzerland, Italy, Belgium, Holland, Spain, the Balkans, Turkey, northern Africa, and the Near East.[35]

Reports concerning the situation near the Eastern Front were judged to be extremely important. Observations regarding military transports provided information not only on the strength of enemy forces, but also on soldiers' morale, offensive and defensive forces behind the front, and the Wehrmacht's successes and defeats in its struggle against the Red Army. Industrial espionage allowed for a more exact evaluation of the German armaments industry and its ability to supply various weaponry to the front lines.[36] This allowed for more effective bombing and destruction of industrial and other centers.

From June 1940 until mid-1944, the number of Polish intelligence outposts and agents in the field rose significantly. At the beginning, the Second Bureau of the PGS had only eight outposts, employing some thirty intelligence agents. But by mid-1944, there were eight stations, two independent intelligence stations, and thirty-three cells, while the number of agents rose to 1,666.[37] The number of positions in the Second Bureau wavered over time, but in April 1944, two months before the Allied landings in Normandy, it was set at 162 officers and 755 soldiers of other rank, at headquarters and the above-mentioned stations and cells.[38]

Unfortunately, the cooperation between the Polish intelligence services and those of the Western Allies did not bring the political results that the Poles expected. The British and the Americans used the information collected and forwarded by the ZWZ-AK and other Polish resistance groups without reciprocating. The Western Allies received valuable intelligence from the Poles for free. The Polish authorities did not capitalize on the difficult military and political situation of the British at the beginning of the war and failed to oblige them to sign a mutually binding political agreement.[39] During the war, new geopolitical realities emerged and it became more evident that the Polish government was unable to change the decisions of the Big Three that were incompatible with the Polish raison d'état.

One of the people who were able to appreciate the work of Polish intelligence during the war was Lieutenant William Casey, who was appointed the chief of the London Secretariat of the OSS in October 1943. It was he who would later be charged with the penetration of the Third Reich by

OSS agents. In his memoir of the secret war against Hitler, it becomes clear that the OSS appreciated Polish intelligence, which he felt was particularly good at locating V-1 rocket installations along the Pas-de-Calais and reporting rocket tests in Poland. Equally important were Polish reports on German troop movements to the Russian Front, on activity in Belgium and northern France, on the bomb damage in cities all over Germany. Casey also praised the Polish radio station that stayed in constant communication with agents and, in his words, "proved to be one of the most valuable information gathering points of the war." He understood the position of the Poles after the revelation of the Katyn massacre and the subsequent Soviet breaking of relations with the Polish government in April 1943, "but the Poles never relented in their efforts to help crush the Nazis."[40]

Casey mentions that in the summer of 1944, chief of Polish intelligence Colonel Stanislaw Gano[41] suggested that the OSS train and send Polish agents into Germany.[42] The idea took hold and developed into an intelligence operation dubbed "Project Eagle." In September 1944, OSS London reviewed its German-speaking personnel and found that only one hundred personnel in the OSS could take part in intelligence activities in Germany. The OSS London leadership found this to be inadequate for the task at hand and decided that the pool could be augmented by agents from the intelligence services of occupied Allied countries. Accordingly, the possibility of co-opting forty Polish agents with the required German language skills was deemed attractive.[43]

THE CREATION OF THE US OFFICE
OF STRATEGIC SERVICES

In the United States prior to World War II, intelligence gathering outside of its borders was the province of the Department of State, the Office of Naval Intelligence (ONI), and the Military Intelligence Division (later Service) of the War Department. The various regional offices of the State Department analyzed the reports forwarded by diplomats, while military intelligence dealt with material sent in by military attachés. The State Department and the military separately and without coordination developed their own intelligence and counterintelligence procedures. The entire system was deemed by one senior diplomat as "timid, parochial, and operating strictly in the tradition of the Spanish-American War."[44]

President Franklin D. Roosevelt, foreseeing the United States' entry into hostilities and prompted by subtle prodding from the British, established a civilian agency reporting to the White House whose chief aim was to coordinate the activities of already-existing agencies and develop strategic approaches to the nation's challenges. He appointed William J. Donovan as the Coordinator of Information (COI). Donovan and his newly established office were empowered to "collect and analyze all information and data, which may bear upon national security: to correlate such information and data, and to make such information and data available to the President and to such departments and officials of the Government as the President may determine; and to carry out, when requested by the President, such supplementary activities as may facilitate the securing of information important for national security not now available to the Government."[45]

America's entry into the war in December 1941 provoked new thinking about the place and role of the COI. Donovan and his new office, with a $10 million budget and six hundred employees, had provoked hostility from the Federal Bureau of Investigation (FBI), the G-2, and various war agencies. The new Joint Chiefs of Staff (JCS) initially shared this distrust, regarding Donovan, a civilian, as an interloper—but one they might be able

William J. Donovan, Coordinator of Information as of July 11, 1941, and director of the Office of Strategic Services from June 13, 1942. (Photo US National Archives)

to control and utilize if COI could be placed under JCS control. Surprisingly, Donovan himself, by now, was inclined to agree. Working with the secretary of the JCS, Brigadier General Walter B. Smith, Donovan devised a plan to bring COI under the JCS in a way that would preserve the office's autonomy while winning it access to military support and resources.

President Roosevelt endorsed the idea of moving COI to the Joint Chiefs. The president, however, wanted to keep COI's Foreign Information Service (FIS), which conducted radio broadcasting, out of military hands. Thus, he split the "black" and "white" propaganda missions, giving FIS the officially attributable side of the business—and half of COI's permanent staff—and sent it to the new Office of War Information. The remainder of COI then became the Office of Strategic Services, or OSS, on June 13, 1942. The change of name to OSS marked the loss of the "white" propaganda mission, but it also fulfilled Donovan's wish for a title that reflected his sense of the "strategic" importance of intelligence and clandestine operations in modern war.

OSS expanded in 1942 into full-fledged operations abroad. Donovan sent units to every theater of war that would have them. His confident approach had already impressed the State Department, which in 1941 had desperately needed men to serve as intelligence officers in French North Africa. Donovan's COI sent a dozen officers to work as "vice consuls" in several North African ports, where they established networks and acquired information to guide the Allied landings (Operation Torch) in November 1942. One of the best sources of information for the Americans was the Polish information network in North Africa, which was well established there.[46]

Major Mieczysław Zygfryd Słowikowski of the Polish Army enlisted several thousand informants and agents to spy on the Axis forces in North Africa. He was an amazing character and real-life hero, as one author described him, who devised a cover for his spy network that provided a healthy profit with which to pay for the spying. Code-named Rygor, the major bought large quantities of oats in Morocco and sold the processed oats throughout Algiers, where his product became popular. The husks from the rolled oats were used to feed the pigs at a farm he purchased near an Axis airfield in Algiers, from which his associates could report on the air traffic in and out of the airfield.

British MI6 never acknowledged the contribution made by Rygor's Agency Africa, which communicated nearly daily with London via a top-secret radio retransmission station in Vichy, and for bulkier reports also via pouch. The Americans were also the recipients of Major Słowikowski's intelligence, and while the success of Torch won the OSS much-needed praise and supporters in Washington, the work of the Polish intelligence network "Agency Africa" was relegated to footnote status in the official history of the OSS.[47]

The reason for the aggrandizement was that as part of a deal with the Vichy authorities to deliver sought-after consumer goods to North Africa, twelve US vice consuls would be assigned there to monitor deliveries. One of them was Colonel William Eddy,[48] who was appointed the US Naval Attaché in Tangier in January 1942 and became the most senior COI/OSS man in North Africa. It was Colonel Eddy who received all the intelligence secured by agents throughout North Africa, including by special arrangement those of its largest network, Agency Africa, whether by pouch or radio, and he forwarded the information onward to Washington.

The official historian of the OSS, Kermit Roosevelt, wrote three decades after the North African campaign that: "The pre-Torch and Torch activities in North Africa . . . were the main reason the OSS survived. Without this evidence to the JCS (i.e., Joint Chiefs of Staff) of its value, it would most probably have been dismembered."[49] A decade later, on the basis of British and French archives and secondary literature, historian John Herman wrote:

> *As Bradley Smith pointed out, Torch had a profound effect on the future of the OSS and "it is obvious that Torch was a major plus for Donovan's organization"; in the latter appraisal, only intelligence escaped criticism since Colonel Eddy had performed his intelligence tasks brilliantly. . . . Undoubtedly, therefore, "North Africa was the testing ground for the OSS. The OSS under General Bill Donovan needed to justify its existence, and must have been under considerable pressure to produce results. In the circumstances the temptation to appropriate the credit for the contribution made by others, especially Agency Africa, must have been irresistible."[50]*

It was to Colonel Eddy. Unbeknownst to him, however, Major Rygor had also been sending intelligence by radio through the Polish Enigma team, code-named Cadix, to the British. The result was that the Allies were kept informed, while OSS claimed the credit for it in Washington and thereby secured its continued existence. It is tempting to conclude that without the quality and quantity of Rygor's intelligence that the efforts of the twelve apostles of the OSS in North Africa might have doomed the organization in the bureaucratic struggles in Washingtonian officialdom. No Agency Africa, no OSS?

Curiously, the British were also plagiarizing Polish intelligence materials. Colonel Ivan D. Yeaton, the head of US Military Intelligence's East European Section, held periodic meetings with his Polish intelligence contact in Washington and in October 1942 complained that British SIS had passed along to Washington a Polish report claiming it came from a trusted London source. Yeaton showed the report to his Polish colleague, who concluded that by sending material to Washington directly, the Poles were strengthening their hand in Washington at the expense of the British.[51] The latter were eager to support the Poles financially in return for their excellent services. In a "Most Secret" letter dated December 10, 1941, from Brigadier Stewart G. Menzies to Herbert Brittain,[52] assistant secretary and treasury officer of accounts, concerning a request for increased funding by Colonel Gano, chief of the Second Bureau of the Polish General Staff, the chief of the British Secret Intelligence Service wrote: "I have examined his request, and in view of the valuable information which has been produced (by far the best of any of our Allies), I consider that, if feasible, the demand should be met."[53] The Polish intelligence chief asked SIS to nearly double the budgetary subsidy the British were paying to support the considerable increase in the Polish network of agents that took place throughout 1941. Both the Americans and the British lagged far behind in the organization of such networks at a time when both Allies were being pressed in Europe and the Far East.

General Douglas MacArthur[54] in the South Pacific and Admiral Chester Nimitz[55] in the Central Pacific saw little use for the OSS, and the office was thus kept from contributing to the main American campaigns against Imperial Japan.[56] Nonetheless, Donovan forged ahead and hoped for the best, tasking Polish intelligence with information collection concerning Japanese maritime matters. Utilizing military cover for the most part, but with some officers under diplomatic and nonofficial cover, the OSS began to build a world-wide clandestine capability. In this effort the Americans were assisted by the British even before the COI was reorganized into the OSS; they helped Donovan's staff organize the first foreign branch in London in November 1941, a month before the United States entered the war.

Between 1942 and 1945, London was the center of Allied intelligence gathering. Besides the British, six other intelligence services used London as their headquarters and base of operations. The Office of Strategic Services was the American counterpart of the British Secret Intelligence Service (also known as MI6) and the Special Operations Executive, with whom it cooperated throughout the war and for a few months thereafter.

In mid-1942, an agreement was signed between OSS Secret Intelligence (SI) and British SOE regarding access to and the exchange of information. Donovan sent his best people to London. William Phillips[57] became branch chief, and among its Special Operations (SO) leadership were Gustav B. Guenther,[58] Richard P. Heppner,[59] and Ellery C. Huntington,[60] while SI chiefs included Whitney Shepardson[61] and William Maddox.[62] Real cooperation started in 1942, when SOE put Donovan's people in touch with their agents in Spain and at Gibraltar to deal with the issue of US prisoners of war who had escaped from detention. The British also gave the Americans access to their radio network.[63]

One of the most important tasks of the OSS in London was establishing contact and cooperation with the intelligence services of captive nations whose émigré governments were housed in London. This was where information collected by members of the various underground organizations operating in German-occupied countries flowed and the place where agents of various Allied countries met. Besides the British, the Americans were also interested in such information and were willing to provide equipment, money, and sometimes their own intelligence information.

The French were the first with whom the OSS established cooperation, via the American Embassy in June 1942. Two months later the OSS established cooperation with the Poles and formed a Polish Section, which in 1944 was renamed the Polish Desk.

Cooperation between the OSS and the Poles appears to have developed with little friction; for various reasons the same cannot be said of American-British cooperation. The British intelligence services—chiefly the Secret Intelligence Service, which was established in 1921 to contend with spying against Great Britain beyond its borders—feared that close cooperation with the inexperienced Americans might threaten intelligence groups already operating in occupied Europe. This somewhat exaggerated caution by the British put the Americans in an awkward position. British intelligence treated their American colleagues as young, inexperienced partners almost to the end of hostilities, for example, during operations meant to disinform the Germans before D-Day, the Allied landings in Normandy in June 1944. As far as the Americans were concerned, the OSS leadership were worried that their newly established branch in London might become too dependent on a foreign intelligence service, even if it was a friendly one. It should also be noted that American diplomats were critically disposed toward the British Empire, and some OSS officers feared that Great Britain had not ceased to strive to expand their colonies. Thanks mainly to their agents' cooperation on all fronts, the fears and ambiguities were slowly overcome and forgotten.

By the end of 1944 at the peak of OSS's development and activities, the organization numbered some 13,000 members, including 4,500 women.[64] This was slightly less than an American infantry division. General Donovan employed thousands of military officers and enlisted men who were seconded from their duty posts, as well as civilians who found appropriate positions in the armed forces. Two-thirds of OSS personnel came from the US Army and the Army Air Corps, a quarter were civilians from various professions, and the remainder came from the US Navy and Coast Guard. About 7,500 employees and agents served abroad, including 900 women. In fiscal year 1945, the OSS spent $43 million, and over its slightly more than four years existence expended about $135 million (almost $1.1 billion today).[65]

These expenditures covered the cost of training agents and prosecuting the war against the Axis on all fronts. OSS scientists developed innovative technologies that agents employed behind the lines. Its Morale Operations Branch (MO) began the use of psychological warfare.[66] Its maritime division was the forerunner of today's SEALs, while its Jedburghs and Operational Groups (OGs) were the predecessors of the Army Special Forces, the Green Berets. Operation Jedburgh was a secret venture in which representatives of the SOE, OSS, and the French Central Bureau of Intelligence and Operations (*Bureau Central de Renseignements et d'Action*, or BCRA), as well as soldiers and officers of the Danish and Belgian armies, were trained and dropped behind enemy lines to engage in diversionary activities and to support local guerillas in their struggles against the Germans. The operation was the first real cooperative action in Europe between SOE and OSS SO.

Members of the Operational Groups were well trained in infantry tactics, guerrilla warfare, foreign weapons, demolition, and parachuting and had attached medical personnel. They always went into action in their uniforms, which in theory afforded them protection accorded prisoners of war. Depending on the country and terrain where they were to be dropped, OGs numbered four officers and around thirty soldiers, but in many cases there were fewer parachutists. The OGs were active in Burma, China, France, Greece, Italy, Norway, and Yugoslavia.[67] The 801st/492nd Bombardment Group ("Carpetbaggers") and other elements of the US Army Air Corps, the air arm of the OSS, were predecessors to the Air Force Special Operations Command. The marines who served in the OSS were succeeded by the Marine Corps Special Operations Command. OSS operational swimmers hailed from the US Coast Guard.

OSS OPERATIONS IN EUROPE AND THE
PENETRATION OF THE THIRD REICH

A year after the OSS was created, SI in Washington and London decided that SI London should prepare and be responsible for intelligence operations on the European continent after the invasion of Europe by American forces. It was felt, however, that SI London was incapable of independent operations from England, among other reasons because of an insufficient number of agents, while the British had earlier established contacts with intelligence services already active on the continent. They also made contact with refugees of various nationalities who could be of help in diversion and intelligence work.

The British were skeptical of the idea of sending American agents into action on the continent. They felt that the Americans might be insufficiently prepared for action among the very complicated intelligence networks in Europe, and feared that through lack of experience, American agents might expose existing diversionary-intelligence networks. Since the British controlled communications and transport between England and the continent, the Americans were in fact completely dependent on the decisions taken by their English ally. In addition, in accord with a June 1942 agreement between OSS SO and the British SOE, in an effort to minimize confusion and duplication, SOE was responsible for diversion and intelligence work in France, Holland, Belgium, Luxembourg, Poland, Czechoslovakia, much of Norway, the Balkans, the Near East, and West Africa.

In January 1943 an annex to the June 1942 agreement was signed in which OSS SO renounced the intention of pursuing any independent operations in Western Europe, and also agreed not to create any independent operational bases in Great Britain whose targets would be in Western Europe. OSS SO London together assisted all resistance movements in Western Europe. The more experienced SOE agents provided their OSS SO colleagues the possibility of training their agents and provided them specialized British communication and other equipment.

Just before the annex was signed, the British requested that OSS SO send an experienced officer to temporarily work with SOE's Polish Section. Its chief was Colonel Peter Wilkinson,[68] and he chose Captain Stacy Lloyd[69] from SI, who, as of November 1, 1942, served as liaison officer between SI and SOE's Polish Section. It was considered that the following advantages would flow from such an arrangement: it would boost the morale of the Poles; it would present both the British and the Poles with a new point of view concerning old conflicts between the Poles and the

British; Polish expectations and demands would be clearer and more logical for the Americans; and finally, if and when American forces entered German-occupied Polish territory, an American liaison officer would be a valuable asset in making contact between the American armed forces and the Polish underground.[70]

In September 1943, things began moving quickly and the Americans asked the British for their views on Directive 406 of the American Joint Chiefs of Staff, which empowered the OSS to engage in intelligence activity in the European Theater of Operations (ETO). Unfortunately, the British voiced their views and objections, which caused the American ETO command to deny the OSS permission to engage in such activities. The negative opinion did not faze General Donovan, who convinced the JCS a month later to allow the OSS to engage in secret intelligence activity in the ETO. From that moment forward, the OSS had a free hand in conducting intelligence collection behind enemy lines in Europe.[71]

The OSS leadership felt that strategic intelligence gathering must be free of the control of even foreign governments. That is why, notwithstanding strong British objections, OSS SI began exchanging (or, more properly, collecting) information from various foreign intelligence services in London.[72] As a result, small, independent operations in France ensued,[73] and the only larger operation SI London planned before the penetration of German territory was Operation SUSSEX,[74] a joint SI/SIS intelligence project of Brigadier General Stewart G. Menzies.[75]

British intelligence weighed various plans to penetrate Germany, Austria, northern Italy, and the Balkans. Among them was a scheme to recruit guerrillas in northern Croatia and infiltrate them into Lower Styria. The plan was to drop two-man groups there whose task would be to prepare bases for additional agents. The idea was dropped because agents sent in without air support and knowledge of the terrain would be virtually ineffective. It was also feared that not all soldiers would be of use in that sort of operation. As a result, British SIS decided to concentrate on a different kind of intelligence action in northern Italy, Yugoslavia, and Central Europe.[76]

The liberation of France did not result, as had been expected, in the immediate collapse of the Third Reich and the end of the war. Consequently, OSS ETO decided to concentrate its activity on the penetration of Germany. It sent its first group of agents, who with the aid of Yugoslav guerrillas crossed into the Third Reich. Unfortunately, on August 5, 1944, after forty-four days in Germany, the members of this group were killed.[77] In total, the OSS in the Mediterranean Theater of Operation sent twelve groups into Germany and nearly all their agents were either captured or killed.[78] These unsuccessful operations discouraged OSS SI in London and its individual sections, such as the French, Belgian, Polish, and German desks as well as the Labor Desk, but the OSS nevertheless began recruiting agents in the United States, England, France, and the Benelux countries.

The Americans, like the British, thought that the penetration of Nazi Germany would be far more difficult than the invasion and liberation of France, because French resistance groups had provided SI with valuable information, prepared landing areas for parachute drops, and secured OSS agents during their time on French soil. The French resistance was in constant radio contact with London, which made it possible to secure parachute drops throughout occupied France. Germany was an entirely different proposition. The Third Reich was an enemy state with a police regime where the Gestapo controlled everything and everyone, and where resistance in large part had been quashed. Agents who would be sent there could count only on themselves, with no local support whatsoever. They could not count on support in everyday situations, or more so, in contacts with London. That meant that agents who were to be sent into Germany had to know the German language and the realities of everyday life there.

Unfortunately, few OSS agents could meet those requirements.[79] A September 1944 internal survey of plans and personnel connected with spy activities in Germany revealed that SI had some eighty people, and SO only ten, that were suitable to be dropped into the Reich to gather intelligence. SI could provide an additional twenty agents once the strength and activity of the Gestapo had weakened.[80]

There were many obstacles to overcome. While the occupied countries provided a large pool of willing people among whom the OSS could recruit and train prospective agents, there were few anti-Nazis among Germans willing to cooperate with Allied intelligence. And for many months cooperation with Communists was banned for purely political reasons. Initially it was decided not to use German prisoners of war as intelligence agents in the European Theater of Operations. They were not trusted and it was thought that there was not enough time to check their credibility. Later, this policy changed and the US Seventh Army and the OSS in the Mediterranean Theater of Operations began to successfully recruit agents among them. Members of Project Eagle were also recruited from German POWs who had surrendered to Allied forces in France and Italy, and who were treated by the Polish government and armed forces as the Polish citizens that they were.

The success of intelligence activities carried out by the OSS in large part depended on the ingenuity, cleverness, and intelligence of its agents.

The OSS understood that its agents needed a credible cover story that they could accept and adopt, and unquestionable documents, shoes, luggage, cigarettes, matches, and so on. Because the cover story had to be coherent and plausible, the work of two OSS divisions—Research and Analysis, and Clothing and Documents—focused on collecting information on and producing these items. In April 1944, five persons in these divisions started their work, preparing agents for their drops, and by the end of the year this group rose to six.

With respect to preparing clothes, the OSS provided a tailor and Polish intelligence a cobbler. Information on German uniforms and various odds and ends that German soldiers might possess were collected from German prisoners held in British camps. In order to gather more German uniforms and various kinds of equipment, the OSS began to send missions to the continent beginning on October 14, 1944. The origins of the minutiae were varied—shoelaces were original and came from Germany, handkerchiefs were from England, and towels from Ireland. In August 1944 a camouflage section was established, which produced additional sundry clothing items such as buttons.

Somewhat earlier, in May 1944, documents and stamps that would lend credibility to the agents' cover stories began to be produced. A British paper mill made paper with counterfeit watermarks, while OSS headquarters printed blank document forms on the paper, and the French BCRA provided information on how to fill them out. In time, the common effort of the tailors, cobblers, and counterfeiters was successful. Only a small percentage of dispatched agents had problems because of their forged documents or clothes.[81] The only agent who was arrested and tortured because of badly prepared documents was a member of the Polish Martini Mission (the report is to be found in chapter 3).

In May 1944, members of the Polish Continental Section (later the Polish Desk) of the OSS in London began to plan for intelligence activity in Germany, whose participants would be Polish soldiers whose German language skills were excellent. A few weeks later, Major Joseph Dasher,[82] the head of the Polish Desk OSS SI in London, suggested to his superiors organizing a group of a few dozen agents whose main task was to be the collection of strategic information in Germany. It was hoped that when hostilities ended in Europe, agents with a native command of German would be useful in intelligence work, including unraveling whatever German secret military activities there might be, or in struggling against a Nazi resistance movement that might become active as a result of the Allied occupation of Germany.

Major Joseph Dasher, head of the Polish Section/Desk of the OSS SI in London. (Photo US National Archives)

The mood in Germany during the war depended on how things were going on the fronts. Early successes gave way to fatalism as the Soviets and the Western Allies fought their way toward Berlin. Soviet advances and a worsening economic situation led to an increasing lack of confidence in the Nazi regime despite a steady diet of propaganda that was falling on deaf ears. Adolf Hitler's popularity had been waning as conditions grew worse, in many places the Nazi Party was hated, and most Germans yearned for an end to the war. The regime was aware of these sentiments during the final six months of hostilities and became increasingly dangerous to its own citizens, especially after intensifying terror in February 1945. People felt greatly intimidated. Military courts dealt out harsh exemplary punishment, mostly death sentences, to those found to be insufficiently patriotic in carrying out their duties. By early March 1945, flying courts martial were active throughout what was still under control of the Reich.[83]

This was what the OSS agents had to face after being parachuted into the Reich in March and April 1945. They were aware of what awaited them in case of discovery. No doubt they also knew that any number of circumstances, like bad weather, Luftwaffe night fighters, the *Volkssturm*,[84] or just plain bad luck could mean capture, torture, and death. Nevertheless, all of the men who volunteered for their missions and completed the training jumped. During the last eight months of the war, OSS London dropped thirty-four groups of two into Germany; four agents were killed in the air or on landing. The agents of sixteen of the thirty-four groups were Poles, whose experiences were unknown until the OSS archives were slowly declassified and made available to researchers.

2

PROJECT EAGLE

WHO WERE THE EAGLES?

The Independent Grenadiers Company of the Polish Armed Forces[1] provided volunteers for the penetration of the Third Reich. Forty soldiers were chosen from among them (twenty observers and twenty radio operators), each with a very good knowledge of the German language and all of whom had served in the German Army. Who were these young Poles who were ready to risk life and limb in a dangerous operation behind the German lines? How had they gotten to England, and how had they joined the Polish Armed Forces there?

In order to address this, we need to revisit the beginning of the armed conflict when on Friday, September 1, 1939, Poland was attacked by its neighbors to the north, west, and south, Germany and Slovakia. At 4:45 a.m., the German battleship *Schleswig-Holstein* opened fire on the Polish Military Transit Depot on the Westerplatte peninsula near the city of Danzig. It is commonly accepted that its gunfire started World War II in Europe.

Despite declarations of war against the Third Reich by Great Britain and France, the Poles were unable to withstand the German onslaught for very long. The German and Slovak armies attacked Poland from three sides, and on September 17 the Red Army invaded Poland from the east. A few weeks earlier, on August 23, Joachim von Ribbentrop and Vyacheslav Molotov, the foreign ministers of the Third Reich and the USSR, respectively, met in Moscow and signed a pact of non-aggression that included a secret protocol establishing the borders of Soviet and German spheres of influence across Poland, Lithuania, Latvia, Estonia, and Finland. On September 28, 1939, with the impending defeat of Polish forces evident, a

28 Chapter 2

supplementary protocol refined the division of territories between the two powers, with 200,000 square kilometers of prewar Poland and some twelve million inhabitants under Soviet occupation, and 189,000 square kilometers of land with twenty-two million people remaining under German rule.

Initially, the German authorities considered various options concerning the future of the Polish areas under German occupation, including the establishment of a puppet state, as, for example, in Slovakia, France, or Norway. Ultimately, the inability to undermine the legality of Polish émigré authorities, first in France and later in Great Britain; the refusal of the British and French governments to recognize an ersatz occupation government; the rejection of any such arrangement by the Soviets; and most importantly, the absence of any Polish politicians or groups that wanted to collaborate with the Germans led the Nazi authorities to reject the idea.

Instead, by decree of the chancellor of the Third Reich, Adolf Hitler, dated October 8, 1939, the prewar Polish *vojevodships* of Silesia, Poznań, and Pomerania and parts of the *vojevodships* of Białystok, Kielce, Kraków (minus the city of Kraków), Łódz, and Warsaw (without the city of Warsaw) were annexed by Germany as incorporated eastern areas. From these lands administrative subdivisions were created. The Reichsgau Danzig-Westpreussen was established and in January 1940 renamed Reichsgau Wartheland. The existing Prussian provinces of Provinz Ostpreussen and Provinz Schlesien were enlarged, and in 1941 a new Provinz Oberschlesien was created. With the occupation of new territories formerly belonging to the USSR, in 1941 Bezirk Bialystok was formally annexed by the Third Reich. Other regions to the east were swallowed by the Reichskomissariat Ostland and the Reichskomissariat Ukraine.

The decree of October 8, 1939, resulted in the incorporation of 91,900 square kilometers of formerly Polish land by Germany and in 1941 an additional 31,100 square kilometers. Approximately 12.3 million people lived on these lands, including about 600,000 ethnic Germans.

Not all Polish territory occupied by the Third Reich was incorporated. On October 12, 1939, Hitler decreed the establishment of unincorporated areas into the General Government (*Generalgouvernement fur die besetzen polnischen Gebiete*, or GG) with Hans Frank as its head and its capital in Kraków. The General Government consisted of four districts: Kraków, Lublin, Radom, and Warsaw. It comprised 96,000 square kilometers with a population of 11.5 million people. Following the German attack on the USSR and the occupation of large areas to the east, a fifth district was added, Galicia, with its capital of Lwów/Lemberg, and the General Government expanded by an additional 47,100 square kilometers and 4.2

million inhabitants. By the end of 1942, the territory of the General Government swelled to 142,800 square kilometers and its population to 15.7 million people.

The annexation of Polish areas did not result from strictly ethnic, racial, or economic reasons. As the war ground on, especially in its later years, the necessity of supplementing the manpower of the German Army with new young recruits forced the German administration to think creatively. And it was from Polish areas incorporated into the Third Reich that the future agents of Project Eagle, most of whom worked in mines and factories early in the war, were later conscripted into the Wehrmacht.

The best treatment of these issues is to be found in a book by Ryszard Kaczmarek, professor at the University of Silesia.[2] Based on German and Polish archival materials, Professor Kaczmarek describes the fates of young Poles who lived in Polish areas (Silesia, Pomerania, Kaszubia, the Poznań region, and Mazuria) before the Second World War that had been incorporated in October 1939 into the Third Reich. Poles living in these areas were faced with the fact that they had become residents of the German Reich and that they were now subject to conscription into the German Army. It is probable that the most common motive for joining the Wehrmacht was simply the urge to survive. Seventy-five years after the end of the war there is still a stigma attached to the forced service in the German military. Kaczmarek notes in his introduction that "today one may look at the issue of Poles' service in the Wehrmacht in a new light: as victims of the German national policy in Polish areas annexed by the Third Reich."[3]

Nearly 90,000 Polish prisoners and deserters from the Wehrmacht, and forced laborers from the Todt Organization,[4] served in the Polish Armed Forces in the West at the end of the Second World War. That is almost 35.8 percent of all Polish soldiers fighting on the western fronts. The Polish government in London considered conscription of Polish citizens into the Wehrmacht as contrary to law and held that those Polish citizens in Allied custody should return to Polish jurisdiction and serve in the Polish Army. As the war drew to its end, on November 28, 1944, the Military Commission of the National Council of the Polish Republic passed a special resolution concerning all Poles serving in the Wehrmacht in which it stated that "the National Council of the Republic of Poland is of the opinion that it is a necessity that full civic rights be returned to former German soldiers, Poles who had been forced into the German Army." This very important resolution for nearly 90,000 Poles, former Wehrmacht soldiers including the members of Project Eagle, allowed them to be treated not as traitors but as persons who had been forced as a result of German policy to fight on the side of the enemy.[5]

The bios[6] of the thirty agents who survived their missions in Germany and returned to London show that, first, most were young men in their twenties; second, seventeen hailed from Silesia, twelve from Pomerania, and one from the Poznań area; third, all of them had been conscripted into the Wehrmacht in 1942–1943 as part of the effort to replenish German losses fighting in the six-month (August 2, 1942–February 2, 1943) siege of Stalingrad; fourth, they were not well-educated men, most having only completed primary school while fourteen completed high school or vocational schools; and fifth, only one deserted from the *Wehrmacht* at the front,[7] with the rest of the available bios referring to surrender or being taken prisoner. Twenty-nine agents were taken into custody by Allied forces in France; Corporal Zbigniew Strzeliński surrendered to the Allies on November 9, 1943, in the Italian town of Cassino,[8] as did Corporal Wiktor Szulik.

It can be assumed that initially, along with all German soldiers captured by Allied forces, the future members of Project Eagle were sent to prisoner-of-war camps, where they were sought out by Polish liaison officers. According to an excerpt of an account by Teofil Biolik of Świerczyniec:

> *The Americans took me prisoner. Several thousand prisoners like me were kept on the bare ground for almost all of April [1945]. Hunger and the cold nights made for tough times. One day a jeep with officers drove into the camp. Using a megaphone, they asked—whoever speaks Polish, step forward! No one did so, although there were many of us there. We were all afraid that during the night the German majority would kill us. . . . The next day some trucks arrived. Once again they used a megaphone to announce: Whoever is a Pole, get in the trucks. About five hundred men got in.*[9]

In order to ensure the safety of the Poles in the camps, the Polish Army came up with a procedure that involved transporting them from the POW camps to nearby barracks where the new soon-to-be recruits discarded their personal items and German uniforms and after a shower received battledresses of the Polish Armed Forces. For the period of the war, their families were informed that they were missing in action.[10]

THE ORIGIN AND PREPARATION OF PROJECT EAGLE

In order to acquaint the reader with the atmosphere and drama of the times when Project Eagle and the abortive Project Eagle II were being organized and agents were being trained, I cite below extensive excerpts of volume 7 of the *OSS/London: Special Operations Branch and Secret Intelligence Branch War Diaries*:

Eagle Project

Early in July 1944 the Polish Section of the General Division headed by Lieutenant Colonel (then Major) Joseph Dasher, proposed that SI, with the cooperation of German-speaking Polish Army personnel placed at its disposal by the Polish Minister of National Defense, operate agents to collect secret intelligence in Germany.

Twenty agents and twenty radio operators, selected from numerous Poles previously impressed for service in the German or in the Todt Organization and who had been taken prisoners of war in the Normandy operations, were to be introduced into Germany as soon as practicable. It was felt that when the military phase of the war in Europe was finished, this personnel, all of whom spoke German, would be most useful for intelligence activities in connection with any clandestine German warfare or in combatting secret Nazi societies which might spring up as a result of the Allied occupation of the Reich.

It was anticipated that the agents would be introduced at predetermined point in Germany, presumably but not necessarily in area in which sizeable Polish colonies were to be found. The agents would, when practicable, make contact with Poles residing in various districts in Germany, and through them obtain information for transmittal by W/T [Wireless Telegraphy]. Intelligence target would be determined by OSS and/or SHAEF at a later date.

Origin of the Project

Early in May 1944 the Polish Section of the Continental Division of SI was giving close attention to long range planning concerning future operations of Poles in Europe. By July, the foundation of the Eagle Project had been laid. This was to be a joint Polish-American project patterned roughly after Sussex,[11] for the procurement of tactical and strategic intelligence from Germany during the period of hostilities and thereafter.

In July, Polish military authorities in the United Kingdom were requested to screen for the project captured Poles, who had already been inducted into the Polish Army. After the initial screening test, further screening was requested for the selection of men qualified for under-cover work in enemy territory. The Polish Section requested the Polish Minister of National Defense and the Commander-in-Chief of the Polish Armed Forces to assign to OSS 40 Polish soldiers selected according to criteria determined by OSS and to appoint a Polish officer, selected by OSS, to cooperate in the execution of the project.

The project provided that of the men selected, 20 would be trained as W/T operators and 20 as agents. W/T training was to be provided by the Poles, employing the facilities they had available. Agent training preferably was to be *provided by OSS, or, if this found to be impossible, jointly by OSS and the Poles, or by the British. Throughout the training period, the Polish Section of SI was to be in close contact with the men. It was expected that W/T training would require 5 months and agent training 3 months. Cover was to be arranged by the Poles. Communication was to be by W/T. Transportation was to be by such medium as available at the proper times. W/T equipment was to be provided by OSS. Clothing and documents were to be provided by the Poles. The budget requested for the training phase of the project was 10,000 British Pounds.*

Approval of the Project

The above project was duly approved by the Chief of SI, Colonel John Haskell[12] and Colonel D.K.E. Bruce,[13] commanding officer OSS/ETO, following which the Polish Minister of National Defense, General of Division Dr. Marian Kukiel,[14] and the Commander-in-Chief of the Polish Armed Forces, General Kazimierz Sosnkowski,[15] were approached and promptly consented to the proposal. Polish authorities gave OSS the highest priority in the selection of the 40 men needed for the project, placing this request ahead of demands from their air force and navy.

Major Tadeusz Szumowski, Chief of the Military Section, Polish Special Operations Office, was appointed to represent the Polish side of the project and to cooperate with OSS in the execution of the project. Major Szumowski was at one time Chief of Polish Strategic Intelligence for Germany.

On 14 July, General Kukiel authorized the detail of 40 men to be used under this project, but retained them under Polish military command and assigned them administratively to the Independent Polish Grenadier Company, a part of Special Forces, operated by the Poles jointly with the British SOE. Because of this situation, it became necessary to obtain the cooperation of the British SOE.

Lack of Cooperation between SOE and SI and the Poles

After considerable negotiations between the Polish Section of SI and the Poles on one side, and the British SOE on the other, an agreement was reached whereby the men selected for the project would be placed in an SOE para-military training center at Aris Aig, Inverness, Scotland, for a course of training for five weeks. In August, during the latter stages of the agents' para-military training, SOE began what some members of the SI Polish Section regarded as efforts to make Polish cooperation with SI difficult.

On 19 August 1944 the following letter from Brigadier E. Mockler-Ferryman,[16] Special Force Headquarters, was sent to Lieutenant General M. Kukiel, Polish Minister of National Defense, Polish General Headquarters:

> *I am a little concerned about the future of the American party of Poles which we are training at our "A" schools at the request of Lieutenant*

Colonel Dasher of OSS/SI. We are, of course, delighted to carry out this work, but we do feel that this is a question which should be completely divorced from the Special Operations Office at Thorney Court. This is an SI matter pure and simple, and it has always been the policy of the British authorities, and we believe it is also your policy to keep SO and SI matters completely separate from an organization point of view.

I would therefore put forward the suggestion that, from now on, the Polish side of this party should be dealt with by your Deuxieme Bureau, i.e., the equivalent of the American SI. We should, of course, continue through the Liaison officer who may be appointed by your Deuxieme Bureau to deal with this matter, to give every assistance within our power.

What I do feel is that both SFHQ and the Polish equivalent i.e., the Special Operations Office, should became completely divorced from matters which concern SI alone.

If you agree with my point of view, I should be obliged if you would issue the necessary orders and I from my side will inform OSS/SI.

The Poles, because of their close tie-up with the British Government, became apprehensive of British displeasure. In the original plan for the project the Poles were to be responsible for the training of the radio operators, while the observers were to be trained by SOE, but such was not possible with the British change of policy. The Poles wished British acquiescence to continue the project. OSS, however, replied saying that the necessity for the agreement of a third party, or country, to an arrangement made by a representative organization of the United States and the Polish Government was not consistent with United States and Polish sovereignty. When the Poles persisted in their desire to have British acquiescence, the Polish Section of SI asked whether, if SHAEF approval of the project were produced, the Poles would agree to continue the project. The solution was deemed satisfactory.

On 19 September 1944 the Eagle Project was approved in its entirety by Brigadier General T. J. Betts,[17] General Staff, deputy assistant chief of staff, G-2, Supreme Headquarters Allied Expeditionary Forces, on behalf of the Supreme Commander. Shortly therefore the Poles organized the radio and observer schools and allotted some teaching and sufficient administrative personnel for their proper maintenance. The 40 men selected for training who had previously been assigned to the Independent Polish Grenadier Company were attached to the School by special order.[18]

Two days earlier William Casey had observed at Gap, forty-five miles south of Grenoble, the surrender of a large garrison of German troops to a handful of American soldiers of Troop A of the 117th Cavalry. "Unable to

The Polish and American leaders of the School of Specialists. (Photo US National Archives)

handle the more than 1,000 prisoners," he later wrote, "Troop A had discovered the Poles pressed into *Wehrmacht* service who were eager to act as military policemen for the Americans. The GIs gave them yellow armbands to wear and sent them south with their prisoners."[19]

A short time after Project Eagle was approved, the Poles organized a special school for the radio operators and observers, and assigned a sufficient number of instructors and administrative personnel to the school. Forty men who had previously been attached to the Polish Independent Grenadiers Company were selected for training and sent to the school by special order.

These soldiers came from middle and lower social backgrounds and were not selected because of their high intelligence. Their task would be to quickly mingle in the large number of Polish forced laborers working in Germany. Initially, the plan was for them to be trained for six months with an end date of April 1, 1945, when they were to be parachuted into Germany. However, the Battle of the Bulge and the Allied need for strategic intelligence before the penetration of the Reich caused a change in plans, and the agents were to be dropped beginning on March 1. As things turned out, the first agents were dropped from Dijon, France,[20] later, on March 18.

<u>*Selection of Agent Personnel*</u>

On 20 July 1944 Lieutenant Colonel Dasher, Major Szumowski and Major Rowinski arrived at the Polkannon camp area, near Edinburgh, where the Poles are encamped following their induction into the Polish Army after release from German prisoner of war camps. On the following day, Major Rowinski,[21] an experienced man in the selection of personnel for intelligence and subversive undercover work, began the task of selecting the forty men for the project, which involved careful screening of every candidate, first through the inspection of the individual candidate's personal record, and secondly through an interview with the candidate. The selection of the forty men involved the close study of more than two thousand individual records and over seven hundred individual interviews.

The Polkannon camp area held about 1500 to 1700 Polish soldiers who, until their recent capture in Normandy, had been serving in the German Army. In accordance with the OSS agreement with the Polish Ministry of National Defense the men selected for the Eagle project were placed for purpose of administration and military command under Major Szymanowski, at that time the commanding officer of the Independent Grenadiers Company. Major Rowinski remained in Edinburgh until the end of July, selecting agents.

<u>*Para Military Training*</u>

As noted above, after considerable negotiation between the Polish Section and the Polish Army officers concerned on one side, and the British SOE on the other side, an agreement was reached whereby the men selected for the project would be placed in an SOE para-military training center. Lieutenant Colonel Hazell,[22] acting for SOE, placed at the disposal of OSS for the purpose of preliminary training one of the SOE training areas at Aris Aig, Inverness, Scotland, which was to be available on 1 August 1944. The proposed program of instruction was drawn up under Lieutenant Colonel F. J. Ingham-Clark's direction by Major McClain, chief instructor for the SOE training areas, and was approved by the Polish officers and by Lieutenant Colonel Dasher. The program outlined a training course for five weeks in military discipline, physical culture, silent killing, quick handling and firing of automatic pistols, familiarity with foreign weapons, map reading, field sketches, route and reconnaissance report, German maps, schemes and projects across country requiring the use of the compass, fieldcraft and minor tactics, and demonstrations of employment and handling of explosives.

The Aris Aig area was fully staffed with instructors and necessary service personnel, and possessed complete training, messing, living and transportation facilities to handle the forty trainees, plus an appropriate number of Polish military personnel who were attached to them. Expenses of the area were to be reimbursed on a reverse lease-lend basis.

At Aris Aig the trainees were divided up into twenty bodies per house, and each house was then subdivided into two squads of ten each for ease in handling instruction. The course of instruction included physical training, close combat, rope work, fieldcraft, weapon training, demolitions, signaling, reports, map reading, and schemes and tactics. In the course of report dated 15 September 1944 the commandant and instructor made the following general remarks on the students:

> *A well-disciplined party who get on very well together. Individuality was slow to appear and it was clear that the majority of the party have never had to do any thinking for themselves. With further training, many of these students will undoubtedly do well. Results have not been altogether satisfactory. Intellectually the students have not been up to the standard of other groups in training courses and many have great difficulty in absorbing much of the lectures. Their practical work has been reasonably good and they certainly have all worked very well.*
>
> *It was evident on arrival that some of these men suffered from inadequate feeding, and were highly nervous of authority. A great improvement in both physical and nervous conditions is apparent, but five weeks is not long enough to build up really sound stamina and there has been a large number of hospital cases due to minor ailments and injuries. Their mental work is very definitely much below their practical. There was a number of students who were so mentally incapable that it was no use to continue their instruction. The majority of the students, however, has greatly benefited from the course. Six students were dropped from the rolls of project at the end of the para-military course. These men were replaced by others with the same background and training.[23]*

Every agent was evaluated in a paramilitary report. Two examples are provided below, on Leon Adrian and Aleksander Bogdanowicz.[24]

S.T.S. No. 25[25]
Name by which known: Adrian, L.–Sgt.
Grade: 2b.
1. *Physical Training: All through the course, he has been a real trier and, although getting on in years, has kept pace with the others. Has plenty of stamina.*
2. *Close Combat: Good at Close Combat; needs to speed up a bit but this will come with more practice.*
3. *Rope Work: Very strong on ropes.*
4. *Fieldcraft: Works very hard and has shown a good mastery of this subject. Good on stalks and has a working knowledge of camouflage and concealment.*
5. *Weapon Training: Very steady, shoots well but needs to speed up. A sound knowledge of most weapons taught.*

6. *Explosives and Demolitions: Shows keen interest and has improved a lot. He handles explosives well and with confidence.*

7. *Signalling and Communications: Average standard sending and receiving—3 w.p.m. Tries very hard.*

8. *Reports, etc.: Although he had difficulty in grasping this subject at first, he has worked very hard and is now reasonably good.*

9. *Map Reading, etc.: On practical map reading he is good, but a test paper seems to scare him.*

10. *Schemes and Tactics: Always a hard worker and takes keen interest.*

11. *Boat Work:* [no note]

12. *Navigation:* [no note]

Instructor's remarks: A good steady student, always reliable and seldom gets flustered. Inclined to a bit slow but is always very thorough.

Commandant's Report: Has gained much from this course and will make a reliable N.C.O. in the field. Has exercised a good and quiet authority over the younger men.

Date: 13.9.44

Signed: [illegible], *Major*
OC
S.T.S. 25

S.T.S. No. 25
Name by which known: Bogdanowicz, A.
Grade: 5b.

1. *Physical Training: Very keen, he has given a good account of himself.*

2. *Close Combat: Very good, he works hard and with practice should become quite proficient.*

3. *Rope Work: He has good technique and can climb all kinds of ropes.*

4. *Fieldcraft: Enthusiastic and keen, he has shown that he has a good practical theoretical knowledge of this subject.*

5. *Weapon Training: Stripping and manipulation very good. He is also a good shot but a little slow.*

6. *Explosives and Demolitions: Very good work indeed. He has really mastered this subject, his practical work is quick and neat and in his examination paper he got 93%.*

7. *Signalling and Communications: Unable to grasp this subject.*

8. *Reports, etc.: Good. He has spent a lot of time on his work with good results.*

9. *Map Reading, etc.: Theoretical and practical knowledge fairly good considering he did little or no map reading before he came here.*

10. *Schemes and Tactics: Leader of the first scheme, he gave a good account of himself. His plan was good and well carried out.*

11. Boat Work: [no note]
12. Navigation: [no note]
Instructor's remarks: A good all around student. He has worked hard and is keen and enthusiastic. He should do well in the field.
Commandant's Report: A keen and hard worker with definite powers of leadership which will improve with experience. Has good brains and is the right type for the work of this organization.
Date: 15.9.44

Signed: [illegible], *Major*
OC
S.T.S. 25

Six men who been chosen for Project Eagle failed to complete their paramilitary training and were replaced by others.

Top left: Hand-to-hand combat training at Aris Aig, Inverness, Scotland, by Project Eagle agents, August–September 1944. (Photo Janet and Stephen Smith)

Top right: Training at Aris Aig, Inverness, Scotland, by Project Eagle agents, August–September 1944. Agent Czogała, right. (Photo Janet and Stephen Smith)

Bottom: Training at Aris Aig, Inverness, Scotland, by Project Eagle agents, August–September 1944. (Photo Janet and Stephen Smith)

Parachute training at Special Training School 51 Ringway near Manchester (No. 1 Parachute Training School), September 16–22, 1944. Agent René de Gaston, third from left. (Photo Krzysztof Marek Barwikowski)

Left and below: Parachute training at Special Training School 51 Ringway near Manchester (No. 1 Parachute Training School), September 16–22, 1944. Agent Edmund Barski, middle. (Photo Janet and Stephen Smith)

Parachute Training

From 16 to 22 September 1944 the forty trainees attended an English parachute jumping school near Manchester. Here they received special physical training exercises for jumping. Three day jumps, in the morning, the afternoon and at dusk, were made. Each agent made one night jump. Jumps were made in slow pairs, quick pairs and quick sticks of five.

After completion of the jump school, the students were given a furlough for one week. They reported to the agent and radio operators' school at 29 and 30 Bryanston Square on 1 October 1944.

W/T Equipment and Training

The buildings at Bryanston Square were supplied by OSS. OSS was to furnish three jeeps, two motorcycles, if possible, equipment for one dispatch rider, two typewriters, one safe, 50,000 cigarettes, and 500 pounds of chocolate. Beds, mattresses, blankets, and office supplies were furnished by the Poles. The Poles also supplied the instructors and the elementary training equipment. Field equipment and additional necessary equipment, valued at about 750 British Pounds, was purchased by OSS.

W/T students lived at the school. There were no messing facilities, but an allowance of 0/7/6 daily for subsistence was paid to each man. The building was policed and guarded by the men themselves.

Personnel for the W/T school consisted of:

Course Director and Assistant Commandant for the Combined Schools	Captain Sobecki
Instructor in Electro-Techniques	Mr. Boleslaw Dulemba
Instructor in Morse Code	Mr. Michal Opiela
Assistant Instructor in Electro-Techniques	Mr. Wladyslaw Majder
Assistant to Course Director	Sergeant Janusz Chłuski

The following summary shows the courses and the number of hours to be completed in each during the five months period of instruction. It was hoped that each student would have a sending speed of twenty words per minute upon the completion of the course.

Subject	Course Hours
Electro Techniques	229
Morse Code	172
W/T Correspondence	62
Ground to Air Communication	60
Ciphers	60
Self Defense and Motor Vehicles	54
Knowledge of Germany	22

Communications Procedure   31
Security of W/T Set, and Defense
   against German Direction Finders   15

Agent Equipment and Training
On 4 September 1944 Lieutenant Colonel Dasher advised that agent training
would have to be given by OSS and Polish authorities in cooperation, because of
the unexpected withdrawal of SOE from this project. It was difficult to procure
training personnel from OSS since no slots were available nor were capable people
available in England at the time. Although Polish authorities had very few training personnel, they agreed to furnish the teaching staff for the agent school. Major
Stefan Szymanowski served as commandant for the agent and W/T schools.
Members of the staff were:

Course Director and Espionage Instructor	Major Stefan Szymanowski
Counter-Espionage Instructors	2nd Lt. Henryk Arwar
	Mr. Winter
	Mr. Adam Lubecki
	Mr. Chmiel
Information on Germany	
Instructors	Mr. Arnold
	Major Raymond Kawalec
	Major Łucjan Makowski
	Mr. Mikołajewski
German Language Instructor	2nd Lt. Edmund Hadrian
Photography Instructors	CSM Francis Sufek
	Sergeant Roman Buzuk
Correspondence and Counterfeiting and	
Documents Instructor	Lieutenant Leonard Łysz
Cipher Instructors	Lt. Tadeusz Rossowiecki
	Lieutenant Koperski
Lock Picking and Concealment Devices	
Instructor	Corporal Stefan Mucha
Electro-Techniques Instructors	Mr. Dulęba
	Mr. Majder
Listening-in Devices Instructor	Sergeant Sobótka
Self Defense and Motor Vehicles	Sergeant Michel Styma (American)
Instructors	Corporal Jan Jakubiak
	Corporal Józef Nowicki
P.T and Close Order Drill Instructor	2nd Lt. Józef Śliwa

Lieutenant A. R. Waters, CMP, served as administrative officer for both schools
and on 18 December 1944, Lieutenant A. W. Wusza, AC, was assigned

to duty with the Polish Section and detailed as plans and operations officer for the project. OSS agreed to supply all instructional aids. Some equipment was procured from the disbanded Area "B."

The curriculum for the agent training course of three months was:

	Theory	Exercise	Total
Technique of Espionage	30	30	60
Technique of Counter-Espionage	20	51	71
Information on State and Military Organization of Germany	80		80
General Information on Germany	70	12	82
Photography	10	60	70
Counterfeiting Documents	5	15	20
Correspondence	10	30	40
Ciphers	6	18	24
Lock Picking	5	15	20
Mail Drops and Construction of Concealment and Devices	4	12	16
Listening-in Devices and Techniques of Other Electrical Devices	36	18	54
Self Defense (Firing of Weapons and Toxicology)	4	18	22
Motor Vehicles	24		24
Close Order Drill		10	10
Hours in Reserve	—	—	31
Total Hours	304	289	624

Field Exercises

A number of field exercises in espionage were held, mostly as whole or half day problems. The students were issued a safe conduct pass should any trouble arise between them and the British police and security forces.

Maps, photographs, diagrams and plans of airports, factories, anti-aircraft defenses and port installations were made by the students. One exercise entailed the collecting and collating of all information of war installations on Edgeware Road between Kilburn Bridge and Marble Arch. Others involved reporting on activities on the London docks, on radio stations and on airfields. The majority of the exercises were combined with similar operations executed by the Polish Counter Intelligence Section, giving the students practice in working under surveillance.

In mid-January, at the request of SI, the training course was shortened thirty days in order to make possible the dispatch of the men in training beginning 1 March instead of 1 April as originally planned.

Equipment and Funds
In July 1944 the following budget outline for the Eagle project was submitted to the Funds Review Committee:

Selection of Personnel	English Pounds 100
Preliminary Training	820
Wireless Telegraphy Course	4,387
Agent Training	3,537
Total Training Course	8,844
Operational Costs	405
Total Training and Operational	9,249
Reserve Fund	751
Grand Total	English Pounds 10,000

On 3 August 1944 the Funds Review Committee recommended that Colonel Bruce approve the budget after deleting certain items of extra pay and prizes for students, reducing the budget to English Pounds 8,399.

In October, Major Szumowski[26] raised the question of additional pay to instructors performing special duties, amounting to English Pounds 1,325. Special Funds took the position that although it could probably pay civilian lecturers at the school for specialists, it could not disburse any money for supplementary allowance for Polish military personnel posted to the school since the United States Articles of War forbid the acceptance by United States military personnel of any additional compensation from any source whatsoever for services in the line of duty, and Special Funds felt that the same rule should apply to allied military personnel. It was stated, however, that if Polish Army regulations did not prohibit such payment, OSS would be glad to re-examine the entire problem. Major Szumowski stated that if the extra pay was not approved the lectures would not be given and the school would have to close. After conferences and an exchange of cables with Mr. Shepardson, chief SI in Washington, the payments were approved by Brigadier General Donovan.

Status of Project as of the End of 1944
At the end of 1944 the Polish agents were in training at the agent and W/T schools in Bryanston Square in London.[27]

Their subsequent activities are described in volume 12 of the *War Diaries*.

On January 17, 1945, a revised plan for Project Eagle was accepted and approved. Of the forty men seconded by the Polish Army, four were trained but not dispatched on missions to the Reich, two were dropped from the school for scholastic difficulties, while another two completed the course but were not considered suitable for work in the field.[28] Thirty-two eventually were dropped in two-man teams into the Reich in March–April 1945. Code names for the sixteen groups were taken from cocktails that were popular in the United States at that time, like, for example, Martini and Manhattan.[29] Code names for five groups of German agents who were being trained for spy missions in Germany were taken from tools, like Hammer and Pickaxe.[30]

OSS SI turned to the members of Project Eagle with a request to provide short bios, but without using their real names. These bios and information on their heirs are provided in the following chapter. Because in the agreement between the OSS and the Polish Armed Forces the Americans stipulated that, if necessary, the agents would cooperate with the OSS in postwar Germany, the Polish Desk at SI London asked the agents to indicate on their bios their familiarity with regions that were well known to them.

Lt. Col. Dasher and members of the Polish Section:

Sgt. Filipkoski, Cpl. Kapustka, Lt. Raczkiewicz, Lt. Wusza, Sgt. Edwards, Maj. Dups, Sgt. Nowakowski.

The Polish Desk, later Section of OSS SI, London Branch. (Photo US National Archives)

Prior to leaving on their mission, individual contracts of employment were signed with each agent, specifying their pay, which was set at the level of an American staff sergeant. The basic monthly salary was US$138, subsistence at $19, and $100 for extra-hazard pay. In total, each agent was to receive US$257 per month starting from the moment he landed in Germany. In addition, each Project Eagle member was covered by an insurance policy that would pay $2,500 to the heirs indicated by the agent.[31] The agents therefore provided the real names and addresses of their closest kin; this was the only document in which the agents provided this data (see the notes regarding the individual bios in chapter 3).[32]

Major Louis P. Dups, the deputy director of the Polish Section, summarized and evaluated the performance of the agents in the Final Report on Project Eagle.[33] However, even before the agents finished their training, the Polish Section of SI was so impressed by their achievements that it proposed to the OSS the organization of Project Eagle II.

THE ABORTIVE ATTEMPT TO CREATE PROJECT EAGLE II

In January 1945, when German armies were withdrawing from the Ardennes following their defeat in the Battle of the Bulge and Soviet forces were crossing the Vistula on their way to the Oder River, the director of a secret intelligence unit of the OSS in London, Lieutenant Joseph Dasher, proposed in a letter to the Polish Minister of National Defense, General Marian Kukiel, a further, intensified form of cooperation that had begun some six months earlier. Dasher informed Kukiel that the representatives of the OSS in London were very satisfied with the results of the training of the Project Eagle agents, and drew the minister's attention to the fact that the situation on the European fronts was changing quickly. The Americans had approached Major Szymanowski, who was responsible on the Polish side for the training, with a request to shorten the training period by one month and prepare the agents at the School of Specialists for action no later than the first days of March 1945.[34]

In his letter, Dasher continued:

> [T]aking into consideration the fact that the School of Specialists as now constituted through your kindness, is such a well-functioning mechanism, and is so expertly directed, we venture to submit to Your Excellency our earnest request for your continued interest and cooperation. On behalf of Major General William J. Donovan, Director of Strategic Services of the United States of America, we

*respectfully ask Your Excellency to authorize Major Szymanowski to select a
second group of forty Polish soldiers, whose training would begin on or about 1
April 1945. In other words, the School of Specialists would continue to function
and the men in training there would remain under your military command and
administrative control in the same manner as at the present time.*[35]

One month later, on February 5, 1945, in a letter to the head of SI
London, William J. Casey, Dasher wrote of his plan, which he code-named
Project Eagle II. He also explained that the commandant of the School
of Specialists, responding to suggestions from the OSS, would reduce the
training program in the school, chiefly due to costs. Dasher wrote in his
letter:

> *The second group of 40 men, all Polish Army soldiers, will be selected accord-
> ing to much higher criteria than those for the first group. As a result, the Polish
> Ministry of National Defense will invest the Polish School of Specialists with
> the status of an Officers' Candidate School. Thus, every graduate of the Pol-
> ish School of Specialists, second group (i.e. "Eagle" Project No. II) will upon
> graduation, be commissioned a Second Lieutenant of the Polish Army. The
> significance of this to the OSS is self-evident. The higher type of individual
> will be eminently valuable for post-military phase intelligence, particularly for
> political and economic observation, and for surveillance of the Nazi underground.
> . . . The continuance of the Polish School of Specialists for another course for
> forty (40) Polish soldiers was verbally approved by the Chief, SI Branch. . . .
> The allocation of a second group of forty (40) Polish soldiers for training at the
> Polish School of Specialists for eventual use by the OSS was verbally approved
> in conversation with the undersigned by Lieutenant General M. Kukiel, Polish
> Minister of National Defense.*[36]

A budget prepared by Major Szymanowski as well as an amended
budget prepared by Lieutenant Colonel Dasher were sent for approval to
William Casey. He was asked to forward an approved budget for further
authorization if necessary by the commanding officer of OSS ETOUSA
and by the Special Funds Commission.

On the following day, February 6, Dasher wrote to the Chief of
Planning and Operational Personnel, Colonel William Harding Jackson,
requesting that he approve Project Eagle II.[37] This was exceptionally quick
action, taking into account military bureaucracy. The reason was obvious:
the Big Three were meeting at Yalta and important decisions were to be
made there concerning Poland's future. In a letter dated February 1, 1945,
Dasher pressured Casey:

In view of the fact that the results of the Big Three Conference have now been made known to the general public and because a resolution of the Polish problem was effected at this conference, it is requested that the Chief, SI Branch, take immediate steps to urge the Plans and Operations staff to take definite action forthwith on "Eagle" Project No. II. In this connection it is desired to point out that as things stand at present, our Polish collaborators here are preparing to proceed with the selection of the second group of forty (40) Polish soldiers to train under Eagle Project No. II. If negative action is to be taken by the OSS on the project, the Poles should be notified accordingly without delay.[38]

The letter probably was the reason why Casey sent a letter to Major C. Brook Peters of Planning and Personnel in which he strongly advocated Project Eagle II, and on February 16 Major Peters sent a letter recommending to his chief that he approve the project. There were, however, caveats:

2. Because of the potential political implications connected with the employment by OSS of Polish Army officers in the post-hostilities phase, it is recommended that the Poles be informed that OSS will review the desirability of continuing the project should hostilities cease before the agents have been trained or employed on mission. 3. It is recommended further that a cable be despatched to Washington and 110 inquiring as to their views regarding the desirability of employing such individuals in the post-hostilities phase. 4. Approval of the project, however, should not await replies to the cables suggested in paragraph 3. It seems desirable to plan for continuation of hostilities into the indefinite future.[39]

Colonel Jackson approved Project Eagle II, and on the same day the chief of OSS-ETO, Colonel J. Russell Forgan,[40] did so.[41]

It is completely understandable that the Yalta agreement had a hugely demoralizing effect on Poles in Great Britain, including, of course, on Polish soldiers. In a report dated February 21, 1945, Dasher wrote to Casey:

1. *Several days ago the undersigned received private information to the effect that the Polish military authorities are delaying the issuance of orders authorizing the screening and selection of the forty (40) Polish soldiers to be trained for the OSS under Eagle Project No. II, pending the clarification of the status of the Polish Armed Forces following the Crimean conference.*
2. *In order to check this the undersigned yesterday, Tuesday, 20 February 1945, conferred with Colonel Lunkiewicz,[42] Officer for Special Assignments to the Polish Minister of National Defense.*
3. *Among other things, Colonel Lunkiewicz told the undersigned that the Polish military authorities continue their lively interest in the project launched by*

Colonel J. Russell Forgan, head of OSS London Branch in 1945. (Photo US National Archives)

them for the OSS and that they are most eager to continue to cooperate with the OSS in the future. The orders for the screening cannot be issued until final decisions are reached at the highest levels of Polish military command as to the future of the Polish armed forces in this part of the world. Colonel Lunkiewicz assured me that, if the Polish army remains, as heretofore, an autonomous force, the respective orders will be published as soon as practicable and, if at all possible, in good time to enable the training to begin, as originally planned, on 1 April 1945.

4. *Therefore, the precise status of Eagle project No. II, at this particular time, may be described as being in the indefinite stage. Its further development is entirely predicated on political events, over which neither the OSS nor the Polish military authorities with whom we are dealing, could conceivably have any control.*[43]

At the close of the training of the Project Eagle members,[44] a lunch was held at the restaurant of Claridge's Hotel. During the ceremonies, which were documented by an OSS photographer, the following remarks by General Donovan were read aloud:

Graduation lunch of Project Eagle members at Claridge's Hotel. (Photo US National Archives)

> *Please extend my cordial greetings and sincere expressions of appreciation to General KUKIEL on the occasion of graduation of the Polish soldiers whom he has so kindly placed at our disposal. The superior spirit of cooperation shown by our POLISH friends on this project is another example of what can be achieved through close coordination of the Allied war effort. My congratulations to the School's Commandant, Major SZYMANOWSKI and his colleagues on the faculty of the AMERICAN–POLISH School of Specialists for the outstanding achievement in organizing the School and training the personnel. I feel confident that the brave POLISH soldiers who will serve with us will make a real contribution to the Allied Cause.*[45]

The Americans at OSS London understood what impact the Yalta Conference and its decisions could have on the morale of the Polish soldiers and their officers. The remarks attributed to General Donovan cited above had been written in reality by the OSS SI chief in Washington, Whitney H. Shepardson, and a group of his associates who were visiting London at that time. Shepardson informed General Donovan on March 19, 1945, that:

1. You will be interested to see, from the attached correspondence, that Joe Dasher's Poles have graduated. 2. Likewise, you will be interested in your cable (and possibly also in my cable!) which Lester and Dasher read at the graduation ceremonies. 3. I have nothing to say except this shows fast footwork on the part of the London boys.[46]

Although the OSS and Donovan could not affect the strategic and political decisions of President Roosevelt, they were ready to cooperate with the Poles to the end. While the members of Project Eagle were getting ready to be dropped into Germany, the armies of the Western Allies were moving eastward, ever closer to the Rhine River, which was crossed at Remagen on March 7, 1945, by the Ninth Armored Division of the US First Army.

While the sixteen missions of Project Eagle were preparing to be parachuted into enemy territory, the Polish Section of SI London continued its efforts to organize Project Eagle II. Its administrative officer, Lieutenant A. R. Waters, sent a report to Colonel Dasher in which he wrote:

1. Major S. Szymanowski, Commandant of the Polish School of Specialists, 30 Bryanston Square, London, W1, in a discussion with this officer disclosed the following information which he requested the reporting officer to relay for your attention. 2. Pressure is being exerted by USSR upon British officials to have Polish units now fighting with the Allies withdrawn. Further pressure is being exerted by this same Power to have all existing relations between Great Britain and émigré Polish authorities broken. 3. The Polish authorities believe that if outward active collaboration between the Americans and Poles is evident in any capacity, the British government will be afforded an excuse for severing relationships and recalling all active and financial support to these Poles. Under present agreements Great Britain would be forced to carry Polish military units fighting with them until the cessation of the present hostilities and for a six months period thereafter. 4. Major Szymanowski believes that if the American-Polish School of Specialists is continued under its present administrative organization, this will be regarded by Great Britain as an act of collaboration between the USA and the Polish émigré government and will thereby afford them the opportunity to comply with Soviet requests for immediate isolation of all émigré Poles and their affiliated divisions. 5. In conclusion Major Szymanowski declared that the secret but highest consideration of the Polish authorities is full and complete cooperation with the United States and that with this in mind, the Poles feel that if financial support could be given to their training cadre without the knowledge of any Allied Power, the present satisfactory schooling could be kept in operation to the mutual benefit of both the American and Polish authorities.[47]

Clearly, the Poles were providing Colonel Dasher with a funding option in the event that British authorities succumbed to Soviet pressure regarding the Polish Armed Forces in the West.

Colonel Dasher was not one to give up easily, and again pressured the Poles to begin a selection process and later training of Polish soldiers for a second group of Project Eagle volunteers. On March 22, 1945, he wrote to Colonel Łunkiewicz:

> *Referring to my letter of 8 January 1945, addressed to Lieutenant General M. Kukiel, Polish Minister of National Defense, and our conversation of this date, may state that the Office of Strategic Services in the European Theater of Operations reiterates its request for the continuation of the Polish School of Specialists, 30 Bryanston Square, and for the assignment of a new group of forty (40) Polish soldiers. Also, we request that the new course of training begin as soon as practicable.*[48]

Despite Dasher's determination and enthusiasm, Washington decided:

> *With Project Eagle No. II not being able to get under way until 1 May and the students not having completed their training until 1 October 1945, and then another month required for briefing and with further reference to Washington incoming cable no. 14724, it has definitely been decided that OSS/ETO will not undertake Eagle Project No. II.*

The memo was signed by Deputy Director of OSS London Captain Lester Armour on March 23, 1945.[49] By that date six of sixteen missions had been parachuted into Germany and one of the twelve agents, Sergeant Antoni Markotny, had been killed. The remaining nine two-man missions were dispatched into Germany during the next two and a half weeks.

PENETRATING THE REICH

The SI leadership in London and their superiors in Washington understood that parachuting agents into Germany to engage in secret intelligence work would mean overcoming enormous obstacles. Germany was an enemy country with frequent document controls, and communication with London was difficult at best. There were no anti-Nazi resistance groups there similar to the French *Maquis*, the Polish *Armia Krajowa*, or Tito's Partisans in Yugoslavia. The Allied intelligence effort was done "in the dark" without up-to-date knowledge of the terrain and with no local assistance. There were very few safe houses, and information on them was often out of date.

SI London knew that all agents dropped into Germany or Austria would be enormously challenged with everyday life as well as with sending information gathered to London. Nevertheless, on September 1, 1944, the first OSS agent was dropped into Germany. From that time until war's end, OSS ETO in London sent thirty-three more missions by parachute into Germany and Austria[50] and organized sixty-six Field Detachment Groups to spy just beyond the German lines. A list of missions dispatched by OSS ETO from London into Germany and Austria is provided in appendix 3.

After the German defeat in the Battle of the Bulge at the end of January 1945, the OSS reorganized its field detachments, whose task became to support units of the US Army rather than gather strategic intelligence. Their tasks, chiefly recruiting and cooperating with the local populace living near the front lines, differentiated them from the goals of the agents who were parachuted further behind German lines. The latter came from various nations that had been overrun and occupied by the Germans. Individuals or two-man groups were tasked with gathering and forwarding information directly to SI London via radio, and failing that, were to give the information to the nearest American military intelligence unit (G-2). A list of the one hundred and one field detachment missions sent into Germany, Austria, and Holland is provided in appendix 2.[51]

The first agent to be parachuted into the Third Reich, on September 1, 1944, was a German named Jupp Kappius,[52] code-named Downend. He was a member of the *Kampfbund* organization that fought against "communism, capitalism, alcohol, meat-eaters etc." He was able to organize an effective intelligence network that penetrated military and industrial objects in the Ruhr region. Downend was not equipped with radio equipment and sent two reports to Switzerland by courier. He was one of seven agents of German nationality recruited by OSS SI among the members of the Free Germany Committee who were organized into five missions. Collectively, they were known at the TOOL missions, with one group being code-named Hammer and another Pickaxe.[53]

Among the remaining twenty-nine missions, the largest ethnic group represented was made up of the sixteen Polish missions of Project Eagle. Of the agents in these thirty-four groups dropped into Germany, Austria, and Holland, four were killed on landing or shortly thereafter.[54]

In the beginning the plan was to train the Polish agents of Project Eagle for six months and end their training on April 1, 1945, following which they would be sent into action around May 1. However, the Battle of the Bulge hastened that plan. In January 1945, Casey, Forgan, and Colonel Ed Gamble met with representatives of the G-2 sections of the Sixth and Twelfth US Army Groups and the US Seventh Army. During that meeting the issue of using the OSS and especially its intelligence agents was discussed:

> *All of these men were very strong in their view that it was of much greater importance to have agents placed the other side of the Rhine in key transport centers than to have agents move a few miles across the line and return. They were acutely interested in what OSS could produce in the way of that kind of intelligence during the first half of 1945. They were planning on the necessity of fighting through to the fall of 1945, and they had been shaken into an acute awareness of the dearth of intelligence by the Runstedt [sic] offensive. General Sibert [G-2 12th AG] said they were going blind into Germany and that they did not want to overlook any bet which might yield intelligence of a strategic nature. General Harrison [G-2 6th AG] . . . protested against an excessive caution, pointing out that we should not hesitate to take risks with our agents while a thousand men a day were being killed along the front. Colonel Forgan was able to assure him that we had already decided to abandon any caution which might have characterized . . . previous [OSS] efforts to penetrate Germany.[55]*

It was, among other reasons, because of this meeting that Casey moved up the date to March 1, 1945, for parachuting the Polish agents. This date was subsequently changed and it was only on March 18 that the first group was dispatched from the Dijon base, which became a favorite place for OSS personnel and agents. It was one of the first of fifty-four such OSS missions to be flown into Germany from Dijon. OSS staff waited sometimes for several days for a mission to deploy agents and spent their time enjoying the good local food and wine.

Prior to leaving London and beginning their missions, agents underwent a short course to reacquaint themselves with the lessons they had been taught during training. Special attention was paid to defensive techniques, obtaining their opponents' order of battle, and transmitting information to base. In other words, instructors tried to remind them of key things they needed to remember in order to carry out and survive their missions.

In the meantime, the quick advance of the Allied forces caused revisions to the list of cities that were the targets for spying. In the end the following locations stayed on the list: Ansbach, Aschaffenburg, Augsburg,

Chemnitz, Erfurt, Giessen, Goettingen, Hanau, Kassel, Magdeburg, Osnabrück, Passau (two groups), Regensburg, Stendal, and Wittenberg. At first the plan called for the first five groups to be dispatched at the end of February–beginning of March, and the rest later in March and April. All of them were to be sent in the dark, with no support group waiting and without knowledge of any safe houses. Agents were ordered to send reports via their SSTR-1 radios;[56] they were charged with locating the electricity that would enable them to do so on their own. They were to report on army movements, fortifications and defensive installations, supplies, and German factories.

Sending information to their base in London was one of the greater problems they had to wrestle with after landing in Germany. Only 20 percent of all groups that SI London dropped anywhere, not just in Germany, were able to communicate with their base. Only one mission, Chauffeure, of the twenty-one missions dispatched to Germany and equipped with the SSTR-1, was able to make radio contact. The radio's problem was lack of electricity. Only in Austria, where agents were able to find small resistance groups with whom they could cooperate and who helped provide security, were the agents able to access a power source and transmit information to base. Without some local support, agents were in danger of being quickly located by the Gestapo or SS units.

In early 1945, the Americans began to equip agents with a new, much lighter radio set known as J-E (Joan-Eleanor).[57] This was the equipment issued to the four missions that were able to communicate successfully with London. Unfortunately, only ten such sets were distributed to agents before war's end, and none of them made it into the hands of the members of Project Eagle. It is interesting that two of four missions dispatched directly from London—including Downend—were issued no radio equipment whatsoever, and were forced to communicate by pouch, a procedure that limited the value of the information being forwarded due to the time it took for the information to arrive in London. Only about 4 percent of agents sent into action by SI London and equipped with the SSTR-1 radio were able to communicate at all with their base.[58] The various issues connected with technical communications problems in the field were duly reported by the Project Eagle members to their Polish and American superiors upon return to England.

Before the missions began, the Polish and other Joes, as the agents who jumped into enemy territory were called in US military jargon, were offered three types of pills: six sleeping tablets, six stimulatory tablets, and one small suicide pill.[59] The agents were dressed in overalls known as the camouflage striptease jumpsuits, made of heavy-canvas mottled dark green and brown cloth, described in an OSS report as "resembling more than anything else an under-water diver minus helmet," with numerous pockets that concealed a sidearm, a knife to help disengage the agent from his parachute in case he got hung up in a tree on landing, a French flashlight with two spare batteries, one can of RAF emergency rations, and a small flask of rum. His head was protected by a helmet with cushions of sponge rubber, and the outfit was complete with leather gloves and protective goggles.[60]

The pressure on the agents and on the dispatchers who flew with them was enormous. Bad weather, German night fighters, and strong anti-aircraft fire resulted in abortive flights that returned to base with exhausted crews and agents such as the members of the Manhattan Mission who were dropped on their eighth attempt. John W. Raczkiewicz, the supervising officer of the Polish Section of SI London, wrote in a report to the deputy director of the Polish Section SI London, Major Louis Dups, on March 26, 1945, about one of the missions that had to turn back without dropping its agents:

1. *The Manhattan team was shot up en route to the target. No one was hurt.*
    The plane returned to base with the Joes.

2. *Lieutenant Waters[61] requests the following:*
    a. Supplies:
        Whiskey
        Cigarettes
        Mail—personal, for himself and Lt. Lysz[62] . . .
    e. *He* [Waters] *would like to go to Paris after his job is completed.*

The flights and drops of other Polish missions that took place according to plan and were successful did not shield the agents and their flight companions from stress on the airfields and on the planes.[63]

In one of his later reports, Lieutenant Raczkiewicz wrote:

I arrived at Area O, 16 March 1945, and took custody of Martini and Sidecar. I received a call to report at the Harrington airfield. Arriving at the field I was informed that the flight was cancelled. I returned to Area "O" with the Joes and awaited further orders.

On 17 March I took off in a B-24 with Lt. Hadrian[64] and the two teams and arrived at the Dijon airport where I waited in an open field for two and a half hours before Capt. Beau came with transportation. The delay was no fault of Capt. Beau as I couldn't reach him by phone because planes were taken [sic] off and it was impossible to get across the airstrip to a phone. . . .

On 18 March I was informed that the operation was to take place that night. We dressed the Joes at home and had them at the field at the designated hour. The plane took off at 21:30 and returned at 0100, completing their mission very successfully. The dispatcher had a little difficulty with Gawor as he hesitated when he gave the order to jump but he overcame that by giving him a push.

The Joes behaved fairly well all the time they were in my custody. I made things as comfortable for them as I possibly could within reason. I fed them enough liquor to keep them satisfied which was my most difficult problem as liquor was very scarce. I slept in the same room with them and never left them out of my sight. . . .

Recommendations:

1. *The Polish officers who go with the conducting officer are unnecessary as they are of no help and at times are detrimental as the conducting officer has to take care of them as well as the men. . . .*[65]

John W. Raczkiewicz
Lieutenant, CAO[66]

In the end, and despite the fact that the Americans wanted to exclude officers from the School of Specialists from accompanying their graduates to waiting stations and then to airfields on the continent, five Polish officers (Major Szymanowski, Major Sobecki, Ensign Łysz, Ensign Arwar, and Ensign Hadrian) were allowed to accompany the Polish parachutists of Project Eagle. The main reason for the change in procedure was the "loss" in transit of four graduates of the school by their American chaperones.[67]

The period from the drop into Germany by the individual mission of Project Eagle until the agents' first contact with Allied forces ranged from a few weeks (the Sidecar and Martini missions) to just a few days (Singapore Sling and Hot Punch). After revealing their identities and their missions to the forces that overran them, they were interrogated multiple times, by military police, by G-2 attached to the liberating army, then at Base X in Luxembourg by representatives of the OSS, and finally by members of the SI Polish Section in London.

THE SITUATION IN GERMANY AND THE REICH'S USE OF TERROR

The evaluations of the agents during their training spoke of patriotism as their most important reason for volunteering for their dangerous missions.

There were other reasons as well. Their records indicate that all thirty-two members of Project Eagle had served in the Wehrmacht, and that an additional ten family members had been or were currently forced to serve in the German Army. Four of their family members were in concentration camps, and a dozen agents had served as forced labor before being conscripted. They were no doubt generally aware of what life in the Reich was like because they had lived part of their adult lives in Hitler's Germany. They knew that in 1942 sterner controls had been introduced by Justice Minister Otto Thierack to meet real or imagined challenges faced by the Nazi state. Faced with drives against the Jews and the churches and military setbacks in North Africa and Stalingrad, the German public had become more subdued and concerned about the future. Opposition to the Nazi regime had emerged at universities and churches and among officers in the Wehrmacht. One group of conservative foes of the regime known as the "Kreisau Circle," consisting of well-known German landowners and prominent Catholic and Protestant clergy opposed to Hitler's regime, met to plan a post-Nazi, postwar state administration.

The German public's mood was changing as well, initially under the impact of the British and American bombing campaign. In 1939 Reich Air Minister Hermann Göring had assured inhabitants of German cities along the Rhine that German air defenses would be strong and prevent British planes from penetrating them; otherwise, the Germans could call him "Meier."[68] Göring's bravado notwithstanding, Germany experienced the horror and displacement of a British bombing campaign that targeted military installations beginning in March 1940 and German cities shortly thereafter. The campaign intensified and expanded when the Americans entered the war and began a strategic bombing campaign that was coordinated with the Royal Air Force.

Over the course of the war, the Allies dropped nearly 1.5 million tons of bombs on Germany or on areas under German control, of which more than one-third fell on larger cities. More than 3.5 million homes were destroyed, and 300,000 civilians died as a result of the raids. Another 780,000 were injured and 7.5 million left homeless. Approximately 5 million people were evacuated. During the final, sixteen-week period of the war in Europe, from January 1 to April 26, 1945, more than 400 air missions were flown against German cities.[69] The damage to railways, roads, bridges, dams, and industrial installations was severe and the authorities responded by engaging between 1 and 1.5 million people in work resulting from air raid damage from the autumn of 1944 on.[70]

The Ruhr Valley, Germany's primary source of coal and steel, produced 80 percent of Germany's coal. The war industry required a supply of no less than 22,000 freight cars of coal per day. By the end of November 1944, the coal shipments had been reduced to 5,000 cars per day.[71] With the loss of industrial Silesia to the Soviets in February 1945, it became the sole producer of coal. The Allied bombing campaign against the vital transportation network was crippling the German war effort. Travel by train was spotty due to the shortage of coal and the bombing and strafing of the rails and trains, which wreaked havoc on the once-legendary on-time schedules of the German railroads. Streetcar transportation in the cities was heavily affected.

Serious shortages of coal for heating and electricity for lighting and cooking made life in the cities especially difficult. Cooking and bathing were subject to the availability of power and water. Life in rural areas was somewhat easier to bear, as families were better able to do with what was on hand. At the same time, people fleeing the bombed cities and populations evacuated by the Wehrmacht in the East and in the West added to the large numbers of prisoners of war, foreign workers, and concentration camp inmates crossing the countryside, creating a sense of overcrowding and unease for rural and small-town dwellers.

Food rations were cut severely during the fall of 1943, affecting such staples of the German diet as bread, meat, potatoes, fish, and cheese. Potatoes in particular were in short supply due to an overabundance of rain and early cold weather. As rations shrank, the black market that had arisen earlier in the war flourished to provide profits for purveyors of food and goods furnished to those who were willing to pay the price. Heavy penalties were imposed on those found guilty. One judge suggested that those convicted of black-market slaughtering be castrated near sausage factories to add to meat supplies. As rations were cut, city dwellers were advised to organize vegetable gardens, while Germans in general were advised to turn to the forests to supplement their diets. Early optimism in the Reich consequently waned as a two-front war resulted in sustained hardship and shortages.

The Nazi Party was aware of public sentiments and tracked what people were saying and doing. Special courts had been established before the war to intimidate the public; their verdicts were not subject to appeal, and sentences were often carried out summarily. By 1940 there were fifty-five of them, managed by younger justices who were more amenable to following Nazi Party directives. By 1943 the special courts dealt with 73 percent of all legal cases, and in 1942 they found only 8 percent of those charged to be "not guilty."[72] An enormous number of soldiers who had lost their units or deserted from them, escaped forced laborers, members of persecuted minorities, "defeatists," and Germans who publicly voiced or showed their opposition to the Nazi regime all faced harsh exemplary punishment.

The campaign heightened after the attempted assassination of Hitler on August 20, 1944, at Rastenburg in East Prussia. A group of high-ranking military officers planned to kill Hitler and overthrow the government and then seek peace with the Western Allies. Hitler survived and the security services rounded up and arrested 7,000 people of whom 5,000 were executed, not all of whom were engaged in the plot but were victims of internal Nazi Party politics. In the aftermath of the attempted coup, extended power passed to a few of Hitler's closest henchmen, who sought every opportunity to prevent a possible rebellion against the increasingly ludicrous orders that were being issued by Bormann, Göring, and Himmler. The security services and regional propaganda offices noted an outpouring of relief among the general public that the Führer had survived the attack. Officers of the Wehrmacht were torn between their oaths of loyalty to Hitler and an increasingly widespread belief in the inevitability of surrender. In the West, where the Allies made efforts to convince Germans not to resist, opposition was palpable.

At the same time, many examples of enthusiastic pursuit of the terror campaign were noted and some observed by the Eagle agents. The men of the Zombie Mission were in close proximity to a mass demonstration in Regensburg on April 23, 1945, where some one thousand men gathered before the office of the county municipal governor, the *Kreisleiter*, to demonstrate their desire for a peaceful end to the war in their city. Arrests ensued, and the cathedral pastor of the city, Dr. Johann Maier, was arrested and executed along with another man.[73] The Zombie Mission was extracted on April 27, 1945.

The Sidecar Mission was dropped in the vicinity of Ansbach on March 18, 1945. They were not present in the city, nor did they report on an incident that took place on April 18 when a nineteen-year-old theology student named Robert Limpert decided to act to prevent his town from being senselessly destroyed like so many other German urban centers. His act of defiance was sabotage: he cut some telephone wires that once but no longer connected the town commandant's office with a Wehrmacht base that had recently moved. He was observed by two Hitler Youth who reported what they had witnessed, and Limpert was subsequently arrested by a policeman who found incriminating evidence and a pistol at the student's home. The town commandant quickly established a summary court to try the young man, and Limpert was found guilty and sentenced to immediate execution.

A noose was placed around his neck at the town hall gate, but Limpert managed to wriggle free and was quickly caught after a few steps with the help of a crowd that had assembled to watch the execution. He was again strung up and hanged, but this time the rope broke and Limpert fell to the ground. The third attempt at hanging was successful, and the commandant ordered his body to hang "until it stinks" and subsequently appropriated a bicycle and pedaled his way out of town. Four hours later the US Army entered Ansbach and cut down the body of Robert Limpert.[74] The Sidecar Mission was recovered on April 24.

The Daiquiri Mission was dropped on the night of March 21–22, 1945, and directed to operate in the vicinity of Hanau. The local *Arbeitsamt* directed them to report to Aschaffenburg for work, where they arrived on the evening of March 23 and found the city devastated. The team spent the night in an overcrowded air-raid shelter, which they described in detail: the toilets were broken and lack of water caused them to issue a sickening odor, those with no beds slept on the cement floor, and the panic during an air raid was said to be indescribable, with people struggling against police guards to try to force themselves to perceived safety. In their written report the team noted that the large factories had been destroyed, and that the first spearheads of American tanks had reached the city on March 25. While the defenders had managed to destroy the concrete bridge over the River Main around noon on that day, they failed to blow up the railroad bridge. The failure to destroy the latter led to the summary execution of a Wehrmacht captain and lieutenant, and their bodies were left hanging for two days. The team further reported that white flags hung by people in the hope that the Americans would spare their homes, shops, and churches were forced to be taken down by party members, local officials, or soldiers dressed as civilians following instructions received from Berlin. On April 3 the Americans overran the team in Wertheim, and the next day they were evacuated to the rear.

The confusion and dilemmas faced by the local populations were widespread and reported in various archival records. After more than fifty years, agent Zbigniew Strzeliński/Paprzycki recalled in correspondence his recollections of this troubled time. He managed to obtain lodging officially with an older gentleman after delivering his injured teammate, Tadeusz Rawski, to a hospital in Osterhofen in April 1945. He lived some three kilometers from the hospital and visited his teammate there two or three times a week until the Americans overran the area. Paprzycki became fond of his host because he had found out that after a few drinks the German was wont to express himself critically about Hitler despite the fact that he had been warned not to do so and had been punished for it. His host had died in the intervening three and a half decades, but the man's neighbor recalled talk of an "English agent" named Karl Essauer (Paprzycki's cover name in wartime Germany) who had lived with the old dissident and subsequently disappeared abruptly at that time. Thirty-five years after the war's end Paprzycki intended to seek out "the good Germans" whom he remembered from his time as an agent, but by 1980 none remained to be found, including his former landlord.[75]

In the East, the Soviet Army enjoyed a five-to-one advantage over German troops facing them in German-occupied Poland, and on January 12, 1945, it launched its Vistula-Oder offensive, which in the course of two weeks battled its way three hundred miles west and crossed the Oder, bringing Soviet and Polish troops to within forty-three miles of Berlin. The German Eastern Front had collapsed and with it, millions of ethnic Germans fled west, along with stragglers, wounded, and deserters from the Wehrmacht. Berlin ordered that approximately 113,000 concentration camp prisoners be marched elsewhere from camps in the path of the advancing Soviet Army to other, unspecified camps further west, in order for them not to fall into the hands of the Soviets. The economic benefit that they represented to the Reich as slave laborers was surely negligible by this time, but they were marched west regardless. Upwards of a third of the inmates who could not keep up in the frigid conditions of January–February 1945 were killed or simply died along the way.[76]

Word of the tremendous disaster that was enveloping an area steadily shrinking in size as Allied armies converged from the east and the west soon spread, and the growing fear among Nazi Party members and Wehrmacht enlisted men and officers alike, and the public in general, resulted in a new wave of terror and repression by those in power. Many Germans exhausted by the deprivations and the terror they were forced to suffer at the hands of a collapsing regime came to view the situation in the closing months of the war via the adage that "an end with terror is better than terror without end."

Summary courts martial had been established by decree of Reich Justice Minister Otto Thierack on February 15, 1945, in order, as Head of the Party Chancellery Martin Bormann wrote, "to ruthlessly suppress every sign of disintegration, cowardice and defeatism with the death sentences of the summary courts martial."[77] A few weeks later they were provided with vehicles and fuel and became "flying courts martial" that could appear any place. They pronounced sentence on the accused after a brief hearing, and the verdict was carried out publicly and instantly. The intended effect was to intimidate a war-weary population who were expected to accept the delusional policies of Hitler and the Nazi elite and, especially in the West, to deter soldiers from surrendering to the Allies. One report noted: "Especially in the course of the rapid withdrawal of German troops from France and Belgium, until the beginning of September [1944] it actually often happened that entire units surrendered to the Allies without a fight. It is therefore hardly surprising that the proportion of 'missing' in the west is 61% of all casualties, in the east it is only 20.3%."[78]

The Allies countered with information that briefly informed the German populace of the situation in their country. Millions of leaflets were dropped over Germany on March 28, 1945, advising people:

> *All German soldiers remaining on the left bank of the Rhine between Switzerland and Holland are prisoners of war of the Allies. Marshal Montgomery's bridgehead near Wesel is 35 kilometers wide and in some areas 20 kilometers deep. New units are streaming without interruption over numerous newly constructed bridges to the east bank. In the Remagen bridgehead General Hodge's troops have penetrated the German defensive front and have advanced 36 kilometers to Limburg on the Lahn. The city itself is in Allied hands. General Patton's advance over the Rhine at Oppenheim led to the fall of Darmstadt two days ago. The advanced armored elements of the Third U.S. Army have crossed the Main near Aschaffenburg. Other American units have entered Frankfurt. Until now more than 10,000 German soldiers have become prisoners of war every day during the month of March. . . .*
>
> *In East Prussia the German resistance in the area of Frischen Haffs has collapsed. During the past two days the Russians have captured 21,000 prisoners of war in this area. South of Oppeln Marshal Schukov's forces have captured Leobschuetz and Neisse and after crossing Upper Silesia have penetrated Czechoslovakia. North of the Plattensee in Hungary the Russians have captured the important transportation network Papa and are positioned 65 kilometers from the Austrian border.[79]*

The goal of the Allied leaflets was to persuade Germans not to resist the invading Allies.

In the East that was an argument that for the most part fell on deaf ears. The mass flight of Germans from occupied Poland was due to both rumors of Soviet atrocities and organized evacuation starting in the summer of 1944 and continuing through the spring of 1945. Still, some chose to remain, and the approximate number of those who fled before the Soviets is subject to wide interpretation. The notion of surrender to the Americans in the West, on the other hand, met with increasing approval by civilians and soldiers alike as the Allies pressed on and the territory still under the control of the Third Reich shrank still further. By the end of April 1945, after two months of fighting, 325,000 Wehrmacht soldiers had surrendered in the so-called Ruhr pocket.

By the time the agents of Project Eagle penetrated the Reich, Hitler had sought to require Germans to follow the example set by the Soviets in 1941 when the Nazis pursued a scorched-earth policy to deny invading forces virtually everything that could assist the Allies in their march forward. He issued a decree on March 19, 1945, that all military centers, transportation, communication infrastructure, and supplies be destroyed before they could become of use to the enemy. The population in these areas was to be evacuated. A few days later, Martin Bormann reiterated the order and followed it up by writing: "The enemy must be brought in the next few days to realize that he has intruded into a hinterland filled with a fanatical will to resist. . . . Any concern for the civilian population can play no role under present circumstances."[80] Bridges that remained operative were ordered destroyed on April 13. As the Western Allies advanced, signs of deep opposition became obvious as people who sought a quick end to the war refused to see their *Heimat* be sacrificed in a last-ditch stand against the Allies. The German population, civilian and military alike, faced a dilemma: remain faithful to their patriotism and various oaths and defend their part of the Reich, or give in without resistance? The agents of Project Eagle reported various reactions to this quandary in their mission reports.

There were indications of army indiscipline. A Party District Leader in the Halle-Merseburg region reported a minor mutiny of two hundred soldiers from a panzer division, and complained about the inability of police checks at stations to pick up deserters. At the fall of Trier, most of the *Volkssturm* defenders were said to have gone over to the enemy. Others did all they could to avoid military duty.[81] By the end of March, only 21 percent of a sample of soldiers captured by the Western Allies still professed faith in the Führer (a drop from 62 percent at the beginning of January), while 72 percent had none. A mere 7 percent still believed in German victory; 89 percent had no such belief.[82]

The agents of Project Eagle were dropped in rural areas near towns with instructions to scout out specific targets such as railroad marshalling yards, factories, and objectives of military importance. As expected, their activities took them into harm's way, and they encountered challenges that some of the teams overcame with ingenuity and determination, as the mission reports in the following chapter demonstrate.

Several teams were dropped far from their dropping pinpoints. The Sidecar Mission had its pinpoint changed before takeoff and landed only 5 kilometers from its newly designated drop site, but 113 kilometers from where its papers were to have placed it. The Highball Mission landed 110 kilometers from its pinpoint, with deadly consequences for one agent and a long hike for the second team member, who gathered no intelligence along the way. The Planters Punch Mission found itself 80 kilometers from its designated pinpoint and across the wide and well-patrolled Elbe River. The Orange Blossom team landed 33 kilometers from where its agents were supposed to have been inserted. The Tom Collins Mission had to cover 65 kilometers to reach its designated drop point. One agent was killed on landing and another went missing, presumed tortured and executed immediately after landing. Another broke his ankle on landing and spent weeks in a German hospital recuperating until liberation by the Allies. In all, six of sixteen missions were dropped in the wrong place; nine men were dropped into enemy hands; eight used their Colt automatics; eight were detained or arrested; and none provided any intelligence by radio.[83]

The mission reports commented on the attitude of the German populace toward the war; the monetary situation; food and general conditions; and, of course, military observations. The reports reflected the agents' blue-collar backgrounds; they were specifically chosen because it was felt that they would more easily mingle with forced laborers, of whom there were approximately 7 million, who took the place of the 18.2 million men who volunteered for or were conscripted into the German armed forces during the war.

By the time the men of Project Eagle were dropped into Germany, the expertly forged ration cards they had been issued by the OSS were practically useless because they were no longer honored by most shopkeepers or by the population at large. In many locales money, which there seemed to be a lot of, was useless as well, and so a barter system evolved. The Eagles each had two small diamonds that some used to obtain food. That meant that eventually the agents had to register with officials to obtain lodging and food and to legalize their stays, which then brought them into contact with police and other officials who checked their documents. All but one of the agents had their papers checked on more than one occasion by the civilian police, the criminal police, the *Volkssturm*, the SS, or the Gestapo. Only Sergeant Czarnecki's papers were never checked.

Why was Sergeant Rawski admitted to a German hospital with a broken ankle on April 13 by a doctor who was certain that his injury could not have occurred by "jumping over a ditch"? Why did the documents of

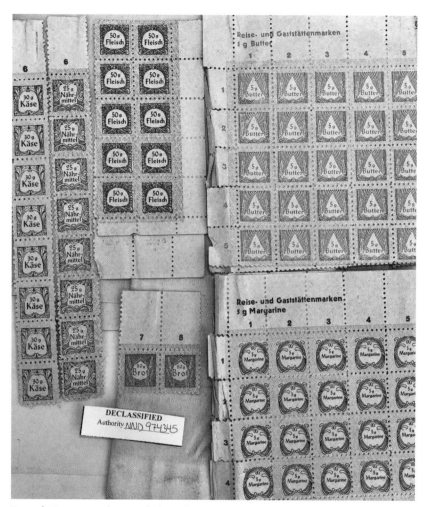

Forged German ration cards issued to Project Eagle agents. (Photo US National Archives)

twenty-nine of the agents, some checked on numerous occasions, not raise any questions by the various police and other officials? Was it sheer luck or war weariness of a society that was going through the motions while waiting for the Americans to overrun them? Perhaps the answer is a little of both. Sergeant Adrian's papers turned out to have been inadequately prepared, and as a result he was taken to a Gestapo prison and tortured, escaping sure death by a fluke: the American bombing of Halle on April 6, 1945. None of the other agents had the misfortune of having been questioned by a German Special Court or Court Martial. Some of the agents had their identities questioned by American, British, and French officers to whom they identified themselves as OSS agents, because their forged documents were deemed to be genuine and therefore, their Allied captors reasoned, they were not the agents they purported to be. Although Sergeant Strzeliński was roughed up by GIs as they searched his room, he and other agents who were initially held by their allies were not treated like Sergeant Adrian had been by the Gestapo. And Adrian's mission report shows that he got his revenge. That may also explain why agent Adrian's documentation disappeared after the war in an effort to shield him from the possible consequences of his application of summary justice.

As the mission reports that follow show, the Project Eagle teams were dropped into a Germany experiencing terror and shortages of transportation, electricity, communications, and food that could not have been somehow remedied by the OSS planners in London and Washington. The reports are divided roughly into the jumps that took place in March and then April 1945.

3

THE AGENTS AND THEIR
MISSION REPORTS

During their selection and training, candidates for Project Eagle were asked to compile a brief bio. They used their pseudonyms and current Polish rank, and responded to a set of questions that were meant to help their Polish and American handlers determine where they might best be used. The bios occasionally contain comments on their qualifications by the OSS staff. The real names of most of the agents were found on their employment contracts with the OSS. The agents' bios are paraphrased below. Each mission report, excised and with obvious errors, follows.

SIDECAR MISSION

The Agents

Private Józef Gawor (real name: Józef Bambynek), 24-year-old observer, born in Janów Miejski in the county of Katowice. His nearest kin was his father, Brunon Bambynek; address: Nikiszowiec, Katowice County, ul. Dolna 18. Gawor had finished eight classes of primary school and three classes of vocational school, and later worked in the mines. He was drafted into the German Army in 1941, but at his father's request was exempted. In 1943 he was conscripted again and sent to Breslau, and then to Normandy. He surrendered to the Americans on June 30, 1944. He knew Silesia quite well.

Corporal Gerhard Nowicki (real name: Gerard Haroński), 26-year-old radio operator, born in Nowa Wieś in Katowice county. His nearest kin was his wife, Małgorzata Harońska; address: Nowa Wieś, ul. 3 Maja 77. Nowicki finished eight years of primary school and before the war worked

DECLASSIFIED
Authority NND 974345

Photographs taken by the OSS for Józef Gawor's forged German military documents. (Photo US National Archives)

in Neuenburg and Beuthen in Germany while living in Poland. At the end of 1939 he was drafted into the German Army and spent a half year in or near Aachen. After France's capitulation he was sent to Normandy and Brittany. Nowicki was a range-finder in an anti-aircraft battery. He surrendered to the Americans with a group of sixteen other Poles on June 30, 1944, near Cherbourg.[1]

Sidecar Mission Report[2]

The members of the Sidecar mission were [text excised] *aged 24,* and [text excised], *26.* [Text excised] *the W/T operator and leader, in civilian life had done a great deal of smuggling across the Polish-German border and hence had an excellent background for his assignment.* [Text excised] *the observatory, had been a* [text excised]. *Both men were given the cover of Czech miners evacuated into their target area from Hindenburg in Prussia and from Beuthen* in Silesia. They were given foreign worker documents. Their target was Ansbach area, where they were to report military traffic and the location of German arms and supply centers.

The men were given 25,000 German Rms [Reichsmarks] and two diamonds, valued at approximately $300 each. They returned to Special Funds 8,500 Rms and reported that they had lost both diamonds, by swallowing them when arrested.

The agents were parachuted from a B-24 based at Dijon on 18 March and overrun on 24 April. Following is the report of the Polish Section on the Sidecar mission, as given by [text excised] W/T operator.

Air Operations
The team was dropped at 23:45 hours, 18 March 1945, from a height of 600 to 700 feet, about 5 kilometers away from the pin-point. [Text excised] landed on plowed field and [text excised] after making several somersaults in the air before straightening out, landed OK near some gardens. They did not meet until about 04:00 hours in the morning because they were searching in opposite directions. Both agents reported the landings were very soft.

First Contacts with People and Authorities
After they found each other they went to look for the container and found it on the edge of the village with four civilians, one armed with a carbine, trying to do something with it, but looking hesitant and perhaps even frightened of it. The agents decided to take the container by force. Gawor took the pistols and went around to one side and started shooting while [text excised] went straight for the container. [Text excised] fired fourteen shots and two of the Germans fell. The rest ran away. The agents then broke up the containers, took out the equipment and ran with it for about an hour, finally hiding in a forest. Later on in the morning, from their hiding place, they saw the container being taken away on a horse-drawn wagon. They were quite certain there must have been a search going on for them so they stayed in these woods for about a week, until 26 March. Wertestrtie [sic] was the name of the village to which they went after hiding out for this week. There they reported directly to the Burgomaster. The Burgomaster gave them food and lodging after looking over their papers and later, the men suspect, he must have called the police. They were taken to Nordlingen and locked up for three days and questioned on why they happened to be in that vicinity since their papers showed they were supposed to be at Nurnberg instead of 70 miles beyond. They were accused of running away from work. Apparently a lot of foreign workers were escaping to the Russians and the police were checking all they could find. The police finally released them to the local Arbeitsamt [Labor Office] where they were given jobs with farmers near Echingen under the condition that they dare not move and if they intended to, they should report to the police first. The two agents worked for different farmers in the same village.

There were some other Poles in the neighborhood where they worked and they got together with them. A few days after being installed with the farmers, the whole bunch went to the place where the radio and suitcases were buried, which was about 7 kilometers away. They brought the equipment in successfully. On Sunday morning, when the farmers went to church, [text excised] set up his equipment in the barn while [text excised] stood guard outside ready to give a warning signal by throwing stones at the barn in case someone should be coming. [Text excised] had established contact and was just changing his crystals to send a message when he heard the danger signal. Two cars of SS men drove up and naturally [text excised] thought they were after him. He quickly covered the radio with some hay and went to the house and tried to appear normal; eating breakfast. As soon as the coast was fairly clear he ran back to the barn, took down the aerial, hid it and stuck the radio deeper into the hay. About two days later the army moved in. The officers searched the house at about 01:30 hours and again [text excised] thought they were looking for him. All they wanted was to find quarters. Four women who were sleeping in separate rooms so arranged by the farmer to keep the army from living in the house, were put into one room and the officers moved in. The men were quartered in the barn for the rest of the time until the Allies came. These German soldiers slept on [text excised] radio equipment, fortunately never discovering it. The whole period was a serious strain on [text excised] nervous system.

Military Observations
Their observation of military operations by the Germans shows that the Germans took advantage of Allied assurances, dropped by leaflets, that farmers would not be hurt. Instead of using trucks for distribution of munitions, horse carts were the chief means of delivering these munitions to the front. No traffic was allowed on roads; railroads were continually under fire, and Allied fighters were strafing every day to the extent that at a neighboring airfield German planes never had a chance to get off the ground. But these horse carts and the barns of the farmers where ammunition was stored, were never touched. This was the first intended message but unfortunately it never came through.

Attitude of the People toward the War
Conditions among the military were not up to standard. Many officers were invalids, with wooden legs or without arms. The men in this particular vicinity were SS troops, composed, however, mostly of foreign elements who had been taken first into Germany as laborers, later put into the GT battalions and finally made into SS troops. They were all on the verge of mutiny, kept running away and disguising themselves in civilian clothes. About a day before the Allies arrived rumors were thick and the soldiers were all deserting their units, everyone look-ing for a job with some farmer. The next day a rumor was spread that the war was over, that Hitler had shot himself, that Berlin had fallen. Some Americans

came along in jeeps instead of tanks or armored cars and that seemed to confirm the rumor and caused a terrific amount of joy among all these soldiers, by then mostly in civilian clothes. The SS corps stationed in this vicinity, as far as this man could ascertain, had all moved to the Danube region. In the opinion of the soldiers it was not much of war, just continual escaping and running away from the Allies all of which indicated that the morale must have been extremely low.

Apparently in those parts the country folk had no desire to participate in the war. Even when ordered to send their 15-16 year-old sons to the army they refused to obey. The forests were hide-outs for many foreign workers and these agents knew some Poles who had ammunition and food. As soon as the Allies came in they took over and cleared out all the Nazis they could find. It must be noted that any city folk who happened to be around were usually ardent followers of Nazism.

The foreign workers had apparently been faithful to orders given by Eisenhower, dropped by leaflets, to desert their jobs and flee to the woods.

Many of the farmers had even prepared food for the coming American Armies and kept it hidden from the Nazis. The one aim of everybody seemed to be to have peace again and the joy of these people seemed to be absolutely sincere.

Food Conditions

The day after the Americans came [text excised] went to the nearby airdrome at Heueberg and asked for G-2. He was told by a captain that there was no G-2 there but he was on his way to the closest one, about 50 miles away, and he would take him along. The next day they fetched [text excised] who, meanwhile, was looking for [text excised]. Gawor in the meantime had been supervising the collection of arms by the Burgomaster and when it was completed, turned them over to the Americans. Also, in a skirmish between some Poles and two SS men one of the Poles was shot, which enraged [text excised] who took out his .45 and shot one of the SS men through the back of the neck when he was fleeing. The other one stopped and pleaded with him not to shoot because he was a Pole. All the other Poles around wanted to lynch him for ever joining the SS and almost succeeded but some Americans took him away.

Both [text excised] and [text excised] were taken to Goettingen and from there to Luxemburg. The evening before leaving for Luxemburg they had a session with American intelligence officers, pointing out various dumps, positions, etc., of the enemy. They were treated very well by the Americans, and well fed.

Attempts at Contact with London

Three attempts at contact were made. The first was before the soldiers took over, the second about a week before the Americans came but there was too much movement all around and they could not risk completing it. The third time was about a day before the Americans came when the German Army was moving out.

Criticisms

Dispatch. They were not dropped on the pin-point. Although five kilometers away is not too bad, still the place they should have been dropped was much better, and no one could have seen them for certain.

Documentation. As to documentation, their cover story did not explain why they were so far beyond the destination named in the letter to the Arbeitsamt at Nurnberg. This aroused the suspicion of the police. Although they were not suspected of being agents, they were accused of being foreign workers who had run away.

MARTINI MISSION

The Agents

Sergeant Leon Adrian, 30-year-old observer, from the village of Siwiałka in Tczew county. His nearest kin was his wife, Marta Markowska; address: Starogard, ul. Średnia 6. Adrian finished a seven-year primary school. He had a father, mother, sister aged 41, and a brother in the Polish underground. His wife and two daughters, aged 4 and 5, lived in Starogard. He was captured by the Russians and exchanged for White Russians in January 1941, then sent as forced labor to the *Kriegsmarinarsenal* (Navy Arsenal), the naval arms and ammunition depot near Danzig. He was a railroad mechanic and electrician. He was conscripted into the German Army and sent to Nauenburg, and then to central France and Marseille. In September 1943 he was sent to Normandy, where on June 19, 1944, he was captured by the Americans. He was familiar with Pomerania and Gdansk.

Private First Class Józef Bartoszek, 21-year-old radio operator, from Wierzyca in Kartuzy county. His nearest kin was his father, August Stark; address: Kościerzyna, ul. Klasztorna 1, Pomerania. He had a father, mother, brother aged 17, and two sisters aged 22 and 13 at home, and a sister aged 25, married. From 1940 to October 1942 Bartoszek worked in a planer's shop in Kościerzyna as a laborer and later as office staff. In October 1942 he was drafted into the German Army and sent to Augsburg, Munich, and later to France. In April 1943 he finished a noncommissioned officers' school in Hohenfels, Bavaria, and was sent back to France, where he was captured by the Allies at Cherbourg in June 1944. He was familiar with Hohenfels, Oberpfalz, Bavaria.[3]

Name:	~~[redacted]~~ Adrian, Leon (agent)
Grade:	Sgt.
Age:	30
Born:	Siwialka, county of Tczew, Poland.
Father's name:	Paul
Father's occupation:	Farmer
Family:	Father, mother, brother aged 34, sister aged 41. Brother is in Polish underground army. Wife and two daughters, ages 4 and 5, live in Starogard.
Schooling:	7 years primary school.
Personal history:	Captured by Russians and exchanged for white Russians in January 1940. Was sent to forced labor. Worked in the Kriegsmarinarsenal, Emden, Altuns Schichu (near Danzig). Was a mechanic and electrician for the railroad.
Army experience:	Drafted into German army 10 Feb. 1943. Sent to Nauenburg, to Central France, and to Marseilles. Sept. 1943 was sent to Normandy. Captured by Americans 19 June 1944.
Territory with which familiar:	Pomerania and Danzig.

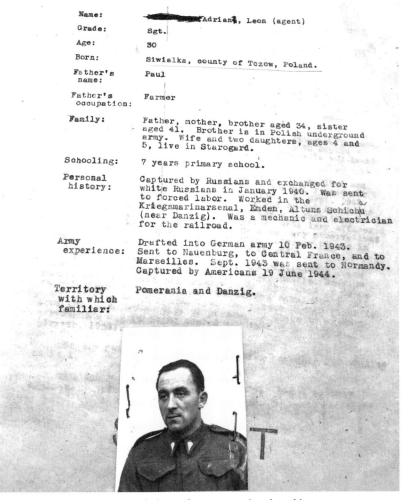

Agent Leon Adrian, Martini Mission. (Photo US National Archives)

```
Name:          Bartoszek, Jozef (radio operator)

Grade:         L/Cpl.

Age:           21

Born:          Wierzyca, County of Kartuzy, Polish
               Pomerania.

Father's       Railroad employee, in Koscierzyna,
occupation:    Polish Pomerania.

Family:        Father, mother, brother 17, two sisters
               22 and 13 at home, and sister, aged 25,
               married.

Schooling:     6 years primary school and 3 years
               secondary school.

Personal       From 1940 to Oct. 1942, he worked at
history:       planing mill in Koscierzyna, as a laborer
               and then as a clerk.

Army           Drafted into German Army, October 1942
Experience:    and sent to Augsburg, and then to Munich.
               His regiment, the Panzerjager Regiment,
               was sent to France.
               April 1943, non-commissioned officers'
               school in Hohenfelz, Oberpfalz, Bavaria.
               After completing this school he returned
               to France.
               Captured 18 June 1944 on the Cherbourg
               peninsula.

Territory      Hohenfelz, Oberpfalz, Bavaria.
with which
familiar:
```

Agent Józef Bartoszek/Stark, Martini Mission. (Photo US National Archives)

Martini Mission Report[4]

The members of the Martini mission were [text excised] *aged 30, observer, and* [text excised] *21, radio operator.* [Text excised] *was a* [long text excised] *before the war, was inducted into the German Army and captured by the Russians, and subsequently exchanged for White Russians* [text excised]. *He again* [text excised] *was drafted into the German Army and was captured by the Americans.* [Text excised] *worked in* [text excised] *before the war, was drafted into the German Army* [text excised] *and captured* [text excised] *near Cherbourg.* [Text excised] *cover story provided that he was a White Russian railroad worker evacuated to the neighborhood of Augsburg from Poznan as a result of the approach of the Russians.* [Text excised] *cover was that of a Lithuanian who had worked in a sawmill in Danzing* [sic] *and had, in February 1945, received orders to report to Darmstadt. He was supposedly travelling to Darmstadt when he arrived in the neighborhood of Augsburg.*

The men were given 25,000 Rms and two diamonds valued approximately at $300 each. They returned 9,300 Rms and one diamond. [Text excised] *diamond was thrown away at the time he was taken by the Gestapo for interrogation.*

The men were dropped into Germany from a B-24 based at Dijon 18 March, into the area of Augsburg. They were recovered in this area on 7 May. [Text excised] *underwent a through interrogation by the Gestapo.*

Following is the report of the Polish Section on the Martini mission.

Air Operation

Two flights. Dropped 18/19 March—landed 00:15 hours. They landed on exact pin-point in the vicinity of an airfield and made a successful landing. The container was found the following morning and was buried without difficulty.

First Contact with Populace

The following day they left the forest and proceeded to the town of Chemnau. On route they met two members of the Feldwacht [sentries] *who stopped them and asked for their papers and where they were coming from. After looking over the papers they brought them to the Burgomaster and asked him to put them up for the night, which he did. The following morning he came with two policemen. The police questioned them and examined the papers and took them to the police headquarters at Jettingen. There they checked their papers again and, being satisfied with their story, procured work for* [text excised]. *As far as* [text excised] *was concerned they could not give him any work since he was considered a German national and a railroad worker. Thus* [text excised] *had to leave and try to find work elsewhere.*

[Text excised] *Story*

After leaving [text excised] *he proceeded to Augsburg to the Eisenbahn* [Railroad] *Bureau to seek work in his line. Arriving there he inquired for work and said that he was from Poznan and was sent to Augsburg to work on the railroad. There they checked his papers and sent him to another office where he immediately saw that he was dealing with Kripo. There they checked his story and demanded a Marschbefehl* [Marching Orders] *which he did not have. He explained that he had lost the paper and when asked why he had not lost the other papers he explained that he kept that paper separately in another pocket because it was always demanded of him wherever he went. He explained again that he was from the Poznan office and they seemed to be satisfied with the rest of his papers, and sent him to the railroad office at Halle. They issued him railroad tickets to proceed to Halle and threatened him that he was to report to Halle immediately—if he did not do so he would be punished. Instead of going directly to the railroad station he went around the city and sometime later to the railroad station and then on a platform to take a train to Ulm, to inform his team mate of his whereabouts. On entering the train for Ulm he was stopped by the two men from the Kripo* [Criminal Police] *and his story was checked again and he was put on the train with two other Kripo men who accompanied him to Halle. They brought him near the railroad office at Halle where they left him and let him go up to the office alone. At the railroad office, he said that he was sent from Poznan to Halle to work. The official there pulled out a list of all railroad workers registered in Poznan, his name was not on there. The official immediately threatened to turn him over to the police but he asked him if it was possible to put him on the list since he didn't want any trouble with the police and to which the official agreed for a sum of 1000 marks. The official had given him papers to go to work in Altenburg and upon leaving the building he was again accosted by the Kripo men who demanded to see what disposition the railroad office had made of him. Seeing that his papers were in order they escorted him to the railroad station and put him on a train for Altenburg. Arriving at Altenburg, he reported to the railroad office to work and he was told to report to the police to register. His papers were checked and he received ration cards and was told to report to the Wehrmeldeamt* [Recruiting Station] *because his soldier's book had expired. Arriving at the Wehrmeldeamt they checked his papers and in looking over his Wehrpass* [Military Service Book] *they noticed that his physical description was not entered. Also they noticed that he had a citizenship which could be revoked and it was impossible for a person of such status to be an official on the railroad and also the fact that he was 41 years old, still single and had not been in the service. They immediately called up the police. When the police arrived and were told his name they immediately pulled out a slip of paper and stated that they had a telephone from the Kripo to keep an eye on him and seeing that some of his papers were not in order took him into custody. They took him to the police station where he was searched and was there four days when four Gestapo men arrived to take him back to Halle. Previous to the trip to Halle he was able to dispose of small items of incriminating evidence which he had on him but did not destroy a large sketch of airfield which he had in his possession. Seeing the four Gestapo arrive he knew his game was up and on the train he chewed that sketch bit by bit. Arriving at Halle he was taken to the Gestapo headquarters where they told him to take off his shoes and they cut them up layer by layer. They then took all of his clothes and ripped them to pieces but could not find anything. After checking his body, they gave him a hypodermic in the arm and in the hip and then gave him a glass of solution which he refused to drink. Upon refusal they hit him over the cheek with the butt of a rifle knocking out five teeth and he was forced to drink the solution in the glass which made him very nauseated and he vomited. Seeing that he did not vomit everything, they used two cylindrical rubber rollers which were pressed against his body and rolled from his knees to his ribs. This process was continued until he had vomited everything out of his stomach. During this process he was hit on the back a few times with the butt of a rifle. Then the contents of his stomach were examined with a large magnifying glass and parts of paper were found. They accused him of being a spy. He explained the presence of paper due to the fact that he had eaten a caramel from which he could not take off the paper. They beat him with rubber clubs and again accused him of being an agent or a deserter. Six to eight hours a day for the next five days the beatings continued but he did not divulge anything. He was given no food and was only given a little warm water with salt. On the sixth day he was told that he was either going to be shot as a spy or was to be sent to Buchenwald, as a deserter. That morning American fortresses* [B-17 Flying Fortresses] *came over Halle and bombed the town. One of the bombs dropped near the prison and blew out the doors of his and other cells through which he escaped with two other men since everyone was underground during the raid. He ran in his weakened condition quite a distance until he reached a small forest where he collapsed from exhaustion. He slept there until the following day. After waking up the following day, he met a group of Russian and Polish slave workers who gave him a little food and place to sleep with them. He explained his condition by telling them that he was beaten up by SS men because he was deserter from the Army.*

<u>*Contact with American Forces*</u>
On 15 April the American Forces arrived and he met a Major Clark[5] who immediately believed his story seeing his condition. He gave him information about enemy troops regarding the direction they were fleeing and their numbers. The major made arrangements to evacuate him to the rear. Immediately a CIC [Counter Intelligence Corps] *detachment learned about him and requested that he be allowed to stay and work with them. Working with the CIC he assisted in the capture of about 20 Gestapo members. Among the captured Gestapo men he recognized the two men who had tortured him. Seeing them he*

pulled out a pistol from one of the nearby soldier's holsters and fired two bullets into each of them. He worked with the CIC until 4 May when a doctor had checked his condition and ordered him to be sent to the rear. He was transferred to the OSS Detachment at Weimar and from there he was brought to Base X Luxembourg.

Comments and Suggestions
The documents that were given him were not complete. He claims that if the documents had been perfect, he would not have fallen into trouble. The Wehrpass was incomplete since there was no physical description and he was not given Marschbefehl to the place where he was going.

[Text excised] Story
After [text excised] departed he was set up at a sawmill where he worked until the Americans came.

Attitude of People toward the War
The people generally had lost hope in winning the war and were just waiting for the Americans to arrive. They also stated that Germany was losing the war on account of too many agents being dropped behind the lines.

Food Conditions
The food situation in Jettingen was very bad and it was practically impossible to purchase any.

Remaining Controls and Functioning Authorities
On two occasions military gendarmes had checked his papers and were satisfied with them. Once he had to report to Gunzburg to the Landsamt [District Authority] where he was thoroughly checked and received his ration cards and permit to travel in the vicinity of Jettingen.

Facility of Movement
Since he was passing as a Lithuanian his movements were not restricted and he had permission to travel alone. He was able to go from place to place and was never bothered by any authorities.

Monetary Situation
It was impossible to buy any food on black market. The only possibility of obtaining food was on the barter system.

Radio Contacts
Upon landing the accumulator was smashed so he made a makeshift accumulator and was able to contact London. When he was ready to shift to give a message

his receiver had failed so he gave up his attempt to contact since the accumulator was exhausted. He later made a contact from Paris and gave messages which he had with him. These contacts from Paris were made to try out the set.

<u>*Contact with American Forces*</u>
He heard that the American Forces were in Burgau so he immediately proceeded there. He met tank spearheads going through the town, and stopped a major, informing him that he was an American agent, but that moment a battle started and the major told him to go to the rear. He returned to the hamlet where he was staying. The following day the Americans arrived at this hamlet and he was immediately stopped and searched for weapons. They found his .45 and confiscated it. He then informed them that he was an OSS agent. They took him to the rear where he was questioned by a major and after he saw his equipment his story was believed and he was immediately taken to an OSS detachment at Dillingen where he was questioned as to what information he had. He told them of the SS divisions which had gone through Augsburg and were on their way to Munich, he also gave them the dispositions of the troops in Augsburg and the reactions of the people in Augsburg. After completing the questioning, the OSS detachment sent him to Paris.

<u>*Practicability of Equipment*</u>
The equipment which was issued to him was excellent except the accumulator. If the accumulator had not been broken he would have been definitely able to make contact with London.

<u>*Names of Nazis*</u>
Peter Hartmann, Jettingen. NOTE: He was offering this information to the American troops but since there was a battle in progress they disregarded his name and evacuated him to the rear. The abovenamed man had a few rifles, pistols and ammunition hidden. He also had numerous letters from SA.

MANHATTAN MISSION

The Agents

Private René de Gaston (real name: Zygmunt Barwikowski), 20-year-old observer, born in Tczew, Pomerania. His nearest kin was his father, Maksymilian Barwikowski; address: Tczew, Marienburgel Str. 20. Gaston finished primary school and three years' high school. From 1939 to 1943 he worked (with interruptions) as a waiter in the Casino in Zoppot and as a docker in the port at Danzig. His father lived in Berlin, his mother in Tczew. One brother was in a convalescent company after being wounded

Name:	DeGaston, Rene (agent)
Grade:	Private
Age:	20
Born:	Tczew (Dirschau) Pomerania, Poland
Father's occupation:	Before the war, government employee in county office at Tczew. In 1939 he was deported for forced labor and in 1942-43 was working as an interpreter in Berlin.
Family:	Father - in Berlin, mother - in Tczew. One brother is in a convalescent company after being wounded on the Russian front.
Schooling:	Primary school, and three years secondary school.
Personal history:	1939 to 1943, was employed as a waiter and as a dock worker in Danzig.
Army experience:	March 1943, drafted into German army and sent to France after training in Thuringia. In the army he worked as a waiter, until apprehended for taking unauthorized leave and sent to disciplinary company at Caen. Captured by British in Caen 6 June 1944.
Territory with which familiar:	A number of places in Germany including Dortmund, Kassel and Berlin. East Prussia.

Agent René de Gaston, Manhattan Mission. (Photo US National Archives)

Zygmunt Barwikowski in the Wehrmacht, standing third from right. (Photo Krzysztof Marek Barwikowski)

on the Russian Front. In March 1943 Gaston was drafted into the German Army and sent for training to Thuringia. He worked as a waiter until he left his barracks without a pass and was sent to a penal company in Caen, where the British took him prisoner on June 6, 1944. He knew well Dortmund, Kassel, Berlin, and East Prussia. Gaston seemed quiet, keen, and intelligent. It seemed that he did not like being trained by the OSS, but he claimed that he would gladly return to Germany to work on behalf of Poland and the Allies.

Private First Class Edmund Barski (real name: Edmund Zeitz), 21-year-old radio operator, born in Kamień, Sępólno county, Pomerania. His nearest kin was his father, Józef Zeitz; address: Tuchola, ul. Karasiewicza 5, Pomerania. Barski completed six classes of primary school and three classes of high school. He was the youngest of the agents. In July 1942 the *Arbeitsamt* sent him to Driesen, and in December 1942 he was drafted into the German Army and seconded to Metz and later to Normandy and Brittany. Together with a friend he surrendered to the Americans on June 19, 1944. He knew the German language very well, but not Germany.[6]

Name:	Barski, Edmund (Radio)
Grade:	L/Cpl.
Age:	21
Born:	Kamien, County of Sempolno, Pomerania
Father's name:	Jozef
Father's occupation:	Bookkeeper, Polish Social Security Bureau.
Family:	Father and mother.
Schooling:	six years primary school, 3 years high school.
Personal history:	After invasion worked as a painter until 1941, then in same office as father. July 1942, sent by Arbeitsdienst to Driesen, on Polish border.
Army experience:	Drafted December 1942, sent to Normandy and Brittany. Surrendered 19 June 1944.
Territory with which familiar:	Native territory.

Agent Edmund Barski/Zeitz, Manhattan Mission. (Photo US National Archives)

Manhattan Mission Report[7]

The Manhattan mission was composed of two Poles, [text excised] aged 20, observer, and [text excised], 21, radio operator. Both men were from Pomerania. The former had been [long text excised] had been drafted into the German Army [text excised] and had been captured at [text excised] had been a [long text excised] had been drafted as a foreign worker [text excised] and was captured in Brittany [text excised] was given the cover of a French worker with the job of visiting French civilian workers camps to check on the condition of the workers. [Text excised] cover was that of a construction worker. The men were to operate in the area of Chemnitz. They were given 25,000 Rms and two diamonds value approximately at $300 each. [Text excised] diamond was taken from him by the Gestapo at Chemnitz. [Text excised] lost his on the day he was cross-examined by G-2 when he was recovered, and stated that he believed it was stolen by a foreign worker.

The men were dispatched on 7 April from B-24 based at Dijon after seven attempts. They were recovered on 7 May. Following is the report of the Polish Section on the Manhattan mission. This team made seven flights over Germany before being dropped. They had been shot up by flak and night fighters, but not once had they faltered in spite of all the difficulties encountered.

Air Operations
This team was dropped the night of 7/8 April from a B-24 and reached the pin-point at 02:03 hours. They were dropped exactly on the pin-point. The drop was made from about 700 feet and the landing was very good. The team was quite satisfied with the air operations.

They found the container easily as it had a white parachute. The radio equipment was buried about 1 kilometer from the place of the drop; the container was broken up and disposed of with the parachutes. They were finished by six-o'clock in the morning. They then got on to the main road and walked to Chemnitz, a distance of 14 kilometers.

Contact with Population and Authorities
During the first day there were no contacts with any authorities and their papers were not checked. About 5 in the evening they met a Pole and got lodging from him in a brickyard just outside of the town. At six in the morning they were more or less asked to leave the place as the SS man, in charge there, would soon be around and their friend did not want any unnecessary questioning.

They went into the town and tried to find something to eat. They had plenty of time as the labor exchange did not open until 9 o'clock. The only place they could find food was the railroad station. [Text excised] wanted to bring food out to [text excised] since his papers were not very good, but thirst on the latter's part caused both to go in.

While in the station they found there was a train 12:45 hours for Leipzig and, should anybody ask, they would say that was the train they were waiting for. A woman, rather elegant in appearance, who spoke Polish well, came up to them supposedly just to carry on a conversation. She was from Lodz posing as a Volksdeutsche. It may well be noted that there were many of these Poles from Lodz who worked hand in hand with the German police. After they sat down at a table and were eating their sandwiches, the Kripo came up to them and asked for their papers. [Text excised]*'s papers were very good but* [text excised] *could not prove he had been working for the past two months and was taken by the police.*

(From this point the stories differ and are reported separately.)

[Text excised] *Story*

[Text excised] *waited for about three hours at the station hoping* [text excised] *might come out again. He noticed many of these phony Poles and also noticed that several Czechs were being arrested. The reason for this police control was probably the mass escaping of Czech workers back to Czechoslovakia, and the police were making all efforts to round up as many of them as possible.*

When it seemed hopeless [text excised] *went into town. He stopped on at the office of the Arbeitsfront and asked for facilities to visit a French prisoners' camp. His story was that now in the sixth year of war there might be efforts at sabotage, escaping, etc., and he had been sent from Berlin to keep an eye on these things. This was where he met Schoener, who was the Kreisleiter* [chief of the county administration (*Landrat*), or NSDAP] *for Chemnitz, in propaganda and political intelligence. He got permission to wander around quite freely and was given instructions to go to HEOF* [Health Emergency Operation Facility]*, which was a branch of the French propaganda unit from Vichy, which had been recently moved there from Leipzig.*

He started wandering around the countryside as he did not want to stay too close to Chemnitz itself and picked up quite a bit of information about underground factories, Panzerfaust factories, etc. Finally after a few days he got installment with a Pole at Glaeser, about one kilometer from Chemnitz. Meanwhile he had made several trips to the brickyard, hoping to meet [text excised]. *They had previously agreed to use that point as a rendezvous.*

After three days he moved to Altendorf. There he went again to the Arbeitsfront and from them got a room in a hotel, the Leipzigerhof. His papers whenever checked, proved very helpful and he was given every possible aid in his "work." Throughout this period he did quite a bit of observing and all the information he gathered was later turned over promptly to the G-2, who use it to take the best advantage. He found that the front was only about 10 kilometers away at Zeitz and he headed in that direction so that he could turn over the intelligence material as quickly as possible, having no communications man to send it through to London. He stayed all night in Zeitz before the Americans moved in. In the shelter he met five American prisoners of war who were supposed to be evacuated with thousands of other people, and kept them with him.

About six the next morning the American tanks rolled in. He went up to a major, told him he wanted to see G-2 and was taken to a village not very far away which was G-2 headquarters for the 6th Division of the Third Army. There he gave them all the information he had and later was sent on to G-2 at Weimar. The G-2 at Weimar employed him for tracking down escaped SS people. He was given a jeep and drove freely around the town, snooping. He got most of his information through liberated Poles and his most important haul was that of eight SS men, who had been guards at Buchenwald, hiding out in Ostmannstadt. All this time he was being used for the interrogation of suspected Germans and when information came for him to go to London, the headquarters where he was employed released him with regret. He returned to the rear with OSS orders.

At a camp where he stayed awaiting transportation, he was confronted by a French officer, supposedly from the Secret Service, who wanted to know what his mission was. This Frenchman tried to get his story and to prove that he was a Frenchman and, therefore, under his control. However, [text excised] *told him he was a Pole, working for OSS and whatever he did was his own business and not the Frenchman's.*

Two days later he got transportation to Frankfurt. At Frankfurt he stayed with the French G-2 and watched them work. The next day he was sent to Luxembourg and from there to London.

[Text excised] *Story*

[Text excised] *was taken to police station where he was given a quick search but nothing incriminating was found. After a few hours he was taken to the Gestapo headquarters at Chemnitz and on the way threw out any incriminating material he had on him. At this headquarters he was given a thorough search and there were three things the police questioned: first, the Benzedrine tablets, which he failed to throw away, second, the diamond, and third, a rather large sum of money, over a thousand marks. He explained the Benzedrine tablets as something for a headache and said he got the diamond with his ration cards from his mother and the marks had been saved up. He was searched twice, the second time still more thoroughly than the first but apparently they believed his story and did no further questioning. He was interrogated by an officer, two non-commissioned officers and a woman, a Czech who spoke Polish. He explained his ignorance of the Czech language by saying he had lived in Poland most of his life and never had a chance to learn the language properly and this seemed OK with her. After the interrogation he was taken to the jail in Chemnitz where he was put in a cell with ten Czechs and one Pole. In this prison he was not fed at all for two days although other prisoners were.* [Text excised] *believes that his story was taken as true and the only reason he was being held was because he was suspected of being a Czech who had run away from work.*

On the third day (12 April) he and his cellmates were told they were going to be taken to work. With about a hundred others they were taken to a village called Neukirchen about 10 kilometers from Chemnitz and put into jail again. They were put into a large room with about 400 prisoners, mostly Czechs, some Poles and some Russians. Before coming to this jail he was given his things back but upon arrival at the new prison they were taken away again and he was left only his soap and towel. The room in which they were placed was about 12 meters long and 8 wide and for 400 people, sleeping had to be done in shifts as it was impossible for everyone to lie down. There were no medical facilities and if anyone was sick he just had to stay sick where he was. Everybody suffered from plague of lice, they could see them crawling on their clothes. The menu for the day was a cup of black dishwater, supposedly coffee, for breakfast, for dinner they had a cup of soup made out of potato peelings and supper was 175 grams of black bread. People who had been there for awhile and couldn't stand it any longer did their best to get outside and those who managed, started eating grass and leaves, anything they could lay their hands on that looked edible. The guards consisted of ten SS men, changed every day at 13:00 hours.

On the morning of 15 April they heard the sound of machine gun fire and very soon after were given back their belongings and told they were going to move to a new place where they would get work. They were to make the trip on foot, marching three days. In the confusion while being let out of the building, [text excised] with another Pole, jumped over a couple of fences and ran in between the houses of the village. Three SS men chased them, firing pistols, but neither of them was hurt. There were plenty of buildings among which they managed to hide.

From this village he got into a forest and the same afternoon went to a village by the name of Leuchtendorf. There they got lodgings from an old German woman where they stayed for a few days. The prison food had given him dysentery and he was so sick he couldn't move. The other Pole, who had escaped with him went to the Wirtschaftsamt [Provisioning Office] where he got ration cards for three days. On the third day [text excised] walked out and was stopped by a policeman who told him that he would be back that evening to take him to Stolberg. He did not wait as he found out the Americans were about six kilometers away and that same day he ran in that direction and gave himself up to the Americans. On his way to the Americans he found very few Germans except for one battalion which was dug in but he bypassed them and reached the American lines.

A lieutenant took him to an MP [Military Police] headquarters; the MPs took him to camp and from there straight to Bad Nauheim, general headquarters for the CIC of the Third Army. As soon as he got to the Americans he gave them the only intelligence he had, about the German battalion and the kind of arms they were using. This battalion was apparently only waiting to surrender as soon as they possibly could, which they did as soon as the Americans appeared.

Before reaching Bad Nauheim, at a French camp an American captain from the CIC had tried to get all the information about OSS from [text excised] what they were paid, what sort of equipment, how many agents were working, etc. [Text excised] refused to give this information, as he had been instructed, and this captain took the attitude that [text excised] was not telling the truth and that he would consider him a German agent. He was then taken to Bad Nauheim where he was treated like a German prisoner, apparently upon the recommendation of this captain. There they sent word to London about him and after four days he was taken to a prison in Wiesbaden. In Wiesbaden he tried to see some American officers but unsuccessfully. He was continually treated as a German and fed the same food the German jails had always given.

Lieutenant Gagnon finally came and picked him up to go to the airdrome at Frankfurt where he was supposed to be picked up. However, they missed the plane and went back to Wiesbaden where he stayed overnight, only not in the prison but at OSS headquarters. At Wiesbaden [text excised] again met the captain who had put him through the works. However, this time the captain apologized for all he had done, explaining that he was entitled to know everything, since he was an American too.

On the way to Luxembourg in a truck the day after the fruitless attempt at meeting the plane from London, they had an accident, a broken axle, and they travelled all night, going through Trier to Luxembourg.

Comments and Suggestions
A very serious criticism was [text excised]'s papers. Several times before being dispatched [text excised] asked for different papers as his were completely unsatisfactory. However, everybody rushed him about, insisting that they were OK and he finally went with them. The results are pretty obvious from the foregoing report. The papers themselves were well made, no German officials had any doubt as to their authenticity, but they were the wrong kind and got him into trouble instead of keeping him out of it.

EGGNOG MISSION

The Agents

Corporal Edmund Czapliński, 31-year-old observer, born May 1913 in Cleveland, Ohio, USA. His nearest kin was his wife, Maria Wysocka; address: Grudziądz, ul. Legionów 55. In January 1914 his parents and he moved to Grudziądz, where they settled. Czapliński completed seven classes of primary school and knew well East Prussia and Pomerania. He was drafted into the German Army on December 30, 1942, and sent to Verdun, France, and then to Caen. He was a tailor in the army. He surrendered to

Agent Edmund Czapliński, Eggnog Mission.
(Photo US National Archives)

Agent Zbigniew Gołąb, Eggnog Mission.
(Photo US National Archives)

the Americans alongside eight other Poles. He spoke German very well. Czapliński intended to regain his American citizenship, especially if Poland were to be occupied by the Russians. He was bright, with innate intelligence, and was expected to handle himself well in any situation.

Private First Class Zbigniew Gołąb, 23-year-old radio operator, born in Grudziądz on February 1, 1921. His nearest kin was his mother, Amanda Kościańska; address: Grudziądz, Marienwerder Str. 28. Gołąb completed six classes at primary school and several classes of high school. His father was in the German Army; he had a mother and one sister. He was drafted by the German Army on February 8, 1943, and sent to southern France, Normandy, and Saint Malo. He surrendered to the Allies on June 14, 1944. He knew East Prussia, Polish and German Pomerania, and Munich. He was reliable and willing.[8]

Eggnog Mission Report[9]

The Eggnog mission consisted of two agents [text excised] *aged 31, observer, and* [text excised]*, 24, radio operator.* [Long text excised] *had gone to Poland with his parents in* [text excised] *1914 and had remained there until* [text excised] *drafted into German Army and stated in* [text excised]*. He surrendered to the Americans on* [text excised]*.* [Text excised] *was born in Pomerania, Poland, and worked as a* [long text excised] *until* [text excised] *he was drafted into the German Army and sent to Normandy, where he* *surrendered* [text excised]. *The cover story for the observer was that of a tailor on his way from Poland to Darmstadt to report for work.* [Text excised] *cover story was that of a concrete mixer deferred from the army for essential work. He was also supposedly on his way to Darmstadt.*

The men were to operate in the area of Aschaffenburg. They were dropped from an A-20 based at Namur on the night of 23/24 March, and were recovered by the advancing American Armies on 31 March. They were given 25,000 German Rms and two diamonds valued at $300 each. They returned 24,915 Rms and the two diamonds.

The men were not able to contact London because of the failure of the radio battery. They were not questioned by the police on any occasion.

Following is a report of the Polish Section on the Eggnog Mission.

The jump was very successful, exactly on the pin-point, with practically no wind and unnoticed by anyone. The only criticism of the air operation the team had was of the time it took place. They would have much preferred to have landed at midnight rather than at 02:05 hours. The plane "buzzed" them after the drop, the men waved an "OK," and the plane flew on, taking a few pictures. (Explanation: The aircraft belonged to a Photo-reconnaissance unit and taking pictures was done for diverse purposes.)

Having just about finished burying their container, the men had to hurry out of sight for a farmer with oxen and a plough had come out to work his field. Not until 5 pm were they able to leave the forest, when the farmer stopped plough-ing. They then dug up the container and after taking out all the contents, broke it up and buried it again.

This team requested a 1:25,000 map of the pin-point vicinity on their next jump. The 1:100,000 had proved inaccurate, either showing non-existent roads, or not showing existing roads. The first example of this inaccuracy occurred when they tried to proceed to the valley of the Kohl-Bach river. After being unsuccessful they turned back and went to Ebenheid. It was late and after eating their supper in the forest, they went to sleep in a haystack on the border of the village. This ended the second night.

The next objective was Eichenbuhl. They walked to it, noting plenty of traffic on the main road, it being Sunday morning. A break in the hike, in order to test the radio, was made. The W/T operator attempted to contact London, fruit-lessly, and he stated that might have been because of the woods surrounding him; also they were in the saddle of a slight valley. An entire afternoon was spent in the forest; the reason contact with London was attempted was that the Germans were taking up defensive position along the road from Eichenbuhl to Reidern. About 4 pm they decided to move on to Eichenbuhl. Coming down a hill lead-ing to a main road the handle of the suitcase broke off, sending the suitcase with all the radio equipment inside, tumbling and rolling clear down to the bottom. Fortunately none of the equipment was damaged.

In Eichenbuhl they found two companies of infantry on the retreat from Miltenberg. Overcrowding by soldiers prevented them from obtaining quarters for the night. On the way out to look for a haystack they were stopped by a military patrol consisting of a captain, two lieutenants and a sergeant. Their papers were examined and found quite in order. The captain then said it was no use going on to Miltenberg. The Americans were almost there and Darmstadt had already been occupied.

After a night's rest on some straw, the W/T operator climbed a hill about three kilometers from Eichenbuhl, on the other side of the stream and again attempted to contact London, unsuccessfully. A suitable place for a hideout was found on the slope of the hill—coordinates 166/217 (GSGS 4416). From there both of them wandered around the countryside for three days within a radius of 10 kilometers.

The main road in their proximity was one of the main routes of retreat of the enemy's Rhine defense units, leading through Hardheim, Tauberbischofsheim to Wurzburg. The latter was supposed to have been the collecting point. It was a sad looking and beaten army with none of the men fully equipped and only about one in ten possessing arms.

On the 27th another and final attempt was made to contact London. Contact was made, but before a message could be sent the battery went dead.

This team is convinced that if the information they had on hand had gone through, the Americans could have gone right through to Wurzburg and captured the city itself intact. The delay had allowed the Germans to offer resistance. Though not much, it was resistance and American lives were lost. On the way a company of SS (about 120 men) completely unarmed could have been caught at Hardheim.

During the eight days spent in Germany, they saw only three pieces of anti-tank artillery—PaK, two drawn by tractors, one by men.

The same day unsuccessful efforts were made at procuring food in the local villages, so the men hiked to Hardheim, a distance of about 17 kilometers where they purchased two loaves of bread and 200 grams of ground meat. The meat was eaten raw.

The next day was spent in efforts to obtain an accumulator for the radio. None were successful and the men retired in the early hours of the following morning.

By this time the Americans were practically "within hearing." All efforts up to date were fruitless and it was decided they would move on eastward with the Germans in hopes of remaining on the enemy side of the lines, perhaps the work could be continued. However, when American pressure began to grow at an extraordinary rate, the radio was buried and the men moved on with some Germans. At Schweinberg three kilometers outside Hardheim, they took up quarters with a farmer.

The Americans reached Schweinberg by the next morning.

It would not have been wise to contact the Americans while in Schweinberg, so the men returned to Hardheim. Two officers directed them to a prisoner of war camp. On the way to this camp an American Lieutenant Colonel who spoke Polish took them in his care, fed them, then assigned a jeep for their use to fetch their radio equipment. On the way back with the radio they took a German prisoner.

Further handling of these agents was OK except for one incident when they were stopped by French Security Police and turned over to the MPs where they waited for Paris G-2 to confirm their identity.

First Contact with Population

The first contact was made near Eibenheim where they stopped a few people on the roads, asking for directions and general information about what was happening. They received news that the Americans were apparently there. Everybody seemed to be waiting. When they got to Hardheim the local Burgomaster was stopping everybody going through and when they saw that they went up to him and asked where there was a baker and butcher. He showed them the way and forgot to ask any formal questions.

Food Conditions

Two loaves of bread and 200 grams of meat was all the food they had been able to purchase because food conditions in that part of Germany were extremely poor.

Attitude of the People toward the War

The attitude of the people toward the war was seemed to be that in eight to 14 days the whole thing would be over. They seemed to be pretty discouraged with the war.

Contact with Authorities

The authorities in these villages were the burgomasters. If the burgomaster happened to be a member of the Nazi party, usually he had run away, leaving somebody to take his place.

Monetary Situation

All they have to say is that the Germans seem to have plenty of money and any bribing was practically impossible unless it was offered in gold or valuable gems. They didn't want money.

Comments and Suggestions

The local people in the vicinity the agents travelled in were not dressed the way they had been briefed. Everybody had very good clothes. All were clean and as far as their clothing having to be dirty since they were to be travelers from Koenigsberg, their clothes would have gotten dirty enough just by handling their equipment after the drop, digging holes and burying the containers, etc., which would make up for their clean appearance.

Practicability of Equipment
Better suitcases must be used in the first place. In the second, two suitcases should be used for the radio instead of one. The equipment was much too heavy to be carried by one man alone.

It did not pay to take just one battery, and the issue of hand-operated generator was strongly advocated. The hand-operated generator, in the opinion of the agents was about the best instrument because it required no petrol and could be used in any circumstances. They tried to get current out of some power lines by throwing wires across them but found the lines completely dead.

Eggnog— "Sidelights"
"After my battery had gone dead we decided to get some sort of power supply—no matter what means we used, so I took a length of antennae wire, a pair of pliers and screw driver and proceeded to the road with my observer. Once on the road we thought it would be a good idea to get farther away from our hideout and moved on about another kilometer. Here I took the handle off the screwdriver, scraped up some of the asphalt and stuck the screwdriver into the road at the forty-five degree angle against the traffic, in a spot where I could see most tire marks. The idea was to cause a flat tire, stop the car, knock out the passengers and take off with the accumulator—or perhaps even with the car. Not many cars went by and those that did, never hit the screwdriver. On the other hand quite a few motorcycles passed by, so we thought we could try another idea—stretch the aerial wire across the road high enough to knock the rider off and then take the motorcycle with its battery. Unfortunately it began to rain. While the vehicles in Germany run without any lights where there is so good weather, they turn on their bright lights when it rains, presuming, I suppose that in such weather they aren't vulnerable to air attack. My aerial wire was bright yellow and in those lights would be seen only too well, so we abandoned that. Our hopes were on the screwdriver after all, and when by four in the morning we had not made any progress, drenched with the rain—we went back to our hideout and went to sleep."

The story of this team regarding the attitude of the German populace toward the war and its progress coincides completely with that of "Daiquiri." As an example they quote the following intelligence:

"At the village of Schweinberg the elder inhabitants had made up their minds that their village was not going to be blown off the map and spread word around to the effect that if they found any enthusiastic youngsters planning the slightest resistance, the first one that fired a shot would be hanged. The whole countryside is extremely religious, all catholic and very much under the influence of the local pastor who about four days before the arrival of the Americans had told his parish the bells would not be rung again until the Americans occupied the village. This was to be a sign that the war had ended for them. The American spearheads were approaching the town, everyone was preparing a white flag and even before the first tanks rolled in, the bells were ringing. The general reaction seemed to be that of relief."

When the agents went into a local shop for some bread, two other men walked in with the greeting "Heil Hitler." They then remembered that they should do the same. After they were served they tried it with "Heil Hitler," everybody looked at them, and the lady behind the counter, with special emphasis, replied "Aufwiedersehen." They decided that was not at all the proper greeting in those parts.

The agents also remarked:

"The area where we were must have had plenty of English spies, the way everyone was talking about them. We even bumped into a pair. One afternoon, while sitting in the woods, we saw a couple of men carrying a small suitcase coming our way. Both were dressed in civilian clothes and we could not figure out what they were up to in the woods, but just in case, we hid in some underbrush. We remained unnoticed even though they passed within six meters of us. My first notion was to follow but as I prepared to do that, I heard them operating a radio. You could hear the code plain as day."

DAIQUIRI MISSION

The Agents

Private First Class Józef Matuszowicz/Ruttkay, 21-year-old observer, born April 21, 1923, in Mysłowice, Katowice county. His nearest kin was his father, Franciszek Ruttkay; address: Cieszyn, ul. Istebna 560. Matuszowicz completed six classes of primary school and two high school classes in Mysłowice. He was conscripted by the German Army on December 8, 1942, and sent to Braunschweig where he served as a translator on the railroad. He served in Belgium and France as a gunsmith, radio technician, and translator. He surrendered to the Americans on June 26, 1944. He was familiar with Germany and Polish and Czech Silesia. He could be dropped anywhere in Germany. He was bright, quick-thinking, and knew how to "play" the Germans.

Private First Class Wilhelm Zagórski (real name: Wilhelm Swoboda), 21-year-old radio operator, born in Wiślica, Cieszyń county in Upper Silesia. His nearest kin was his father, Rudolf Swoboda; address: Skoczów, ul. Wiślica 64. Zagórski completed six classes of primary school and three

Agent Wilhelm Zagórski/Swoboda, Daiquiri Mission. (Photo Swoboda family and Rafał Niedziela)

classes of high school. In December 1939 he was taken for forced labor, returning to Bohumin at the end of 1940, and worked on the railroad until January 1943. He was conscripted thereafter into the German Army and sent to France, where he was captured by the Americans at Cherbourg on June 28, 1944.[10]

Daiquiri Mission Report[11]

The Daiquiri Mission agents were [text excised] aged 21, observer, and [text excised] 22, radio operator. [Text excised] had worked in civilian life [text excised] in Poland where he was born. Drafted into the German Army [text excised] he served in Poland, and France as [long text excised] he surrendered to the Americans. [Text excised] was born in Upper Silesia, was drafted [long text excised] into the German Army [text excised] received military training in France, and was a member of the [text excised] Regiment when captured by the Americans [text excised].

The observer's cover was that of an armament worker being evacuated from Breslau to Darmstadt to report for work. The radio operator's cover was that of man who had worked in a firm manufacturing floors of airplane hangars in Breslau who was also on the way to Darmstadt from Breslau.

The men were to operate in the neighborhood of Hanau. They were dropped from an A-20 based at Namur on 21 March and recovered by the American Armies on 8 April. They were given 25,000 German Rms and two diamonds. They returned 20,210 Rms but lost both the diamonds. [Text excised] *said he lost his diamond out of his watch pocket one night while he was sleeping in hayloft.* [Text excised] *said that he lost his diamond out of a hole in the lining of his coat where it was hidden. The men were not able to contact London and were not questioned by the police on any occasion.*

The following is a report of the Polish Section on the Daiquiri mission:

"In line with orders received on 28 February, we landed on 22 March 1945 at 00:15 hours on Germany territory in the vicinity of Ebenheid, coordinates 188/258 (exactly on the pin-point planned).

"We landed without being noticed by anyone. The radio equipment was put inside the container which in turn was hidden in the nearby forest. The parachutes were buried right in the field. We took all the other equipment with us. It was impossible to carry the radio equipment because our suitcase had cracked, probably from the impact on landing. Our intentions were to fetch the radio after getting properly installed. At 10:00 hours the next day an approaching group of lumbermen forced us to leave the forest. We did not want them to see us.

"The road to Miltenberg was traversed without incident. About one kilometer east of the city there were about 400 barrels of unidentified fuel. Arrived at Miltenberg at 14:00 hours and found quarters for the night at the NSF [NS Frauenschaft, a German women's organization affiliated with the NSDAP], *a barracks building used by travelling soldiers. The soldiers and civilian population were awaiting the arrival of the Allies. Everyone seemed very much afraid of the Party, which kept everything under strict control. From a local woman I found that in the vicinity of Darmstadt there was an underground factory for arms and ammunition, manned by prisoners of war and criminal offenders, without regards for sex or age. These people never saw daylight. They were kept under strict guard by the SS.*

"The railroad station at Miltenberg was practically undamaged and that day was only one train, half freight and half passenger, that left for Wertheim. There was no traffic in the Aschaffenburg–Frankfurt direction. The main reasons were lack of locomotives and continuous air attacks.

"On the third day, in the morning, some passing soldiers told me that the night before an Allied aircraft containing two civilians had been shot down and the wounded were probably taken to the hospital. During the day we went to the Arbeitsamt where we found that Darmstadt (to which we were supposed to go according to our evacuation orders) was under artillery fire. The local Arbeitsamt could not give us any aid since it now contained about 20,000 inhabitants as

compared with a pre-war 4,000. Our papers were examined and found in order. Then we were sent to the main Arbeitsamt in Aschaffenburg. A military vehicle was our means of transport. An officer riding in the same vehicle told us that Darmstadt had been entered. From my conversation with him I concluded that even this officer was anxious to be overrun as that would give him peace of mind. All the factories on the way were bombed out and inactive.

"We reached Aschaffenburg on 23 March in the evening. The city was already destroyed. We were sent to the cellar in the castle, used as quarters for the homeless.

"Description of the shelter: The cellar which was designated by the Hitlerites as an air raid shelter made a horrible impression. There were no ventilators except for two small windows which were shut anyhow. In front of the entrance in the corridor was space designated for Poles and Russians. In the cellar itself near the entrance there was a pile of rubble (bricks, sand, clay, plaster, etc.,); four tier beds were used by women, children and old people. The toilets in the shelter were broken. The lack of water for flushing caused toilets to give forth a sickening odor, therefore, the space in their proximity was designated for such nationalities as French, Italians, Belgians, Dutch and prisoners of war. The center was occupied by German families. Especially constructed space with ventilators were occupied by the police, firemen and local party people. The shelter was over-crowded so that people who had no beds were forced to sleep on the cement floor.

"The panic during an air raid was indescribable. The excited people in the corridors pushed and shoved against the police guard, trying to get into the shelter. A Ukrainian woman had tried to get into the shelter to find her child and was slapped in the face and thrown out by a Baurat [Building Officer] from Aschaffenburg (I do not remember his name).

"On 24 March we went to Arbeitsamt in order to legalize our sojourn in the city. Our papers were examined, we told them our story and demanded some place to get installed. We were sent from one clerk to another and none of them could give us any help. In the end we were shown in to the director of the entire exchange, who, upon learning our story and examining our papers, was very sympathetic. He found us a place to work at the firm of Paul Ostheimer. I was to be a lathe operator and my W/T operator a mechanic's helper. This firm was situated next to the gas works which was still working. The owner told me that his firm was not active, that part of his equipment and machinery was evacuated to Wertheim from 20 to 24 March. He still had in the cellar of his home a second shop consisting of four automatic lathes, about seven meters long, with which he made parts for artillery shells. In view of the fact that the Allies would soon arrive we were not accepted. We then decided to wait until Monday 26 March. Meanwhile we wanted to see what was happening in the city.

"All the large factories were destroyed and only the smaller shops were working. Many of the people never left their shelters. Everywhere you could see general confusion and excitement.

"On 25 March at 10:00 hours news was received that the first spearheads of the American tanks were reaching the city. The civilian population was immediately shoved into the shelters. Some of the people were joyful, others sad; emotions were varied. The army and Volkssturm began excitedly to prepare defenses, which was not received well by the civilian population. Shortly before 12:00 hours the concrete bridge cover the Main was blown up. The city's water supply lines were cut, depriving it of water. At 3 o'clock the first tanks crossed the river on the railroad bridge which the Germans had not had time to blow up. For failing to blow up this bridge a captain and a lieutenant were hung and left hanging for two days. The tanks took up their positions at the southern railroad station. If they had immediately entered the town I am sure the Germans would not have put up any resistance because all they had at their disposal was one platoon of Pioneers without arms, in training only four weeks, and all of them were over 40, about 50 Volkssturm with French carbines and a platoon of the penal company who had carbines and 5 rounds each. These soldiers had not eaten for three days and were fed by the civilians. On the night of the 26th one company of infantry had come.

"The next morning all foreigners had to leave the city toward Lohr—Wurzburg. We were also forced to leave. Entering the village of Goldbach we witnessed this scene: There was a white flag on the first house. A few minutes later a Parteigenosse [party member] drove up in a car, tried to shoot the white flag down or get the inhabitants out of the house. Having been unsuccessful he swore and departed. In another village, Hosbach, a white flag was twice displayed on the church tower but the burgomaster had threatened to shoot and it had to be taken down. This was done by soldiers dressed as civilians, as I found out from the villagers.

"This same day we separated from a column of foreigners and found quarters at a farmhouse. In this barn this farmer had six lathes. This leads me to believe that German industry was transferred to the country. The next day we returned to the city via a round-about way to wait for the armies since all other roads had been cut off. We waited for the surrender of the city in one of the houses. On the morning of 3 April the city surrendered.

"On the 4th we found a CIC officer in Wertheim from where we were sent to Tauberbischofsheim and from there to OSS in Darmstadt. After handing in our report, we were sent to Paris.

"We never had enough time to make contact with London."

OLD FASHIONED MISSION

The Agents

Private Aleksander Bogdanowicz (real name: Aleksander Banaszkie-wicz), 21-year-old observer, born in Ostrawa in the province of Poznan. His nearest kin was his wife, Bronisława Banaszkiewicz; address: Bydgo-szcz, Bergkulonie Str. 18. Bogdanowicz completed primary school and four classes of high school majoring in business. He had a father, mother, brother aged 22 at home, sister aged 20 in a concentration camp, and sister aged 17 at forced labor near Berlin. In 1942 he was sent as forced labor to Hamburg. He was drafted into the German Army in 1943 and in May 1944 was sent to Cherbourg, where he was taken prisoner by Allied forces on June 24, 1944. He was quite familiar with Hamburg.

Private Julian Sobiechowski (real name: Zygfryd Kowalski), 22-year-old radio operator, born in Bydgoszcz. His nearest kin was his wife, Helena Kowalska; address: Bydgoszcz, ul. Bronikowskiego 5/7. Sobiechowski completed seven classes of primary school. He was conscripted into the German Army in February 1943 and sent to France, where he surrendered to the Allies in Cherbourg on June 16, 1944. He was familiar with Bydgo-szcz and its environs.[12]

Agent Aleksander Bogdanowicz/ Banaszkiewicz, Old Fashioned Mission. (Photo US National Archives)

Agent Julian Sobiechowski/Zygfryd Kowalski, Old Fashioned Mission. (Photo US National Archives)

Old Fashioned Mission Report[13]

The Old Fashioned team consisted of [text excised], *aged 23, observer and* [text excised], *32, radio operator.* [Text excised] *had worked as* [text excised] *up to 1942, when he was drafted* [text excised] *into the German Army* [text excised] *and captured in Cherbourg.* [Text excised] *had worked in* [text excised] *Poland until [text excised] and then was drafted into the German Army, surrendering near Cherbourg* [text excised]. *The observer's cover story was that he was a Lithuanian working in the reproduction and drafting department of a firm making cables and other technical devices in Bromberg. He was allegedly ordered from there to Danzig in 1945 and was at Danzig told to go to Diessen* [Giessen] *in western Germany, to report to the Arbeitsamt.*

The men were given worker documents, 25,000 German Rms and two diamonds. As will be noted from the following account the container of this team was seized by the Germans. It contained [text excised] *diamonds and money, which were therefore not recovered.* [Text excised] *was still missing in July 1945. A personal search made in Germany by Lieutenant Colonel Dasher failed to find any trace of him, and inquiries conducted by CIC and the British military government authorities also had no result.*[14] *The men were parachuted from an A-20 plane based at Namur on 25 March near Giessen, a little bit south of Homberg. The radio operator was picked up by the American Army in Rheinbach on 28 March. They were supposed to work in Giessen, reporting on military traffic and the location of German troops and supply centers. The most interesting experience of the radio operator occurred when he was overrun by the Americans. The CIC did not believe that his papers were faked, claiming that they had checked them with a German expert who said they were genuine.*

Following is a report of the Polish section on the Old Fashioned mission as given by Sergeant [text excised], *surviving member of the team.*

Personal Report of Radio Operator

On 25 March, at approximately 20:00 hours, we left the airfield for the pin-point south of Homburg. We arrived at the pin-point about 21:13 hours. Before my observer, Sergeant [text excised] *jumped, I looked out and saw a village below us. At 21:15 hours Lieutenant Gagnon, our dispatcher, gave the "Go" signal. It was much too early, the moon was very bright and we were spotted at once by the village people. I heard them shouting something about paratroopers. As soon as I hit the ground, on the border of the village beside a large woodpile and home, two civilians, one of them armed with an old rifle, ran up to me and shouted "Hande lang ziechen" ("Spread your hands on the ground"). They then searched me and took my knife, pistol and extra clips of ammunition. It was too difficult for them to take off my parachute harness so they ordered me to do it. Next they took off my "strip-tease" and relieved me of all the chocolate and cigarettes I possessed. This was being done by one man while the other stood guard, pointing the rifle at me. The one who searched me dropped one of the articles he had taken, and the other stooped to see what he was looking at. I took advantage of this, slugged him behind the ear, he fell and I took off as fast as I could in an easterly direction, ran close to a house in which there seemed to be much noise, turned south and kept running until I reached the banks of the river Lahn. There I found a bush partly in the water so I got behind it up to my knees in water. While I hid some civilians came by, one of them asked "Habt er ein Maschinengewehr?" ("Has he a machine-gun?"). He received no answer and they went on, returning again after a while for the second and last time. About 01:30 hours the moon went down and it got dark enough for me to continue on my journey. I followed the river bank until I came to a ploughed field, crossed it into a woods and headed west, using the compass the Germans failed to find on me. I oriented myself and decided we were not dropped on pin-point which was to be 8 kilometers to the left of the river. We dropped on the right bank in a village. Needless to say, I have no idea of what happened to my observer and the container.*

I walked until 05:00 hours then lay down in the woods and slept until 09:00 hours. I was never sure of my location but continued steadily westwards. Soon I heard some firing and proceeded in its direction. On the way I came upon a sign saying this was the county of Wiesbaden. It was not possible to travel on the roads. Our Allied aircraft were shooting anything they saw moving along them. I stopped about 1 kilometer from the firing, took cover in the woods and waited. Two roads skirted this wood, both were full of retreating Germans. The village below the woods was full of white flags of surrender as soon as the German troops were evacuated. I then entered that village, spent the night in a billet formerly used by French slave laborers. The following morning the Americans came. I immediately asked for G-2 and was unable to find them, so I moved on to the next village. There I met an American Lieutenant who spoke Polish. Upon hearing my story he told me to wait and see him again about 13:00 hours. He had no news for me when we met again and advised moving on until I found someone. So I went on to the next village, still not knowing where I was. About 4 kilometers down the road I came upon a guard with a Russian slave laborer who had been freed. The guard spoke Polish and again I asked for G-2. He took me to an American major. No questions were asked of me. I was put in a convoy with an MP escort. We travelled quite some distance and arrived at some forward position about nightfall. Here they took my papers, stripped me naked and searched me, and locked me up for the night with some German prisoners. I went all this time without food.

The following morning my papers and watch were returned and I was told everything was in order. Then I finally got some food and was allowed to wash and shave. Later I was recalled to MP headquarters where a 2nd lieutenant again questioned me, took my watch, wallet and papers and told me I was just another Hitlerite. He refused to believe my papers were fake, that he had checked them with some German. I was removed to another location and confronted with an American major and three assistants. Again I told my whole story, was put up for the night. Next morning, the 28th, I was taken to German prisoners collecting point at Rheinbach, since they classified me as another German. The 29th a Polish-speaking lieutenant questioned me and said he'd send me back, where he wouldn't say. I was then put on a vehicle with two Germans, one an SS man in civilian clothes, and the other a "Kreis-Bauern Fuhrer [Farmers' Circle Leader]." We arrived in Rheinbach where I was locked up with these Germans until 12 April. On the 4th I was photographed. On the 6th I was questioned and brought before the CO who listened to my life story and said he would contact London. I requested some shaving articles and cigarettes but no one paid attention to me and I was locked up again until the 12th when Lieutenant Gagnon arrived. My papers were returned to me, but I never saw my watch or wallet again. I let that go, glad to be set free.

Lieutenant Gagnon, who was my dispatcher, said the navigator gave him the signal to drop me, insisting it was the correct pin-point. We reached Brussels where I was finally given proper treatment and well taken care of.

HIGHBALL MISSION

The Agents

Corporal Wiktor Czarnecki (real name: Wiktor Szulik), 21-year-old observer, born in Szyny Jankowice, Rybnik county in Upper Silesia. His nearest kin was Alojzy Szulik; address: Jankowice Rybnickie, ul. Górnicza 18. Czarnecki was drafted into the German Army in July 1942 and served in Silesia and Frankfurt am Oder. He fought in Russia, where he was wounded in December 1942. He convalesced in Frankfurt am Oder, following which he was sent to France and Italy. He was captured by Allied forces near Cassino on October 2, 1944. He was very familiar with Silesia and Frankfurt am Oder.

Corporal Antoni Markotny (real name: Antoni Myszor), 37-year-old radio operator, born in Świętochłowice in Katowice county. His nearest kin was his son, Kazimierz Myszor; address: Bytom, Górny Śląsk, ul. Krakowska 30. Markotny was a widower with three children, probably taken by the Nazi Party. He was arrested and put in a forced labor battalion. He was drafted into the German Army in 1943 and sent to the south of France, and in September of that year to the 24th Infantry Division stationed in Normandy. He was captured by the Allies on July 18, 1944. He was very familiar with Katowice.[15]

Name:	Czarnecki, Wiktor (agent)
Grade:	Cpl.
Age:	21
Born:	Szyby Jankowice, county of Rybnik, Upper Silesia.
Father's occupation:	Coal miner.
Family:	Brothers, 23 and 17, sister 24, mother and father.
Schooling:	8 years primary school.
Personal history:	March 1940, drafted for forced labor and sent to Rittergutkolln Kreis Rothenburg Oberlausitz, Lower Silesia. - worked in a distillery. Fall 1941 - transferred to a farm in Reichenbach Kreis Görlitz. He ran away, returned home, was apprehended by German police and returned to the farm.
Army experience:	Drafted into the German army, July 1942. He served in Gorlitz and Liegnitz in Silesia, and at Frankfurt-am-Oder. He fought in Russia an was wounded in December 1942. Was in a hospital in Frankfurt-am-Oder. Was sent to France and then to Italy. Captured by the Americans in Italy, 23 October, 1943.

Agent Wiktor Czarnecki/Szulik, Highball Mission. (Photo US National Archives)

Name:	Markotny, Antoni (radio operator)
Grade:	Cpl.
Age:	37
Born:	Swietochlowice, county of Katowice, Poland
Father's name:	Franciszek
Father's occupation:	Miner.
Family:	Is a widower with three children, one boy and two girls. His wife died last April and the children were probably taken by the Nazi party. He has three brothers, 34, 32 and 30, and two sisters, 40 and 23.
Schooling:	8 years of primary school.
Personal history:	Was a railway employee before the war. In 1939 he was in the Polish Army, but was not captured. Was finally arrested and put in a forced labor battalion in Lower Silesia. During 1942 he worked as a railway dispatcher on the border between the Government General of Poland and Germany.
Army Experience:	Drafted into the German Army in 1943, sent to Southern France. Sept. 1943 sent to Normandy to the 243rd Inf. Division. Captured in Normandy 18 July 1944.
Territory with which familiar:	County of Katowice.

Agent Antoni Markotny/Myszor, Highball Mission. (Photo US National Archives)

Highball Mission Report16

The Highball mission was composed of [text excised] aged 21, observer and [text excised] 27, radio operator. *Czarnecki was born in Upper Silesia and drafted [long text excised] into the German Army [text excised] fought in Russia, was sent to France and then to Italy, where he was captured by the Americans.* [Text excised] born in Poland, was [text excised] before the war, during 1942 working as [long text excised]. *He was drafted into the German Army [text excised] and captured in Normandy [text excised]. The observer's cover story provided that he was Silesian, had worked as a concrete mixer in Ratibor and, in February 1942, was ordered by Arbeitsamt to evacuate to Kassel. The radio operator's cover story was that he worked as a stoker on the German railway and was transferred to Kassel in January 1945 for further duty as a stoker. He was supposed to be a Lithuanian.*

The men were given 25,000 German Rms and two diamonds. [Text excised] *returned 12,528 Rms and one diamond. In July 1945 [text excised] was still missing. The two men were directed to cover the Kassel area. They were dispatched by A-20 from Namur on 23 March 1945 and the observer was picked up three days later on the 26th.*

The Polish Section made no formal report on Highball. However, it is clear that the observer lost his nerve when he failed to contact his radio operator and set out immediately for the Allied lines, walking 110 kilometers before he was picked up. He reported as follows:

"The next time I go I want to make sure I have a decent pin-point. Instead of being dropped on a field, I and the container landed in the woods, my W/T operator, Sergeant [text excised] landed on a rooftop in the village. If it is true that he hesitated, it still was wrong because he also would have landed in the woods. The pilot should have flown along the field and not across it. I never found my container. It might still be in the treetops, or lying in the thick underbrush."

The observer's documents were never examined throughout the whole of his 110-kilometer trek.

ALEXANDER MISSION

The Agents

Private First Class Jan Czogowski (real name: Jan Czogala), 21-year-old observer, born in Stara Wieś in Pszczyna county in Upper Silesia. His nearest kin was his father, Jan Czogala; address: Stara Wieś, Pszczyna county, Upper Silesia. Czogowski completed seven classes in primary school and one high school class. His father was arrested by the Germans

Agent Jan Czogowski/Czogała, Alexander Mission. (Photo Janet and Stephen Smith)

and held at Oranienburg concentration camp for three years, then put to work in Blechhammer. In 1941 he was employed in the building of a large factory in Oświęcim[17] and in 1942 was called up by the German Army and sent to Czechoslovakia and later to southern and central France. In August or September 1943 he was sent to Normandy, where on August 10, 1944, he became an American prisoner. He knew Upper Silesia well.

Private First Class Józef Pająk (real name: Jan Masłowski), 23-year-old radio operator, born in Kochcice, Lubliniec county in Silesia. His nearest kin was his father, Jan Masłowski; address: Lubliniec, ul. Podmiejska 9. Pająk completed eight classes of primary school. In 1939 he was sent for forced labor, and from November 1942 until January 1943 was imprisoned in a concentration camp. He had a father, mother, two sisters, and three brothers, one of whom was killed in a concentration camp. Pająk was drafted by the German Army on January 14, 1943 (he probably agreed just to get out of the camp), and was sent to France. He ran away from the German Army on June 9, 1944, and surrendered to the Americans on June 22, 1944. He knew all of Silesia very well.[18]

Alexander Mission Report19

The members of the Alexander mission were [text excised] aged 20, observer
and [text excised] 23, radio operator. [Text excised] was born in Upper
Silesia and was employed [text excised] until drafted into the German Army
[text excised]. He was captured by the Americans [text excised] worked [text
excised], when he was sent to forced labor by the Germans. He [text excised]
was then drafted into the German Army and captured by the Americans [text
excised]. The observer's cover story was that of a railway track repair man evacuated to Osnabruck because of the Russian advance. The radio operator's cover
story was that he was also a railway worker evacuated to Osnabruck from Gorlitz
for the same reason. Both men were given Polish foreign worker documents.

The men were given 25,000 Rms and two diamonds. They returned 15,295
Rms, but lost both diamonds. [Text excised] had to burn his suit and in the
process he forgot about the diamond sewed into his lining. [Text excised] kept
his diamond with his radio which was lost.

The men were parachuted from an A-20 plane based at Namur on 23 March
near Osnabruck. Both men were recovered on 7 April by the advancing British
Army.

Following is a report of the Polish section on the Alexander mission.

Air Operations

This team was not dropped according to plan. To begin with the pin-point
selected was not a good one, but rather difficult to identify and locate. Further,
they were dropped from a height of about three thousand feet and definitely at too
high an airspeed. The following is the story as told by Sergeant [text excised]
the observer:

"I moved up immediately after my partner had dropped and had just barely
stuck my feet outside the plane when I was violently yanked out, and flipped
about a half a dozen somersaults before my chute opened and stopped me. It was
a clear, moonlit night and I could see Sergeant [text excised] and the container
going down but getting farther and farther away. My descent lasted for several
minutes, I had plenty of time to get untangled (after making all those somersaults
I was in a mess) and then to watch my landing. To my horror, I saw I was
going to land in a village; however, I hit the ground about 25 yards before the
first house, rushing madly I picked up the chute, harness, and ran in the direction of woods where my partner fell, for on the way down I had seen people run
about and heard someone shouting and quite naturally expected to be shot at
any minute. Somehow nobody chased me. Later I found out that the villagers
saw the three chutes, and believing it was three men, became frightened and hid.
Luckily, there were no soldiers or police on hand. My partner worried me, I saw
him land in the trees about 400 meters away. When I got to him, he was up
to his waist in slime, still hooked up to his parachute, pointing his gun in my

direction. We exchanged signals by whistling and then I helped him to get out of his predicament."

The story of Sergeant [text excised] the radio operator, was equally interesting. It follows:

"We must have been dropped at a terrific speed. I was yanked out of the plane so fast I couldn't collect my senses until the plane was pretty far away and I found myself violently swaying, my chute was open and had no rips, so I stopped my sway and prepared for landing. I must add, the plane never cut its engines and seemed not to have slowed down at all when he dropped us and, further, he certainly was out of sight and hearing in no time at all. To continue with my landing, I saw the container go down faster than I and it seemed to be drafting far away. I looked down and saw a wonderful field—nice and long, seemingly smooth. 'Good show' I thought, I was so high and drifting speedily, this field was out of sight before I hit the ground. I watched my partner for awhile—he was settling farther and farther away, but I could see he was heading for a village and then saw myself heading for a road. 'Looks like we've had it,' I thought, 'if there is anyone on the road, I'll shoot it out,' so I pulled out my .45 and held it prepared. Luckily, I passed the road and headed straight for the woods. I quickly put away my pistol and covered my face. The next thing I knew I was dangling about 5 or 6 meters above the ground. I looked up—my parachute was spread out over the tree top like a roof. 'Well,' I thought, 'the only way to get down is to climb up the lines and down the tree.' I shook myself into position and was going to hit my buckle, when suddenly I crashed down into some water, slimy mud and water, sunk up to my waist. There were some roots on the bottom, my foot hit them and gave me some pain. I had no time to start getting out when I saw a man coming toward me, so I whipped out my .45 again, then watched and waited. He came up closer and whistled—it was my partner."

The men took down the parachute with great pains, trying to make the least amount of noise. Having done that, they found the container by planning the drops.

Trek to Osnabruck

The team was given instructions to proceed directly southwards from the pinpoint. They did and found themselves in a marshland. They changed directions to go through the woods which they were told were absolutely clear and safe, and walked into an airplane dispersal area. They got out on a main road by asking questions of a pretty German girl, an employee at the aerodrome.

From her they found out about the defenses and equipment of the aerodrome and had they not heard that the area was being searched for some spies, would have sent that information to London. This information came in handy later on, when the British were attacking the field. To show them the defenses were poorly manned, these men went 500 yards forward of their lines, drawing very little fire. Upon their return the British attacked successfully.

Once on the road, with their suitcases on their shoulders, they marched along, singing gaily, much to amusement of the soldiers and people they passed.

Except for the few times they had to duck Allied air attacks, they ran into no further difficulties and reached Osnabruck in good condition.

<u>Documentation: Contact with Authorities in Osnabruck</u>
In Osnabruck, a thoroughly bombed out city, the team had considerable difficulty in finding the Arbeitsamt and police offices. The British night attack had left the city burning for three days, dislocating all the authorities and control. The clerk at the Arbeitsamt furnished the men with a tense moment. He took their "Kennkarten" [identity cards], laid them side by side and mused over them for about ten minutes, muttering to himself, looking very suspicious. Meanwhile the men were preparing for the worst. Sergeant [text excised] was gradually working his way back of the clerk ready to slug the man at the first indication of hostile intentions. Sergeant [text excised] had his hands on the edge of the table, ready to grab the documents and then to turn the table over—onto the clerk. The clerk apparently was satisfied for he looked up finally and said, "All is OK." Then he gave them papers with the RR.

The men gave their documents a going over after leaving the office to see just what had aroused such suspicion. It seemed pretty obvious. Although one was to have been issued in Breslau and the other in Gleiwitz, they could swear that the photographs were made by the same photographers and furthermore, the handwriting was the same on both and looked it despite the fact that different ink was used.

At the RR employment office, the men ran into difficulty again. Their cover story stated them to be RR workers of roughly 3 years experience, yet questioned on how much they earned, were not able to offer a satisfactory reply. They got around this by playing dumb and unintelligent, which, as they stated, seemed to get them out of every kind of trouble.

The RR furnished them with Reichbahn Ausweise [Reich Railroad ID cards] which gave them splendid freedom of movement, together with RR worker's uniforms which they bought out of operational money.

The only two items for criticism were the two Kennkarten, as mentioned before, and their lack of information about their previous jobs.

It is interesting to know that as "Protektorat-Sangehoeringer" [inhabitants of the Protectorate of Bohemia and Moravia] they had equal if not more privileges than German citizens, also, that the German RR uniform gave them absolute freedom of movement and they were unmolested even at times when the Volkssturm, SS, or Parteigenosse were checking on every civilian on the street.

The same uniform inspired confidence of their environment in social activities causing a free flow of comments on the war, the Party, the Allies, etc.

Comments on War by Germans
This team had much contact with the ordinary Germans. It was quite apparent that so-called "Good Germans" were extremely rare. A summary of the team's conclusions can be given thus: When Allies front was still distant all the Germans were pro-party, with plenty of faith in their strength and the much advertised "Secret Weapon" and further that in case they did lose the war, the next time would not end in a failure.

On the other hand, when evacuation was imminent with Allied tanks almost in sight, the Nazi Party was being renounced by all the very same who had expressed such faith before. SS and SA uniforms were disposed of, arms and ammunition, of which there was plenty, were hidden and anti-Nazis were every-where loudly condemning Hitler and all he stood for.

Later, after the territory had been occupied, these men gathered two jeeploads of pistols, rifles, machine guns and ammunition. The technique used is described thus:

"*Haben Sie Waffen*" [Have you any weapons?] one would ask, and keep him occupied, while the other would enter the house, ignoring the owner, and search. Not in one case did they come out without arms of some kind, and plenty of ammunition to go with it.

It is the contention of this team that every German family is well armed and that searches are essential. Along with arms there is plenty of food stored away in secret hiding places.

When handed over to Americans the team was able to lead the GI's to enor-mous supplies, or if the GI's were hesitant about looting, they'd go out in a jeep or truck and bring back full loads.

Billets
Although entitled to private billets, the team had to live in RR billets because there were absolutely no rooms or flats available, due to bombing. They shared a room with a "*Bahnschutzpolizei*" [Railroad Police], a man who worked nights.

Attempts at W/T Contact
This team made no W/T contact with the London Base. After the drop one radio was buried with the container, the other in another location, near an aero-drome. After they had established themselves, attempts were made to retrieve this equipment, unsuccessfully because of the proximity of the Allies and restrictions imposed on the inhabitants of Osnabruck.

PINK LADY MISSION

The Agents

Private Wacław Chojnicki (real name: Wacław Kujawski), 21-year-old observer, born in Chojnice, Pomerania. His nearest kin was his mother, Klara Kujawska; address: Chojnice, ul. Warszawska 7. Chojnicki completed seven classes of primary school and was an apprentice before the war. He was sent as forced labor near Stettin, from which he escaped. Around Christmas 1941 he was caught and sent to Danzig. In September 1943 he was drafted into the German Army and served, among other places, in France. On June 16, 1944, he surrendered to the Americans near Cherbourg.

Private First Class Zygmunt Orłowicz (real name: Zygmunt Tydda), 26-year-old radio operator, born in Dortmund, Germany, but living in Poland. His nearest kin was his brother, Wacław Drzewianowski; address: 58, MU Squadron RAF, Station Newark, Lincoln Rd., Notts, England. Orłowicz finished seven classes of primary school and three classes of high school, majoring in business. He served in the Polish Army and was taken prisoner by the Germans in September 1939, but managed to escape. He was arrested four times and jailed from March 1940 to October 16, 1942. He was drafted into the German Army on February 8, 1943, and stationed in southern France, and then posted to a naval unit in Cherbourg. He was captured by the Americans on July 1, 1944. He knew Pomerania well.[20]

Pink Lady Mission Report[21]

The members of the Pink Lady mission were [text excised] *aged 26, radio operator and leader, and* [text excised] *aged 21, observer.* [Text excised] *was in* [text excised] *in 1939 when he joined the Polish Army. He was taken prisoner but escaped, was later arrested and* [text excised] *was drafted into German Army. He was captured by the Americans near* [text excised]. [Text excised] *was* [text excised] *before the war, was sent by the Germans to* [text excised] *whence he escaped but was later caught and drafted into German Army. He surrendered to the Americans on* [text excised]. *The radio operator was born in* [text excised] *Germany, of Polish extraction, and the observer was born in* [text excised].

Both men were given a cover of Polish farm laborers evacuated to the neighborhood of Erfurt because of the approach of the Russians. They received 25,000 Rms, and two diamonds, of which they returned 13,690 Rms but lost both diamonds. They had given the clothes in which their diamonds were sewn to a Polish girl to launder. When they were overrun they were unable to return to the

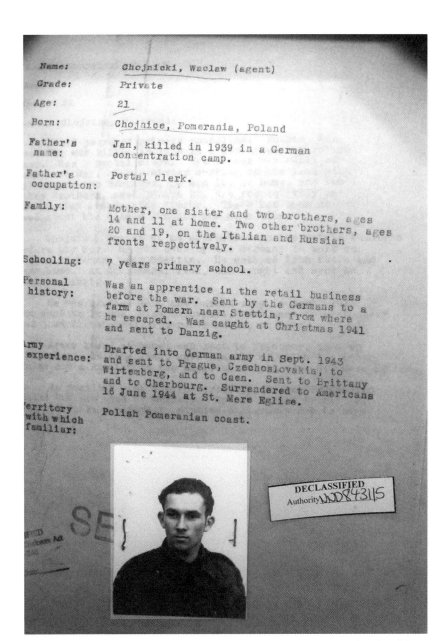

Name:	Chojnicki, Waclaw (agent)
Grade:	Private
Age:	21
Born:	Chojnice, Pomerania, Poland
Father's name:	Jan, killed in 1939 in a German concentration camp.
Father's occupation:	Postal clerk.
Family:	Mother, one sister and two brothers, ages 14 and 11 at home. Two other brothers, ages 20 and 19, on the Italian and Russian fronts respectively.
Schooling:	7 years primary school.
Personal history:	Was an apprentice in the retail business before the war. Sent by the Germans to a farm at Pomern near Stettin, from where he escaped. Was caught at Christmas 1941 and sent to Danzig.
Army experience:	Drafted into German army in Sept. 1943 and sent to Prague, Czechoslovakia, to Wirtemberg, and to Caen. Sent to Brittany and to Cherbourg. Surrendered to Americans 16 June 1944 at St. Mere Eglise.
Territory with which familiar:	Polish Pomeranian coast.

Agent Wacław Chojnicki/Kujawski, Pink Lady Mission. (Photo US National Archives)

Orlowicz, Zygmunt (radio Operator)

L/Cpl.

26

Dortmund, Germany

s   Stefan

       Blacksmith on railroad.
ion:

       Father and one brother in Poland.
       Mother and one brother in England, one
       brother in the RAF.

ng: 7 years of primary school, 3 years of
       business school.

       Sept. 1939, was taken prisoner but escaped.
y: He was arrested, for the fourth time, and
       stayed in prison from 3 March 1940 to
       16 October 1942.

       Drafted into German army, 8 February 1943.
ience: He was stationed in Southern France.
       4 September 1943, put in naval unit at
       Cherbourg. Captured by the Americans
       1 July 1944.

Agent Zygmunt Orłowicz/Tydda, Pink Lady Mission. (Photo US National Archives)

farm on which they stayed and recover their clothes, despite representations to the Americans authorities to allow them to do so.

The radio operator made one contact with the base but unfortunately his batteries were insufficient. He was unable to find any alternative source of power.

The team was parachuted from an A-20 plane based at Namur on 30 March and was recovered on 16 April. The men were supposed to work in the Erfurt area and were able to move around quite freely in this area.

Following is the report of the Polish Section on the Pink Lady mission:

Air Operations

The team was dropped at about 23:45 hours on 30 March, the drop being made from about 300 to 350 feet. The two men and the container all landed in a line within 50 yards. The pin-point was OK, the container being dropped about 50 yards from the forest. The only criticism was that they were dropped too close to the road and were seen by some SS troops.

First Contact with the Population

They did not go into the forest immediately. The container was seen by the SS men who came up to it but did not touch it. Meanwhile the agents ran towards the village in the opposite direction and when they saw the troops return to the road, they came back to the container, took it into the woods and covered it up with the parachutes. The troops meanwhile headed for the village, where they saw the agents headed. A whole company of SS troops looked for them. While this was going on the men came out of the forest, took everything out of the container, buried the chutes, broke up the container and buried it. They could work without being seen because they were in the shade of the woods with the trees as a background. After packing they went back on the road, saw no one and so they went on and marched about 8 kilometers until dawn and finally stopped in some woods. Meanwhile an air raid was going on; Erfurt was being bombed and the alarm was sounded all over the countryside. This added confusion and probably aided them to a certain extent. One of the radios was buried in the woods. They stayed there for about two days and on Easter Monday around noon they sallied out. Wandering around they ran into some lumbermen, decided to go to them to see if they were wise to anything. These people asked them who they were, what they were doing in the woods and their answer was that people around there were not very cooperative, that they had been roaming around the woods all morning after having been told that the shortest way to Erfurt went that way. They were finally put onto the road to Erfurt by an old man, where they found the 71st Communications Regiment setting up a new telephone line about 50 yards from the road and parallel to it. The old man showed them which way to go to Erfurt and that seemed OK with the working troops as they did not interfere. They continued on to Erfurt through Schellrod where they ran into some Poles and decided to find out about the local conditions from them. The most important thing was to find out whether there had been an alarm given about parachutists. There had been and strict control was set up at all bridges and intersections. In the villages and small towns everyone was being checked.

<u>*Contact with Authorities*</u>
Crossing the Autobahn on the way to Erfurt they were stopped by a patrol of two officer candidates, one from the 71st Regiment (which seemed to be spread all over the countryside) and the other from Air Force Communications. This was their first document check and after seeing their papers OK by this patrol their confidence was established. They asked for the way to Erfurt, which led directly through a prisoners' camp, housing mostly Russians and Italians, and were directed to go to one side of it.

Along this whole road to Erfurt this communications regiment was cutting down the old telephone poles and setting up a new line away from the road itself. Mines were being laid at each point where the old telephone poles had stood. These poles were later taken by the local people directly into their homes. The team could not establish the purpose of this but surmised that they might be prepared for use as anti-tank defenses or barricades, etc., later on. At Windisch-Holzhousen they were stopped again by some SS troops and the villagers also came up, all anxious to know who these men were and what they were doing there. They had to show their papers again. The papers were OK and they were told it was all right to go on to Erfurt but it was doubtful whether they could get the work they were looking for. When asked why they think they looked so suspicious to everyone, the team answered it was probably because they were travelers with suitcases, were dressed very much alike, and most important, both of them were young and most probably were suspected of being deserters from the army.

Before reaching Erfurt they tried to hide the radio just south of the city. When they got there they found it was all military barracks and defense positions and the bombing of the previous night had not touched any of these. Most of the bombs fell in the open field to the east of the forest. In Erfurt they tried to get some food but did not have potato ration cards and bread could not be had until the next morning so they satisfied themselves with beer. The same day they saw the jail. Prisoners from it were being marched to Buchenwald. It was impossible to take all of them, according to a local German, and all of the most insane were being shot on the spot. These men saw trucks going into the jail through a hole blasted in one of the walls by bombing, being loaded with dead bodies and then driven away. The local civilian populace seemed to be quite happy about getting rid of these prisoners, about their being shot and disposed of, said all they had was trouble with them.

The agents tried to find a safe address given to them by one of the boys in the school, which was his aunt's home, but it was getting late and the entire population of the city moved out at night so they had to do the same. On the way they found the Arbeitsamt and it had been bombed the previous night They figured, correctly, that they would not have to report there. They moved out to Melchendorf for the night. The next day they marched from village to village looking for work but finally ended up in Klettbach. On the way they noticed the mining of the road which was mentioned in their message received in London. At Klettbach they ran into some girls dressed in German uniforms, with armbands marked Reichsschule SS [an SS school], who however, spoke little German and consisted of French, Flemish and chiefly Luxembourg citizens. They were headed east, marching with their baggage on tracks. It was impossible to find out what their duties were.

They arranged to settle down as quickly as possible in the immediate neighborhood so they could send their message and get established. Both were very tired. Just before the village of Nauendorf they were stopped by some SS man who became very suspicious and threatened to shoot them right on the spot if he had any doubts at all about their papers. They were turned over to the burgomaster in the village, who, after looking at their papers at least 10 minutes, finally decided they were OK. Meanwhile, the men had been getting ready to shoot it out. At the village they were told to keep on going to Bad Berka where they would find some work.

Morale of Population

This section of Germany could be classified as one under conscientious German rule and strongly influenced by the Nazi party. The Volkssturm was rather active until it came to the actual fighting. The fifth paragraph of the report contains a good illustration of how the Germans in Erfurt felt about prisons, concentration camps, and prisoners.

When the arrival of the Allies was imminent, the people became frightened, expecting the worst. When the retreating Germans came to Tonndorf just a day before the Americans occupied the village, arms and munitions were dropped into a pond. Most of the soldiers were put into civilian clothes, and after the Allies had arrived none of the local population made attempts to expose these bogus civilians, in contrast to the contrary experience of the "Sidecar" team. Conversations among various circles from military through labor and farm elements revealed that the Germans had not expected the Allies to advance the way they did and that confidence was expressed that if they did they would be thrown back.

Food and General Conditions

As in most reports, the food situation was extremely severe. It was hard to obtain and much red tape had to be overcome to get it. Apparently large stores of it were hidden, and these were opened just prior to the Americans' arrival. Work and money were plentiful, but there was nothing to spend the money on. The people could not be bribed.

Military Observations

The area covered by this team was mostly under the control of the 71st Nachrich-
ten (Communications) Regiment. Discipline was good and morale at an average
level. Many of the officers and troops were invalids as classified under normal
military circumstances. They took advantage of their shortcomings later when
the Allies arrived and in this way tried to prove that they had never been in the
army. This team made many observations on the disposition of troops. They
made reports on the following units of this vicinity to the G-2: 11th Panzer
Division (minus panzers and armored cars), a battalion of Hungarian volunteers,
a battalion of Cossacks, the 71th Nachrichten Regiment and artillery defenses at
Erfurt. Some of this intelligence was sent directly to London.

Facility of Movement

This team moved around much more than most of the teams; however, it was all
done by foot. Transportation was difficult to find anywhere and it was avoided
even by the Germans on account of the constant air attacks. Although they
moved around considerably, it was by no means a simple job because they were
constantly being checked by the military of Volkssturm units.

SS and Special Troops

The only large unit of SS troops which this team ran into was one composed of
Hungarian volunteers. SS troops were in charge of the evacuation of prisoners
from Erfurt. A special unit composed of about 80 women in army greatcoats
with SS armbands went through one of the villages where the men stopped.
They suspected that these women were the guards of prison camps but had no
way to confirm that. Most of these women were not Germans—but predominant
nationality seemed to be Luxembourg, some French and Dutch. (They probably
were used for their knowledge of the respective languages.)

Attempts of Contact

This team made contact and sent a message through to London. They had quite a
bit of information to report; however, they ran up against the same difficulties that
most of the teams had, namely, shortage of the power supply. After their battery
had run out they stole two accumulators from wrecked cars and tried them out by
hooking the batteries together in parallel, but it was insufficient. The men found
a running German car and just after they had taken out the battery they were
noticed, had to drop it and run, for they were being shot at with a machine gun.

Recovery

This team was at the village of Tonndorf when the Americans occupied it and
they made contact with an American officer the same day when he came to their
home to look for quarters. They were sent through the offices of a major, a colonel,
the G-2 and finally the CIC. The next day they were taken to headquarters at

Arnstadt. The following day, for some reason they were unable to explain, they were sent to the FFSS [French Intelligence outpost] *in Frankfurt-on-Main. This French outfit treated them rather contemptuously, and the boys were highly dissatisfied. Fortunately they had a radio which they used to contact London, and with the instructions received in reply managed to convince the French to treat them as members of the American Army. They stayed at this unit for six days and were sent to Luxembourg where they were taken over by the advanced base of the Polish Section.*

<u>*Comments and Suggestions*</u>
The team was dropped on its pin-point, which was a good one, but they criticized the operation for being dropped too close to a main road, a circumstance which made them visible to some passing troops. The equipment they had was good, but the idea of using a battery was severely criticized. The life of a battery is much too short for extensive use. Electric current in Germany was either missing or, if it was to be had, the voltage was much too high. Both men praised the issue of special shoes for jumping. They used them in their cross-country runs, mainly, because, having a wide and flat sole, they left no footprints.

This team suggested that any future operations take into account bad weather and either furnish a pair of good raincoats or still better some tent flaps with which to arrange a shelter. It is possible that the circumstances were rather extreme due to the large number of refugees in the vicinity, otherwise they would have been able to obtain quarters. However, as a precaution for future use a team should be outfitted with a semi-camping outfit with plenty of food rations that can always be buried in the container.

PLANTER'S PUNCH MISSION

The Agents

Private First Class Leon Górski (real name: Jan Prochowski), 23-year-old observer, born in Nowa near Grudziądz, Pomerania. His nearest kin was his father, Jan Prochowski; address: Nenenburg Wjw., Horst Wesselstr. Górski completed seven classes of primary school and between 1937 and 1942 worked as a carpenter. He was drafted into the German Army in December 1942 and sent to France. He first served in Brittany and then in Normandy, where he was captured by the Americans on July 17, 1944. He knew Pomerania and Danzig.

Private First Class Bolesław Gajewski (real name: Bolesław Wiśniewski), 23-year-old radio operator, born in Gajewo in Świecie county, Pomerania. His nearest kin was his father, Józef Wiśniewski; address: Espenwerden

Name:	Gorski, Leon (agent)
Grade:	L/Cpl.
Age:	23
Born:	Nowe, Pomerania (near Grudziadz) Poland.
Father's occupation:	Carpenter
Family:	Father, mother, one brother and one sister.
Schooling:	7 years primary school.
Personal history:	1937 to 1942 - carpenter. 1939 - interned for 6 weeks.
Army experience:	Dec. 1942 - drafted into German army, and sent to southern France. August 1943 - sent to Brittany, then to Normandy. Captured 17 July 1944.
Territory with which familiar:	Pomerania, Danzig.

Agent Leon Górski/Jan Prochowski, Planter's Punch Mission. (Photo US National Archives)

Name:	Gajewski, Boleslaw (radio)
Grade:	L/Cpl.
Age:	23
Born:	Gajewo, county of Swiecie (Pomerania)
Father's name:	Jozef
Father's occupation:	Farmer and fisher.
Family:	Father, mother, six brothers, one sister.
Schooling:	4 years primary school, one year evening classes.
Personal history:	Had started apprenticeship in carpentry.
Army experience:	Drafted into German army Dec. 1942. Sent to Normandy. Surrendered 19 June 1944 near Cherbourg.
Territory with which familiar:	Native territory - Pomerania.

Agent Bolesław Gajewski/Wiśniewski, Planter's Punch Mission. (Photo US National Archives)

Post, Hardenberg, Kreis Schwets, Westpreussen. Gajewski completed four classes in primary school and one evening course. He was drafted into the German Army in December 1942 and sent to Normandy. On June 19, 1944, he was captured by Allied forces near Cherbourg. He knew Pomerania.[22]

Planter's Punch Mission Report[23]

The Planter's Punch agents were [text excised] *aged 23, observer, and* [text excised] *23, radio operator.* [Text excised] *was born in Pomerania, was* [text excised] *drafted into the German Army* [text excised] *and subsequently captured by the Americans* [text excised]. [Text excised] *also born in Pomerania, had just started his* [text excised] *before the war when he was drafted into the German Army. He surrendered* [text excised].

The cover stories of both men provided that they were skilled carpenters refugeeing from the Russians in the neighborhood of Stendal. The men were given 25,000 Rms. and two diamonds, of which they returned 16,760 Rms., but lost both diamonds.

Parachuted on 9 April from an A-26 plane based at Harrington, the agents never made any contact with base. When they got set up to do so they noted that the American trips were close and therefore decided not to risk themselves. They were recovered on 13 April.

Following is the Polish Section's report on the Planter's Punch mission.

<u>Air Operations</u>
The team left Harrington on 9 April 1945, at 18:00 hours, by A-26, for dispatch over Germany after refueling at Brussels. The trip was smooth. It was past the moonlight period and the night was pitch-black, making it difficult to observe the terrain over which they flew. Reaching their dropping point, the container was dropped first, followed by Gorski and then Gajewski [unexcised]. *The descent was satisfactory for both men.*

This team was dropped at the wrong pin-point but did not realize it until they started for their destination, Stendal. They were dropped near Rathenow, on the east side of the Elbe river and about eighty kilometers from the original pin-point which was on the west side of the river near Stendal.

<u>First Contact with Population</u>
After a twenty-minutes search, the container was found in a fruit tree in a nearby orchard. It was necessary to be very careful in removing the container because the owner's house was very near. The container was taken immediately to the wooded area where everything was buried with the exception of one radio set and their personal belongings. The next morning they noticed a man, apparently the

owner of the orchard, with a dog, snooping around where they had hidden the equipment. The man left immediately before they were discovered.

Getting onto the road they started in what they assumed to be direction of Stendal, still believing they had been dropped at the correct pin-point. From a civilian met on the way they discovered that Stendal was in the direction from which they had come and that the population was already evacuating that city due to the nearness of the Allies armies. They then decided to go back toward Rathenow.

First Contact with Authorities

At Rathenow they went to the Arbeitsamt to inquire about transportation. They were told that transportation from Rathenow was difficult but that they probably could get on at the next station, about 9 kilometers away. As it was already late evening they slept that night in the woods.

The following morning they walked to the station where they boarded a train from Stendal. On the way to the station they were stopped several times by civilian police and questioned but each time asked about the Arbeitsamt and were allowed to continue. Stendal was reached at 15:00 hours the next afternoon.

At Stendal they were interrogated by civilian police who obviously thought they were partisans or anti-Nazis. They explained that they were coming from Hannover and persuaded the police that they were patriotic and willing to help in the war effort. They found an older couple in Stendal who gave them quarters and food during their stay.

Comments on War by Germans

Most of the German people seemed to be tired of the prolonged war and willing to be taken by the Americans, but not by the Russians. They say that their dictator, Adolf Hitler, was a very fine man and had done what he could for the German people. But Himmler and Goering were not favorites. The Germans seemed to think that Goering, while in command of the air force, had spread a lot of propaganda about the strength of his Luftwaffe and that now German cities were being bombed continually without the slightest bit of opposition by the German Air Force.

The "Hitler Youth" were just the reverse. They were willing to fight on and believed that they would still win the war. They had not the slightest idea of losing their Fatherland.

Many of the SS troops dressed in civilian clothes as soon as the American Armies came near, and pretended to be ignorant of military activity.

Contact with Allies, Recovery

Friday, 13 April, at 11:00 hours the Allied tanks rolled into Stendal and began occupying the city. There was very little opposition and white flags had been hung up that morning over Stendal. The people welcomed the occupation as they felt their troubles were partly over. All the arms and ammunition were gathered up and taken away by the Americans. Four days later the infantry marched in and began keeping order.

[Text excised] and [text excised] then asked for G-2 and were taken to a major who interrogated them. They were asked to prove their identity. Definite proof was established after the major communicated with proper authorities of the Allied governments.

From the time the agents met the major they were treated very well. They received meals and suitable sleeping quarters at all headquarters at which they stopped on their journey back to Luxembourg. The agents said that on the whole the Americans treated them well except for the long periods of waiting while trying to contact authorities for their proper identification.

CUBA LIBRE MISSION

The Agents

Private Józef Jankowski (real name: Józef Parlich), 25-year-old observer, born in Giszowiec, Katowice county. His nearest kin was his wife, Maria Parlich; address: Giszowiec, Schlagester Str. 18. Jankowski finished eight classes of primary school and three evening classes, and worked as a miner. His father was at forced labor in Germany and he had a mother; four brothers, one in the German Army; and two sisters. He was drafted into the German Army the first time in May 1941 but sent back to work in the mines; he was drafted a second time in March 1943 and sent to southern France and then Normandy, where on June 30, 1944, he surrendered to the Allies. He knew Silesia very well.

Private Józef Jasiak (real name: Józef Kowalski), 25-year-old radio operator, born in Gruden in German Silesia near Oppeln. His nearest kin was his father, Piotr; address: Grudzice pod Opolem. Jasiak completed six classes of primary school and four classes of high school. He was conscripted into the German Army on June 24, 1943, and sent to France. A year later on June 25, 1944, he surrendered to the Allies. He knew German and Polish Silesia well.[24]

Cuba Libre Mission Report[25]

Introduction
The Cuba Libre mission was composed of [text excised] aged 25, observer, and [text excised] 25, radio operator. [Text excised] was born in [text excised] Poland, had spent 8 years in primary school, [text excised]. He was

drafted in [text excised] *the Germans but released to work in* [text excised]. *He was drafted again in* [text excised] *and served in France and Normandy, surrendering* [text excised] *in Normandy.* [Text excised] *was born in German Silesia* [text excised] *went 6 years to primary school and* [text excised]. *After the invasion of Poland he ran away to work in a* [text excised]. *He was drafted in* [text excised] *sent to France and captured* [text excised]. [Text excised] *was given the cover of a Czech foreign worker refugeeing from the Hermann-Goeringwerke* [Reichswerke Hermann Göring] *to Gottingen.* [Text excised] *cover was also that of Czech worker who had been employed in a synthetic gasoline plant in Czechoslovakia and had been ordered to evacuate to the Reich.*

The two men were given 25,000 Rms and two diamonds worth about $300 each. Most of the money and one of the diamonds were used in obtaining food and special privileges in a prisoner of war camp after the two men were recuperated. The other diamond was used by [text excised] *to bribe a man to take him across the Elbe. Considerable doubt was thrown on the men's stories by Major Jacques Beau, in charge of the liquidation of the agents, and further investigations were ordered to check on the men's statement of their disposal of the money and the diamonds.*

The two men were dispatched on the night of 1/2 April and were recovered separately. [Text excised] *on 11 April and* [text excised] *on 3 May.*

<u>*Agents' Accounts of Their Experience*</u>
On the night of the 1/2 April 1945, the two agents jumped out of a Harrington-base A-26 to a pin-point near Gottingen. According to the men's story the pin-point was changed when they arrived at the airport. They were given very little time whatever to study their new pin-point, the pilot simply saying that he knew a better spot that the one for which they had originally been briefed.

The men were separated immediately upon landing and their stories therefore are completely different. The two stories are given below:

<u>[Text excised] *Story*</u>
[Text excised] *did not find either the container or his partner when he landed. He dropped in a garden about 3 meters from a house. In front of the house there appeared to be a main highway, which* [text excised] *first intended to cross. He noticed that cars were continually passing and, furthermore, there appeared to be people about.* [Text excised] *stayed in the garden therefore until it got light and then went into a neighboring wood where he buried his parachute and strip-tease and then moved on deeper into the wood. It was raining very hard and he could not sleep. By 9 o'clock he came to a main road where he met a group of Polish slave laborers. They had come from Kassel and he mixed with them until he got on the road to Gottingen. On the afternoon of 4 April he reached Gottingen where he was supposed to meet* [text excised] *in case the two men had not met*

at the landing point. He waited for three days and then went to the Arbeitsamt to get work and quarters. They called the police as soon as they saw his evacuation order from Katowice but he did not wait to be handed over. He jumped out of the window of the Arbeitsamt and made his way to Northeim. On the way he slept at an inn in the village of Norten where he hid most of his money, keeping only enough to live on.

At Northeim a little further on he reported to the Arbeitsamt and was taken by the police with a group of other foreign workers to Goslar. Escaping from the group he stayed free for about a week until the police caught him sleeping in a factory. The Americans were already approaching Goslar and the police took all the remaining foreign workers directly to the railroad station. [Text excised] travelled with the foreign workers to Magdeburg where they expected the Americans at any moment. However, the Americans did not come immediately and [text excised] again escaped from the group and went to work with another Pole watching cattle in the pasture. This was near the village of Wornalitz.

The foreign workers who were hiding in the woods regularly stole food and items of value from the surrounding farms and in one of the police punitive raids [text excised] was again caught. Presumably he had been stealing food too. He was transported to the city of Burg where he remained in camp until the Russians were close by. He then escaped and crossed the Elba river on 3 May, was almost put back into the Russian zone by an American officer, but managed to mix in with some Italian prisoners, with whom he was marched to a prisoner of war camp where he joined a group of Poles. He made several attempts to contact OSS through officers of the prisoner of war camp, but then the Americans left Hillersleben and the English took over, no disposition had been made of his case. He finally contacted a Polish tank brigade and through it was able to get to Bremen, where he contacted G-2 and through G-2 OSS. He arrived back in London early in August after nearly 3 months in various prisoner of war camps.

During the entire time in enemy territory he did not make any attempt to collect intelligence. He said that since he had no communication facilities he considered mission quite futile.

[Text excised] *Story*

[Text excised] *was descending in his parachute he noticed that he was heading right for the roof of a building. By pulling the forward shroud lines he managed to miss the house and land safely alongside the fence of the village yard. He landed on the other side of the road from his companion and immediately assumed that the activity on the road was caused by their descent. He packed up his parachute and strip-tease and crawled to a clump of trees. After things quieted down he whistled the prearranged signal for his companion but received no reply and went into a nearby wood where he buried his equipment and afterwards fell asleep. He did not find the container.*

The next morning he crept back to the village where he had landed and saw the straw with which the container was packed but did not find the container. He assumed that it had been discovered by the police and he moved off quickly in a southerly direction to reach Gottingen. He followed the woods until he reached a small town called Uslar where he met a game-keeper who told him there was no sense in going to Gottingen. This proved true because at the first cross-road he was stopped by the NSKK [Nationalsozialistisches Kraftfahrkorps (National Socialist Motor Corps)] his papers were examined and he was turned over to the local burgomaster. His papers were taken away from him and examined and then returned. He was placed with other foreign workers in a schoolhouse under guard. He was taken eventually with the group from village to village and at Bad Gandersheim with four other Poles managed to leave the group and set out for the front line. He succeeded in contacting the Americans after ditching his four companions and was ordered to Seesen by an MP lieutenant. At that place he was mixed in with a lot of Czechs and interrogated, but such was the confusion that he was not specially dealt with. He was told that when he reached the rear area he could present his case again and he would be taken care of. He stayed with this group for some time until he reached Rheinberg where after three weeks separation of foreign workers began. At the end of three weeks he was sent with other Poles to Chalons in France, where after staying a week he got to see the camp CO. On the same day he had a fight with one of the foreign workers and was sentenced to 30 days on bread and water. He explained his plight to the first Polish lieutenant he saw and after seven days in jail he was sent to Paris, where he arrived on 23 June and contacted OSS. He left for London on 15 July and arrived on the 28th.

Like his companion he made no effort whatever to collect intelligence.

<u>Comments</u>
Commenting on the reports of both of the men Lieutenant Wusza of the Polish Desk remarked that neither man tried very hard to complete his mission. In particular he mentioned his disappointment with [text excised] of him he said:

"This man has been trying to put himself into as clean a light as possible, but obviously has made many untruthful statements, which I have checked by having several talks with him before his report was officially taken down. It is this officer's opinion that the man is, first of all, of extremely poor intelligence; second, he took the opportunity offered by the loss of his companion to use up as extravagantly as he could the money given him for operational purposes, satisfied his lust for adventure by ganging up with some other Poles and, armed with his Colt, indulged in some rough looting sprees. An individual wholly undesirable for this kind of work—for any kind of work with the OSS."

Disposition

The final financial settlement with the Poles was not made immediately on their return to London. The staff of OSS did not believe either of the men had told an honest story about the disposition of the money, and investigations were instituted to check the story. In the meantime the men were kept in London. Eventually they were returned to the Polish Army.

ORANGE BLOSSOM MISSION

The Agents

Private First Class Władysław Leszko-Sokołowski (real name: Władysław Kocur), 23-year-old observer, born in Rybnik, Silesia. His nearest kin was his wife, Adela Kocur; address: Godow O/S Kreis Rybnik, Bahn Str. 120. He had two brothers, both discharged from the German Army. He was drafted by the German Army on March 22, 1942, and was sent first to Upper Bavaria, then to Holland, and later to Normandy in France. Leszko-Sokołowski surrendered to the Allies on June 28, 1944. He knew Upper Bavaria and German Silesia well.

Private Józef Talarek (real name: Józef Herzyk), 20-year-old radio operator, born in Czech Silesia, Karwina county. His nearest kin was his mother, Stefanie Herzyk; address: Karwina Str. dSA Krs. Teschen 217/OS. Talarek completed six classes of primary school and two years of vocational school. In 1942 he was sent to forced labor at Namburg, German Silesia. He was drafted by the German Army on August 29, 1943, and sent to France. In July 1944 he surrendered to the Allies. He knew his native region.[26]

Orange Blossom Mission Report[27]

The Orange Blossom team members were [text excised] aged 23, observer and [text excised] 20, radio operator. [Text excised] was born in [text excised] Poland and, before the war, had worked [text excised]. Drafted into Germany Army in 1942, he surrendered on [text excised] to the Americans in Normandy. [Text excised] was born in Czechoslovakia and, after the German invasion, was [text excised]. He was drafted in 1943 and surrendered in France [text excised].

The cover stories for both men provided that they be Czechs. The observer, according to the story, had been a clerk in an electrical industry in Slovakia, but because of the Russians advance had been ordered to Magdeburg. The radio

Name:	Leszko-Sokolowski, Wladyslaw (radio operator)
Grade:	L/Cpl.
Age:	23
Born:	Rybnik
Father's name:	Franciszek
Father's occupation:	Died in 1943. Had been a mail carrier.
Family:	Mother, two brothers - both discharged from German army. Is married.
Schooling:	7 years primary school, 3 years commercial school.
Personal history:	Worked for city technical works in Rybnik in office. 1940 was discharged and sent by Germans to Altweile, as soil tester.
Army experience:	Drafted 22 March 1942, and sent to Upper Bavaria, then to Holland. Then sent to Normandy. Surrendered 28 June 1944.
Territory with which familiar:	Upper Bavaria, Frankfort-am-Main, all of German Silesia - Ratibor, Gleiwitz, Oppeln.

Agent Władysław Leszko-Sokołowski, Orange Blossom Mission. (Photo US National Archives)

Name:	Talarek, Jozef (radio)
Grade:	Private
Age:	20
Born:	Karwina, county of Cieszyn (Czech)
Fathers' name:	Jozef
Father's occupation:	miner
Family:	Mother; one brother in communications school in England.
Schooling:	6 years primary school, 2 years technical.
Personal history:	After German invasion, was apprentice in a mechanics shop. 1942, sent by Arbeitsdienst to Namburg, near Gruenberg, German Silesia. Had been a boy scout.
Army experience:	Drafted 29 August, 1943, and sent to France. Surrendered July 1944.
Territory with which familiar:	Native territory.

Agent Józef Talarek/Herzyk, Orange Blossom Mission. (Photo US National Archives)

operator, according to his story, had been an apprentice in a mine in Upper Silesia and had been evacuated to Magdeburg because of the Russian advance.

The men were given 25,000 Rms and two diamonds. They returned 18,200 Rms and reported both diamonds lost. [Text excised] lost his diamond when he buried his equipment on landing. He said it must have fallen out of his pocket. [Text excised] had put the diamond in his strip-tease and forgotten about it until after he had buried the strip-tease.

The men were not able to make contact by radio because of their short time in Germany. The mission was dropped on 9 April from an A-26 plane based at Harrington and recovered on 13 April. The team target was Magdeburg.

Following is the Polish Section's report on the Orange Blossom mission:

Air Operation
The team left Harrington on 9 April 1945 by A-26 for Brussels. The take-off from Brussels for final dispatch over Germany was at 21:35 hours. A few minutes before departure from the plane the bomb-bay doors were opened and the men were told to look down and observe the surrounding terrain which could not be seen very well because of the very dark night. The container was dropped first, followed immediately by [text excised] and then by [text excised].

The weather for jumping was satisfactory except for the pitch-dark. Nothing at all could be seen until the men hit the ground and their eyes got accustomed to the night. While dropping, [text excised] parachute lines were tangled so that he had very little time to straighten out and made a most unexpected, early landing. [Text excised] made a beautiful landing and while descending heard peoples' voices below him where he was to land. Fortunately, they landed quite a distance away from these people. [Text excised] landed about 40 meters from [text excised] and approximately 5 meters from the woods in which they later took cover.

First Contact with Local Population
[Text excised] *told* [text excised] *about the people being in the vicinity and then they noticed two persons, silhouetted against the horizon, moving toward them. The team was prepared to shoot if necessary. When they came within sight, the team recognized them as two civilians who lived in Oschersleben, a town about 500 meters away. The civilians noticed the team standing near the woods but apparently were frightened and passed by without speaking.*

The team assumed that the population and the police would be alerted so hurriedly began to look for the container, in order to hide it before anyone else appeared. The container was found after a twenty minutes search. The hatchet and shovel attached to the container, had been thrown off, probably by the impact on landing and were not found. The two radio sets and the equipment were taken from the container. The equipment could not be buried in what had seemed the most satisfactory spot as the ground was rocky and could not be penetrated without a shovel. The best alternative seemed to be to camouflage the radio and parachutes, which was done by putting them about a hundred meters apart covered with brush. A few moments later gunshots were heard in the neighboring woods so the team quickly dragged the container to a clump of bushes and camouflaged it. While they were working on the container a guard on horseback rode past on the road but did not notice them. Later they discovered that most of the civilian population slept in the wooded area where they had landed.

At about 01:45 hours the team left the forest, proceeding toward their destination, Magdeburg, about 33 kilometers distance. They encountered nobody until they reached Wanzleben where they met two civilians evacuated from, and coming from the direction of Magdeburg. The civilians advised them it was useless to continue as almost everyone was evacuating and the enemy was very near to the city.

First Contact with Authorities

They then returned to Oschersleben, being stopped several times by the Volkssturm and asked for their identification. Each time the papers proved satisfactory and they were allowed to continue.

Comments on War by Germans and Local Conditions

Oschersleben was reached by early morning (about 10:40 hours). On arriving at the place where the equipment was hidden they found German civilians still there. A great percentage were Auslanders [foreigners], Czechs, Poles and Italians. These people told the team about the hardship they had gone through under German rule and how they were continually escaping from their enemy the Russians. The older folk of the town were more than happy the Allied armies were so near and soon they would fear no more bombardments; but the younger ones, the "Hitler Youth," were persistent in their belief that Germany would win the war and were sincere in fighting for their Fatherland. They knew very little about Germany losing the war up to this date. Half of the older people were also ignorant of this fact.

Later that day they went to the Arbeitsamt in order to secure some sort of work, preferably in one of the many factories in the locality. They were asked where they were coming from and what they were looking for. The team told their pre-arranged story, and the clerk laughed and said, "You're escaping from the Russians and running straight into the Americans." The staff had already evacuated the town and there wasn't much help they could give. The men were told to go to the burgomaster, but instead went back for the radio in order to move on. Arriving at the woods they again found civilians with their personal belongings as the air raid alarm had just sounded. Some of them were very close to the set and the team was rather frightened about possible discovery of them.

Artillery was heard early the next morning, by which they knew the Allies were near. The same morning about 10:00 hours American tanks rolled into the town of Oschersleben and took over. There was not much opposition and so they did not stay long but left a few troops to keep order. At first there was a lot of commotion and people began robbing food stores and ammunition dumps but the troops later forced them to proceed to their homes by firing shots in the air.

That night they slept in the barracks (Auslandarbeiterlager) [foreign workers' camp] with the remaining people. The following morning American infantry occupied the town from 09:00 hours on.

<u>Contact with Allies</u>
After the occupation the team went into the town to find S-2 or G-2. They met a lieutenant and told him that they were Allied personnel working for the OSS. Obviously he did not believe them and to prove their identity they took a captain and sergeant to the place where the radio and parachutes were hidden.

Two days later they were taken to G-2 which was located near Wanzleben. Their identity was checked after communication with proper authorities. G-2 turned the team over to the Nine Army whose subsidiary headquarters at that time were in Bielefeld. After being there two days they were taken to OSS Detachment and then to Maastricht, where they waited for transportation to Luxembourg. All transportation was by jeep. A few days later they arrived at Luxembourg and later in the United Kingdom.

On the whole the Americans treated them well, although they were treated better by the front line troops than by the armies. At least they got good food at the front after the occupation but as they travelled further to the rear they received K-rations.

ZOMBIE MISSION

The Agents

Private Władysław Piotrowski (real name: Władysław Wolny), 20-year-old observer, born in Wędrynia, Czech Silesia (the part annexed by Poland in 1938). His nearest kin was his father, Ludwig Wolny; address: Kr. Teschen, Wendrein 232. Piotrowski completed five classes of primary school and four classes of vocational school. On January 15, 1943, he was drafted by the German Army and stationed in central and southern France and then in Normandy, where he surrendered to the Americans on June 17, 1944. He knew Silesia.

Private First Class Władysław Turzecki (real name: Władysław Gatnar), 23-year-old radio operator, born in Turza Śląska in Rybnik county. His nearest kin was his father, Franciszek Gatnar; address: Gross-Turze, Wala Strasse, Kr. Rybnik. Turzecki completed eight classes of primary

Agent Władysław Turzecki/Gatnar, Zombie Mission. (Photo Elżbieta and Piotr Gatnar)

school and worked in the Polish Tax Office. He had a father; mother; four brothers, one in a concentration camp, another three in the German Army; and three sisters. After the September Campaign he was sent to forced labor, from which he escaped several times. On January 24, 1943, he was drafted by the German Army and sent to the south of France and later to Normandy, where on June 16, 1944, he surrendered to the Allies. He knew German and Polish Silesia well.[28]

Zombie Mission Report[29]

The two Zombie mission members were [text excised] *aged 20, observer and* [text excised] *was born in Czech portion of Silesia taken over by Poland in 1938, had worked in* [text excised] *and* [text excised] *was drafted into the German Army, subsequently surrendering to the Americans on* [text excised]. [Text excised] *was born in Poland, had worked* [long text excised]. *He was drafted into the German Army* [text excised] *and surrendered in Normandy* [text excised].

The observer's cover story was that of a machinist in a German factory, while that of the radio operator was of an interpreter for the Germans in Czechoslovakia. Both men were supposedly evacuated to the vicinity of Magdeburg because of the approach of the Russians. The men were given 23,000 Rms and two diamonds. They returned 19,440 Rms and the diamonds. The team was not able to contact London because their batteries had been smashed on landing. The power they did find was too weak, although they were able to hear the London call signals.

The team was dropped from a B-24 based at Dijon on 31 March 1945. Their target was changed from Magdeburg to Regensburg at the last moment. They were recovered on 27 April.

Following is the Polish Section's report on the Zombie mission:

Air Operations
One flight. They were dropped at 23:55 hours on 31 March 1945 at the exact pin-point. The flight was very peaceful and the plane had circled the area three times before dropping. Both dropped successfully and immediately made contact with each other. They had difficulty in finding their container as they had jumped a bit late after it. After location the container, it was buried in a nearby wood, where they spent the night.

First Contact with Populace
The following morning both men walked north and met old people and inquired the way to Kelheim. Walking a little way they came upon a little village where they had asked for food and lodging but the people refused to take them in and refused food since they were very short themselves. With regard to work, it was absolutely impossible to find anything in that immediate area. The first two nights were spent sleeping in the woods since the whole area was filled with evacuees.

Contact with Authorities
On the third night they met some Volkssturm troops who, when asked for a place to sleep, referred them to the burgomaster of Viehhausen. They started to the burgomaster but were later called back by the Volkssturm men who escorted them to burgomaster. There they were asked numerous questions, where they came from; where they were going. At the end of the interview, he asked for their papers, which they produced. After examining the papers he was satisfied, found a place for them to sleep and informed them that they were to report to the Arbeitsamt at Regensburg the following morning. Next day they did not wait for the burgomaster to go with them but left early in the morning and proceeded to Regensburg on foot. They reported at the Arbeitsamt and were informed that the only work available was farm work which they took. Generally in their contacts with the authorities they had no trouble whatsoever with their documents.

Food Conditions
The food situation in the Regensburg area was very bad. Food could not be obtained with ration cards by black market. They had offered large sums of money for food but could not get it. The only food available was at the place where they worked.

Remaining Controls and Functioning Authorities
Generally in the Regensburg area the controls were very lax. They were questioned only once at a bridge by a police man who just glanced at the papers and passed them on. The vicinity was mainly patrolled by the Volksturm who would make an attempt to check on some people, but it was impossible for them to check on all since there were a lot of evacuees coming through.

Facility of Movement
From the 1st to 15th April movement was very simple and there were no restrictions until about 15 April when cadets from nearby officers school built barricades in that area. Then it was impossible to get around since the whole area was restricted. When the restriction came into effect all inhabitants had to remain in the vicinity of Regensburg and wait until they had been evacuated.

SS and Party
Eight kilometers west of Regensburg there was an SS supply dump for Auslanders. The dump contained mostly clothing which the SS troops in the vicinity were taking and discarding their uniform. In Regensburg there was an officers school which was taken over by Kampfkomandant Bekel who directed the defenses around the school. He was not an SS man but had a few SS troops under his command.

The Monetary Situation
Money was plentiful but had no value whatsoever. A barter system mainly existed.

Radio Contact
An attempt was made to contact London but they heard the call sign only once and it died out since the power they were using was too weak. Their accumulators were smashed on landing.

Contact with American Forces
The American troops arrived on 25 April and on 26 April they were told to evacuate with the rest of the populace. They did not want to report to the American authorities immediately since there was too much shooting going on but finally when they could not find a place to sleep they saw a major and informed him that they were Polish soldiers working as agents for the OSS. At first the

major was very dubious about their story but when they told him that they had radio sets hidden, a jeep was dispatched to pick up the radios. Upon examining the radio sets, their story was believed by the major. He asked them questions about the troops that were in the vicinity and also if there were any SS men. They informed him that there was one SS soldier hiding out and then they sent them to CP of the 104th Division. At the CP whey were questioned by a lieutenant colonel who did not believe their story at all and told them that they were German agents. They had shown him the radio, their signal plans and told him what organization they worked for. He examined their clothes, and equipment very carefully and refused to believe that their documents were made here in London and still doubted the story of the men. Then they informed him that they had parachutes and other equipment hidden about 20 kilometers away. Then he was convinced a little that they were legitimate agents but still doubted them. He asked them about the artillery positions and troops in the vicinity. They showed him artillery positions in Regensburg and told him of the troops and fortifications that were in the area. The following morning they sent them out with one soldier to retrieve the container which was still in the battle zone. They succeeded in getting over the line and found the container and returned to the CP. Then the lieutenant colonel was thoroughly convinced. He then started to ask about the OSS organization as to who the officers were, what pay the officers were receiving, what pay the agents were receiving and also wanted addresses of OSS officers. They replied that since he was an officer of a higher rank, he had his secrets and they had theirs and they refused to divulge any information. The lieutenant colonel was quite perturbed about their refusal to answer his questions. He told them that they had no military discipline since they refused to answer questions asked by an officer of higher rank. To that the men answered that he should only ask tactical information as to troops in the vicinity which they had answered and nothing else. The lieutenant colonel ordered a vehicle and sent them to the rear.

Practicability of Equipment
The radio equipment was practically worthless to them since the accumulators were smushed on landing as they were not packed properly. If they had been able to get sufficient power, the radio would have been operating and contact would have been made.

Comments and Suggestions
The men felt that if pin-points were not changed at the last minute they would have been able to operate more efficiently since in their case they were prepared for a different pin-point and did not have time to study the new one as well as they wanted to. The documents that the men had were excellent and they had no trouble whatsoever with them. Their main complaint was that the accumulator was smashed and they were unable to make contact. Otherwise everything went smoothly for them.

SINGAPORE SLING MISSION

Private Jan Prądzyński (real name: Jan Dumka), 23-year-old observer, born in Prądzona, Chojnice county in Pomerania. His nearest kin was his father, Paweł Dumka; address: unknown. From March 1940 to January 1943 Prądzyński worked on a farm in German Pomerania. His brother, aged 25, was confined to a German concentration camp in Oranienburg. In January 1943 he was drafted by the German Army and stationed in Holland, Belgium, and France. On June 25, 1944, he surrendered to the Allies at Cherbourg. He knew Polish Pomerania and especially the Chojnice area well.

Private Ernest Grimmel (real name: Ernest Musiol), 28-year-old radio operator, born in Królówka in Pszczyna in Upper Silesia. His nearest kin was his father, Emanuel Musiol; address: Królówka, Pszczyna county, Upper Silesia. Grimmel was a baker and after 1939 directed a bakery in Germany. He had a father, mother, four brothers, and two sisters. Three brothers were in the German Army, in Yugoslavia, Russia, and France. He was drafted into the German Army in January 1942, but exempted because of his work. In December 1942 he was again drafted and sent to the south of France and later to Normandy, where he surrendered to the Allies on June 22, 1944. He knew all of Silesia very well.[30]

Singapore Sling Mission Report[31]

The members of the Singapore Sling mission were [text excised] *aged 23, observer, and* [text excised] *28, radio operator.* [Text excised] *was born in Polish Pomerania, and worked* [text excised] *until* [text excised] *1943 when he was drafted into German Army. He was captured* [text excised] *at Cherbourg.* [Text excised] *born in Poland, was* [text excised]. *Drafted into the German Army* [text excised], *he surrendered* [text excised]. *Their cover stories specified that they were Czechs evacuated from Silesia to Passau, on their way to Kassel.*

The men were given 25,000 Rms and two diamonds. They returned 13,240 Rms. [Text excised] *reported his diamond lost. Bradzynski* [sic, unexcised] *used his to buy food from a farmer in Altmark, on the way to Passau.*

The agents were dropped by B-24 based at Dijon on 12 April 1945 and recovered on 6 May. Their target was Passau. Five attempts at radio contact were made but they failed because of the lack of power. They produced some intelligence, which they turned over to the United States Army. [Text excised] *turned out to be the leader.*

Following is the Polish Section's report on the Singapore Sling mission:

Air Operations

Two flights. 11/12 April at 00:35 hours. The men dropped about 500 meters from the original pin-point making a successful landing. After discarding the "strip-tease" they found the container which they buried immediately. They helped another team to bury it since one of the members had broken leg. The team then proceeded to a forest where they remained all night, since it was raining.

First Contact with Populace

On their first contact with the civilian population they caused some curiosity since both men appeared to be very young and most of the civilian population consisted of middle aged and older people. Since they aroused so much attention they stayed hidden during the day and only walked at night in the direction of Passau. Arriving in the vicinity of Passau they buried the radio which they had with them.

First Contact with Authorities

During their stay in Passau their papers were examined only once by an officer of the military gendarmerie. The papers were well scrutinized and were returned to the men and they were sent on their way. The papers evidently were very satisfactory.

General Attitude of Population toward the War

The people in Passau were generally worried about the Russians coming, they were just waiting for the American troops to arrive and were glad that the war was at its end. When the Americans were about 30 kilometers away they were burning all pictures of Hitler.

Food Conditions

The food situation was very acute in Passau. Food was unobtainable even with ration cards. People waited for hours and received practically nothing.

Remaining Controls and Functioning Authorities

Before the arrival of the Americans the SS troops controlled all governmental agencies in Passau.

Facility of Movement

Generally in that area there were no restrictions of movements. Both men were able to wander around in the city quite extensively and were never asked for their papers.

Monetary Situation

Everyone seemed to have plenty of money but it was impossible to buy anything for German marks. The only way food was obtained was by barter.

<u>Radio Contact</u>
They made three unsuccessful attempts to contact London. They believe it was the fault of the accumulator. Later two attempts were made using house current but still they could not contact London. On the last attempt they sent a message blind in the hope that London could hear them. In all these attempts they had heard the London signal but could never get contact with the London operator. All contacts were attempted at night since it was impossible to operate during the day. They believed that the radio was in working condition.

<u>First Contact with American Forces</u>
When the Americans arrived they first contacted an American sergeant who at first refused to listen to their story. When he finally did, he took them to a major who looked over their codes and sent them back to the factory where they were staying and said that he would return in the afternoon. The following day they reported again to the same sergeant who called up the major who finally arrived and took them to a Battalion CP, where they were not questioned at all but sent to an OSS Detachment in St. Martin, Austria. At the OSS Detachment they were interrogated and they gave all the military information they had. From there they were transported to Regensburg, from Regensburg to Erlangen, then back to Regensburg where they were picked up by a plane which took them to London. Both received excellent treatment by the Americans. The forces they reported to were very familiar with OSS operations.

<u>Comments in Practicability of Equipment</u>
Their main complaint on the equipment issued for the operation was about the accumulator. They suggested the use of a hand-operated generator as more practical.

HOT PUNCH MISSION

The Agents

Corporal Zbigniew Strzeliński (real name: Zbigniew Paprzycki), 21-year-old observer, born in Kępno, Poznan province. His nearest kin was his mother, Gertruda Paprzycka; address: Konarzyny, Chojnice county in Pomerania. Strzeliński completed six classes of primary school and three classes of high school. In February 1940 he was sent to Germany as forced labor, and from March 1941 worked in a factory in German Pomerania. He was conscripted into the German Army on July 24, 1942, and stationed first in Germany and then in Italy, where near the town of Cassino he surrendered to the Allies on November 9, 1943. He knew Poznan and Frankfurt on the Oder well.

Name:	Strzelinski, Zbigniew
Grade:	Corporal
Age:	21
Born:	Kepno, county of Kepno, Poland
Father's name:	Kazimierz
Father's occupation:	Customs officer (died 1941)
Family:	Mother and one sister, whereabouts unknown.
Schooling:	6 years primary school, 3 years high school.
Personal history:	Feb. 1940 sent to forced labor at Gulpin, near Deutsche Eilau, county of Rosenberg. March 1941, returned home and worked in factory making farm implements at Zampol, county of Schlechau, German Pomerania.
Army experience:	Drafted 24 July 1942. Sent for three months to Danzig, and for three months to Wanden near Frankfurt-am-Oder. Dec. 1942 sent to Southern France, and to Italy. Surrendered at Cassino, 9 November 1943.
Territory with which familiar:	District of Poznan, and Frankfurt-am-Oder.

SECRET

Agent Zbigniew Strzeliński/Paprzycki, Hot Punch Mission. (Photo US National Archives)

Name:	Rawski, Tadeusz (radio)
Grade:	L/Cpl.
Age:	22
Born:	Warsaw
Father's name:	Henryk
Father's occupation:	Highschool teacher before the war, then in business for himself.
Family:	Father, mother, one sister aged 19, one brother aged 16.
Schooling:	5 years of primary school, four years high school.
Personal experience:	After Polish campaign joined his father (in Mlawa) and helped in his business.
Army experience:	Drafted 24 March 1942. Stationed in East Prussia, and on Russian front. Sent to Bitche, and to Normandy. Surrendered 16 June 1944.
Territory with which familiar:	East Prussia, native territory, Bitche and Metz.

SECRET

Agent Tadeusz Rawski/Hahn, Hot Punch Mission. (Photo US National Archives)

Private First Class Tadeusz Rawski (real name: Tadeusz Hahn), 22-year-old radio operator, born in Warsaw. His nearest kin was his father, Fryderyk Hahn, and his mother, Maria Hahn; address: Mława, ul. Warszawska 54.[32] Rawski completed five classes of primary school and four classes of high school, and after the September Campaign he left for the home of his father, who lived and worked in Mława (from October 26, 1939, Mława was incorporated into the Third Reich). He was drafted into the German Army on March 24, 1942, and initially stationed in East Prussia and later sent to the Russian Front and then to France. He surrendered to the Allies on June 16, 1944. He knew East Prussia well.[33]

Hot Punch Mission Report[34]

The Hot Punch mission was composed of [text excised] *aged 21, observer and* [text excised] *22, radio operator.* [Text excised] *was born in Poland and, after 1940, worked in a* [long text excised]. *He was drafted into the German Army in* [text excised] *and surrendered at Casino.* [Text excised] *was born in Warsaw, son of a* [long text excised] *help his father until* [text excised] *when he was drafted into the German Army. He surrendered in Normandy on* [text excised]. *The observer's cover story provided that he had worked in a railroad car factory in Danzig and had been evacuated to Leipzig, and from there to Passau. The radio operator's story was that he had been a purchasing agent for textile for foreign workers in Danzig and had been evacuated from there to Leipzig and thence to Passau.*

The men were given 25,000 Rms and two diamonds. They returned 18,420 Rms and the two diamonds.

Unfortunately [text excised] *broke his leg when he landed, incapacitating the team. The observer made no attempt to work alone and gather intelligence that could have been of use to the United States forces.*

The team was dispatched by B-24 based at Dijon on 12 April 1945, with the Singapore Sling mission. The four men landed together and the Singapore Sling members helped [text excised] *to a hospital. The team's target was Passau. They were picked up on 6 May 1945.*

Following is the Polish Section's report on the Hot Punch mission.

Air Operations
Two flights. 11/12 April at 00:30 hours both men were dropped 1/2 kilometer from their pin-point in a plowed field. [Text excised] *dropped in a plowed field which had hardened and upon hitting the ground broke his leg.* [Text excised] *sprained his ankle slightly.* [Text excised] *was unconscious for a moment but returned to consciousness and took off his "strip-tease" but he was unable to get*

up at all due to the broken leg. [Text excised] *came to his aid and carried him into the nearby woods, where he made him comfortable. The container was found very easily and was buried with the help of the Singapore Sling team members.*

First Contact with Populace

The morning after the drop [text excised] *left* [text excised] *in the woods and went to several hamlets trying to find a place for* [text excised] *but was unable to find anything because of the overcrowded conditions. Everyone referred him to the burgomaster and said that he must register there. The following day* [text excised] *saw that he had to take* [text excised] *to the hospital; so he reported to the burgomaster, who checked his papers and sent a wagon to pick up* [text excised] *who was brought to the hospital. At the hospital* [text excised] *was asked his whole history and X-rays were taken of the leg, which showed Trimall joint dislocation* [trimalleolar fracture]. *The doctor seemed to surmise that this wasn't an injury from jumping over a ditch as they had told him but he let it go at that and didn't bother to make any report.* [Text excised] *remained in the hospital until the Americans came.*

Food Conditions

Food was generally scarce in Osterhofen area since it was overcrowded. They were only able to get meager subsistence with the ration cards.

Remaining Controls and Functioning Authorities

Generally in the town of Osterhofen the burgomaster was the only authority. There were a few troops but they never bothered the civilians.

Facility of Movement

[Text excised] *was able to move around in the vicinity without any trouble whatsoever. He was very seldom asked for his papers.*

SS and Party

There were no SS men in the vicinity until a few days before the Americans arrived when a few SS officers came in and insisted that the Volksturm in that vicinity defend the town, but they refused to do so. There were constant arguments between the SS officers, the Volkssturm and the burgomaster. When the Americans were at the gates of the town the SS officers fled.

Monetary Situation

Money was absolutely worthless and it was impossible to buy anything. Everyone seemed to have plenty of money. Exchange of goods and food was on the barter system.

Radio Contacts
No radio contacts were made because of the injury sustained by [text excised], the operator.

Contact with American Forces
After the Americans arrived they burst into the house where [text excised] was living and found a pistol in his possession. They threw his belongings all over the floor and when he attempted to pick them up the US soldier hit him over the right eye with the butt of a pistol. Then he was brought to the MP station where he requested that he be allowed to talk to an officer, to whom he explained that he was an OSS agent. He then requested to be brought to an intelligence officer. Since there was none available he had to wait a few hours, when transportation was made available for him and he was brought to the 64th Infantry Division headquarters. At the headquarter they asked him his complete story, the dates he dropped, etc. and also asked him if he had any valuable intelligence, which he did not have since this small town had no activity whatsoever. He then was taken to corps headquarters where he went through the same process. Corps sent him back to the original place where he had lived in Osterhofen and later returned and took him to the woods to find the equipment, which was already gone since another team which had landed in the same vicinity had been there a day before. He had notified the American authorities that [text excised] was in the hospital with broken leg. He then was taken to Regensburg where he met [text excised] and boarded a plane for Base X, Luxembourg.

TOM COLLINS MISSION

The Agents

Private First Class Franciszek Synowiec (real name: Fryderyk Jarosz), 21-year-old observer, born in Mysłowice in Upper Silesia. His nearest kin was his father, Zygfryd Jarosz; address: Birkental, Kr. Kattowitz, O/S Moltkestrasse 72a. Synowiec completed six classes of primary school and in 1940–1942 worked as a miner in a coal mine in Mysłowice. In July 1942 he was drafted into the German Army, and from November 1942 until the Allied invasion he was stationed in France. On June 9, 1944, he surrendered to the Allies at La Chappelle. He knew Upper Silesia well.

Corporal Józef Celer (real name: Józef Piecha), 21-year-old radio operator, born in Hażlach, Cieszyń county. His nearest kin was his mother, Zuzanna Piecha; address: Hażlach, nr 100, powiat cieszyński. Until he was drafted into the German Army in August 1942, Celer worked in the iron-works in Moravia. During his military service he was stationed in various places in France, and surrendered to the Americans at Cherbourg on June 9, 1944. He knew Polish Silesia. He spoke and read German but had problems with writing. Generally, he had big problems with studying, a very limited German vocabulary, and a strong Silesian accent.[35]

Tom Collins Mission Report[36]

The Tom Collins team members were [text excised] *aged 21, observer, and* [text excised] *21, radio operator.* [Text excised] *was drafted into the German Army* [text excised] *and was captured* [text excised] *in Normandy.* [Text excised] *worked in* [text excised] *Poland until he was drafted by the Germans* [text excised]. *He was captured by the Americans* [text excised]. *Both men were born in Silesia.*

The observer's cover story was that he had worked as a lathe operator in Kattowitz [Katowice] until ordered to evacuate to Wittenberg upon the advance of the Russians. The radio operator also, according to the story, had been a lathe operator evacuated from his job in one of the branches of the Herman Goering Works to Wittenberg.

The men were given 25,000 Rms and two diamonds, of which they returned 20,775 Rms and one diamond. [Text excised] *lost his diamond when he had to flee suddenly upon an alarm that the Gestapo was coming.*

The men were dropped on 10 April 1945 by A-26 based at Harrington and were picked up on 24 April. Their target area was Wittenberg. Unfortunately they lost their container so were never able to make radio contact. However, they gave intelligence to the US forces on recovery.

Following is the Polish Section's report on the Tom Collins mission.

Air Operations
One flight. The men were dropped at 22:55 hours 10 April. They were dropped 65 kilometers of their designated pin-point, and landed in the large forest. The men saw each other in the air but upon landing they were completely separated.

[Text excised] Story
On landing [text excised] *was hung up in a tree. The parachute ripped and he fell about 15 meters to the ground, injuring his ankle. He hobbled around all night and the next day in search for the container and his teammate, but due to movements of police and soldiers on nearby road from a bivouac area 4 kilometers away he was forced to abandon the search.*

First Contact with Populace
On leaving the woods he went to a road and met a German soldier who asked him for a cigarette, which he gave. The soldier departed. When he proceeded to a nearby town there was an air raid on, so he immediately turned back and went

into the woods. Later he proceeded by another road to a town 7 kilometers away from the woods. Reaching the town he found it filled with troops. He asked two civilians if they could show him the way across the Elbe. The civilians dissuaded him from going across the Elbe, stating that he would be returned or taken into Volkssturm. He observed what troops, artillery and transport were in that town and proceeded to a nearby hamlet. Arriving at this place he inquired for work. A woman referred him to the burgomaster. At the burgomaster he showed his documents, which were checked and returned to him with some ration cards. A woman hired him, and he stayed there 10 days until Americans arrived.

General Conditions
The people generally were just waiting patiently for the Americans to arrive and were definitely anti-Nazi. In the city of Dannenberg there was a definite short-age of food. People were continually in queues trying to obtain food since the soldiers who had arrived there had cleaned out the whole city. In small hamlets surrounding the city food was plentiful since most people had buried their food.

Generally in the Dannenberg vicinity the controls were very lax and [text excised] wasn't troubled at all for any identification papers. Around the small hamlet there were only a few local policemen who did not bother anyone at all. When the Americans arrived they immediately made a thorough check of every-one in the hamlet and the controls were very strict.

He had no trouble moving around since he was dressed as a farmer.

In the vicinity of Luchow there were scattered remnants of SS troops who immediately fled upon the arrival of the Americans.

In Luchow it was possible to buy food with money but after the Americans arrived money was worthless.

No radio contacts were possible since the container was not retrieved.

Contact with American Forces
When the Americans arrived they went through the house where he was living and questioned him. He immediately asked to be taken to G-2. A lieutenant there questioned why he wanted to go to G-2. He then informed him that he was an American agent. Arriving at G-2 he was questioned and his story about being an OSS agent was believed. G-2 asked detailed information about the enemy which he promptly gave. He gave the number of troops, vehicles and artil-lery that had gone through, also information about the bridges across the Elbe. He then was taken to another headquarters and further questioned as to where he was from, what equipment he had and how much money he had on him. He told them that he had a pistol, a parachute and a "strip-tease" buried in the woods but they disregarded that and evacuated him to Braunschweig where he was further questioned by the CIC and then taken to Maastricht to the OSS headquarters where he stayed three days.

Finally he was taken to Base X, Luxembourg.

Comments and Suggestions
The team received its pin-point one hour before taking off, since it had been changed, and they had no time to study the terrain. Also, since the pilot was not given enough time to study the drop zone, they were dropped about 65 kilometers from the designated location.

[Text excised] Story
[Text excised] landed on the tree which was about 15 meters high. While hanging there he was able to catch a branch and shimmed down the tree to the ground. He searched for his partner and the container the whole night and the following day but was unable to find either. After orienting himself he found that he was 60 kilometers from pin-point.

First Contact with Populace
After giving up his search for the container and his partner he proceeded to a road and saw an old man on a bicycle from whom he inquired the way to Wittenberg. The man immediately told him that it was on the other side of the Elbe and that it was impossible to get across since the bridges were mined. The old man asked him where he was coming from. He told him that he was coming from Braunschweig and had walked for three days and was very hungry. The man gave him food and questioned him as to what he was going to do now. He said that he would like to find some work so the old man offered him work cutting down trees. He replied that the work was too hard for him since he was not used to such heavy work whereupon the old man departed. He then proceeded along the road.

First Contact with Authorities
Walking along the road he was stopped by two Gestapo men who asked him where he was going and for his papers which he produced. They checked his papers and returned them to him after seeming satisfied with them and sent him on his way. He then walked for a few hours and reached a smaller hamlet where he reported to the burgomaster and stated that he wanted to get some work. The burgomaster asked him for his papers, which he checked carefully and returned to him. He then gave him food and directed him to a labor camp, where he fell asleep. The same evening he was awakened by two policemen, who evidently were sent by the burgomaster. His papers were checked and he was questioned as to where he came from and where he was going. He answered all their questions and, being satisfied with his story, they let him sleep on. The following day he got some work on a farm where he worked about 9 days. As the Americans were coming close, a car with Gestapo men pulled up to the labor camp where he slept, coming into the barracks, they informed all of the occupants that they were to be evacuated. [Text excised] immediately hid in the corner of the barracks and escaped through a hole. Then he hid in the nearby wood where he waited for the Americans, who were a few kilometers away.

Attitude of the People toward the War
Generally the people had known of the German reverse but were confident they were going to win the war eventually.

General Conditions
For a while food was very bad but when Americans got closer the food was a little-bit better. In a few instances [text excised] was able to buy food on the outside.

At the labor camp where he stayed, control was mainly by Gestapo men. Two days before the Americans came the Gestapo had all fled and the camp was in charge of the local burgomaster.

His movements were restricted since he was mainly confined to the camp. He was able to go out to the village but had to be back at a certain time. There were no SS troops in that vicinity.

Radio Contact
He could not make radio contact since all equipment was lost.

Contact with American Forces
When the Americans arrived he informed them that he was an American agent. They questioned him and searched him and took him to Luchow which was 8 kilometers away. At Luchow he was taken to a CIC detachment, where he was questioned and his story was not believed. He stayed there two days and was further questioned by a major who spoke Polish. He questioned him as to the complete story and when he informed the major that he belonged to an OSS organization he was taken in a jeep and driven from town to town in search for an OSS detachment. They finally found some OSS personnel who took him over and delivered him to Maastricht, from where he was sent to Base X, Luxembourg.

Comments and Suggestions
[Text excised] stated that one hour prior to the takeoff he was given his pin-point, which he was unable to study. He was completely ignorant of the terrain in which he was dropped. He also stated the pilot was not given enough time to check over the area in which they were to drop, causing them to drop about 65 kilometers from their original pin-point.

4

ASSESSMENTS OF PROJECT EAGLE
AND POSTWAR REALITIES

EVALUATIONS BY OSS LONDON

Major Louis P. Dups, Deputy Chief of Project Eagle, wrote a final report concerning Project Eagle in which he summarized and evaluated the missions.

Cover Story and Documents

Generally speaking, the cover stories and documentations stood up very well. The only difficulty encountered by the agents was that some of the papers could not be changed when, at the last moment, the pin-points were changed. Letters of introduction mentioning certain destinations could not be rewritten. In four cases out of the 28 the documents were detected as frauds. Men were not accused of being spies but merely deserters from either the German Army or the Labor Units. In one case the documents of both men of one team, although ostensibly originating in widely different localities, appeared to have the same handwriting. A third man had a military document on which the physical description was missing. A fourth man unfortunately parachuted into a region full of Czechoslovakian escapees who were being rounded up. His papers, which proved him a Czech, caused him immediately to be arrested.

Equipment and Supplies

Clothing passed adequately in all cases. The men suffered from lack of food. Although they had ration cards the food shortage was such that they could not buy anything with them. All the radio sets landed safely with the exception of two containers in which batteries were broken. Since no reception committees were available it was mandatory that the weight of the radio sets be kept to a minimum; hence the batteries did not have very much capacity. It was intended that the power would be supplemented from local sources, but this turned out to be impossible. In almost all the areas in which they operated, the electricity systems

149

had been knocked out by Allied bombing. Agents on several occasions had just managed to make contact with Station Victor when their batteries died.

Briefing

The briefing was, on the whole, adequate. The men returning expressed great satisfaction with the accuracy of the information given them, particularly as to conditions in general life in Germany.

Dispatching

Many of the teams were dispatched in the inter-moon periods as a result of the urgency of the work they were to do. Of the 16 teams dispatched, 10 dropped at or adjacent to their pin-points, five were dropped at distances varying up to 80 kilometers from their pin-points, in two cases on the wrong side of the river Elbe. Three types of planes were used in the operations. B-24s from Dijon, A-20s from Namur, A-26s from Harrington.[1]

William Casey, OSS SI London chief from December 1944 to August 1945, wrote his own evaluation of Project Eagle. The future CIA chief assessed SI's cooperation with agents from various occupied nations, including the Poles, in a measured and restrained fashion. Casey had been interested mainly in strategic, long-term intelligence and his agents had been trained appropriately. In July 1945 he evaluated the penetration of Germany and the Poles' part in the operation.

The Poles provided and joined with OSS in training 40 recruits who finally boiled down to 16 teams. OSS prepared and operated these teams entirely on its own as soon as the training was completed. Major diplomatic victory was gained in persuading the Poles to curtail the training presented for their agents by a month and 10 of those Poles were graduated with formal exercises on February 2 and on March 1 were over Germany in B-24s which unfortunately ran into weather which made their departure impossible on that trip. The Poles were generally unproductive. Though excellently trained, they were generally inferior in native intelligence and ability. They had difficulty with batteries and power for their radios and many of them were overrun before they had a chance to get settled.[2]

In his analysis, Casey overlooked the fact that the members of Project Eagle had been selected precisely for the job proposed and failed to note that they were neither officers nor civilians with a higher education. They were lower- and middle-class laborers whose task was to melt into the large numbers of forced laborers that had been forcibly deported from their homes by the Third Reich. Casey does mention the problems that his agents had with the SSTR-1 radio:

Considerable power trouble was encountered. Because there was no reception and weight had to be kept to a minimum, a generating apparatus and additional batteries were not furnished as it was considered feasible to procure batteries locally or to play wireless sets into local current. The batteries taken by the initial W/T teams were good for only an hour and a half and in some cases the operator just managed to make contact with Victor when the accumulator died. Allied air raids had so crippled the German electricity system that the men were not able to reactivate their sets. Attempts to steal batteries from automobiles did not work.[3]

Later, exceedingly brief accounts by Kermit Roosevelt[4] and authors who followed[5] claim that none of the Project Eagle groups were able to make contact with London base. The truth is that contacts were made but the batteries discharged so quickly that no substantive information—if any was available so soon after landing—was transmitted. As mentioned previously, one of the biggest problems the agents had was making radio contact. The entire "suitcase radio," the SSTR-1, consisted of a transmitter, receiver, and two batteries that together weighed nearly thirty pounds. During hard landings the electronic tubes and batteries were prone to break, and in such cases, agents understood immediately that they would be unable to complete their missions, that is, to transmit information to London. Ten of sixteen groups of Project Eagle experienced such problems.

Nevertheless, radio operators tried to make contact with London. The radio operator of Mission Sidecar tried three times to contact his superiors without success, until the batteries ran down completely. Mission Eggnog had similar problems, and at much risk to their lives and unfortunately without success, attempted to connect to the local electricity network. The Zombie and Singapore Sling Missions tried many times to use their radios, and also failed. Only two groups succeeded in making contact with base. The Martini Mission managed to send a very short message to OSS London and Paris before its batteries were discharged. Mission Pink Lady's radio operator, at great risk to life and limb, stole two car batteries that he used to contact London. In neither case were the Polish agents able to transmit any important information, but they continued to try to do so many times.[6] According to Kermit Roosevelt, only one of twenty-one SI London groups active in Germany successfully made contact with base.[7]

All the issues, including communications, that plagued the missions dropped into Germany were well known to Project Eagle members. In their reports they criticized the radio batteries, flight delays, and last-minute changes in targets that resulted in agents' being dropped into areas that were completely unknown to them. During their missions they were frequently stopped and questioned by the *Volkssturm* and Gestapo, but were able to talk their way out of any serious consequences. Even Sergeant Leon Adrian, who was awaiting death in a jail cell in Halle, survived thanks to the fortuitous bombing of his jail by American bombers. Unfortunately, first contacts with the invading Allied forces were not always friendly. Some Project Eagle members were jailed by Allied military police or G-2 because the latter did not believe that they worked for the OSS.

In this author's view, William Casey's July 1945 assessment of the penetration of Nazi Germany was objective with respect to the Poles in Project Eagle. They comprised the largest Allied group among the agents trained and parachuted into Germany by the OSS, and they knew that there would probably be little chance of their returning to Poland. In an unpublished work, Casey wrote in 1976 that when the Yalta agreement handed Poland to Stalin, "overnight the morale drained right out of our Poles, I could see it happening before my eyes. After [Yalta] they just went through the motions. They weren't worth a damn. I never forgot what caving in to the Russians did to those people."[8] Yet three decades later in his wartime memoir, Casey recalled, as noted earlier, that "the Poles never relented in their efforts to overcome the Nazis."[9]

The Yalta agreement had a similar impact on Polish soldiers fighting elsewhere on Western European fronts, as General Stanisław Maczek[10] wrote in his wartime autobiography: "At that time, winter in Breda, Yalta came to us. First, in whispers, fragments of conversations, rumors, until it revealed its terrible and tragic face. Its impact on the army was enormously disheartening. What next? . . . Of course, we're going to fight on."[11]

According to the *War Diaries*, during the penetration of Germany about 5 percent of all the agents sent by SI London were casualties. Some agents were sent without documents or with imperfect documents. That was not the case with the agents of Project Eagle, but they suffered losses for other reasons. Two agents were killed and one other was injured during landing, making Project Eagle's casualty rate about 9 percent.

From a technical point of view, Project Eagle was assessed by its leadership as a success. However, none of its agents were able to transmit any worthwhile intelligence to London, and although they did provide tactical information directly to the Counter Intelligence Corps, their intelligence-gathering missions were deemed a failure. Major Louis P. Dups explained why in his Final Report on Project Eagle:

> *The primary factor was lack of time. The first two teams were dropped on 18 March and the unconditional German surrender occurred on 8 May. In the intervening seven weeks our armies advanced at such a rapid rate that most of the*

men were overrun in a matter of days. On the average a team was in the field between 10 and 15 days only. This obviously did not allow them sufficient time to establish themselves, let alone organize an intelligence reseau [intelligence network].

Secondary factors which proved to be major deterrents, might not have handicapped the men to the extent they did if more time had been available to solve these difficulties. They were as follows:

It is not practical to dispatch teams on missions into enemy occupied territory involving a blind drop without safe houses or safe addresses. Even assuming the men are dropped immediately on or adjacent to their target, too much time is lost through the necessity of burying their equipment, pending such time as they are established locally. Then their equipment has to be recovered before they can commence transmitting the results of their intelligence work. In the case of the Eagle Project their dispatch and their being overrun in many cases was only a matter of days.

The communications equipment issued the teams must be entirely self-sufficient and must not depend on using local facilities of any nature whatsoever. Again in the case of the Eagle Project the teams were not furnished with sufficient batteries as it was mandatory to save weight and it was thought feasible to augment their current needs locally. This anticipation did not materialize and several teams who made initials contact were unable to send intelligence due to complete failure of their electricity supply.

In no way can any aspersions be cast on the activities of these agents while in Germany Their interrogation reports proved them to have performed their assigned tasks with merit. They encountered a great many obstacles and exhibited a considerable amount of native intelligence and ingenuity in surmounting them.[12]

What intelligence did the men of Project Eagle pass on to CIC and OSS SI following their recovery? They were "to act as pathfinders and reception committees for further personnel and will be briefed to report on German rail and road movements."[13] The OSS records include brief assessments that included each team's accomplishments and results. The results are as follows:

Sidecar: *This team was caught by police, questioned but not identified as agents and released. They reported on the strength, armament, etc. of divisions stationed in the vicinity of Ansbach, direction of retreat and final collecting point of retreating armies.*

Martini: *Radio Operator: Reported on troop movements through GUNZBURG and AUGSBURG, local defense and supply dumps.*

Observer:	*Caught by Gestapo, tortured and escaped during bombardment of HALLE. After reaching American lines, he cooperated with CIC, identifying SS troops and guards, soldiers in civilian clothes, etc.*
Manhattan:	*Observer: Reported defenses, counter-espionage units, strength of divisions passing through CHEMNITZ, and their destinations. After being overrun, cooperated with French Hq. in rounding up and interrogating SS troops, Nazis, and soldiers in civilian clothes.*
Operator:	*Caught by Gestapo and imprisoned as deserter from labor unit. Escaped and succeeded in reaching American lines where he reported on conditions in the Gestapo prisons and position of an enemy battalion near his point of junction with Americans.*
Eggnog:	*Reported on the condition of retreating German Rhine armies, armament and destination; sketches of anti-tank emplacements, Volkssturm defenses.*
Daiquiri:	*Reported on defenses of ASCHAFFENBURG, uncovered plot to blow up bridge across the Main; results of bombardment and strafing at ASCHAFFENBURG.*
Old Fashioned:	*The operator was caught on landing but escaped by use of force and cunning. Without equipment and his observer, he headed immediately for American lines. He was treated as a German spy and imprisoned for 12 days and was unable to report the information he had.*
Observer:	*lost.*
Highball:	*The observer lost his partner and equipment on landing and headed immediately for American lines. No intelligence was procured.*
Operator:	*lost.*
Alexander:	*Reported extensively on troops and supply movements, evacuation schedules and plans, defenses in vicinity of OSNABRUCK. Helped British forces in capture of an airdrome.*

Pink Lady:	*On landing the team evaded capture by German patrols who had observed their descent. Reported extensively on troops and defense emplacements within 20–30 kilometer radius of ERFURT. Uncovered upon recovery, spies left behind by 71st Communications Regiment, uncovered underground airdrome; supplies of hidden arms and ammunition. Reported to London on road mining operations South of ERFURT. Gave descriptions of conditions and mass murders of prisoners in Gestapo prison in ERFURT.*
Planters Punch:	*Team landed 60 miles from target and were unable to develop intelligence procurement due to being overrun almost immediately.*
Cuba Libre:	*This team recovered 10 July 1945 and as yet not deprocessed or interrogated. Were believed lost.*
Orange Blossom:	*Team unable to reach target and was overrun four days after landing. No intelligence procured.*
Zombie:	*Reporting on training activities, later turned into defense, of SS School near REGENSBURG, artillery positions, troops, fortifications.*
Singapore Sling:	*Reported on retreating German armies through Danube Valley and attempted contact with London, although German radio station, transmitting and receiving, was within 30 yards of their own.*
Hot Punch:	*Radio operator broke his leg on landing and observer got him into a German hospital successfully and legitimately. He did no intelligence procuring, but merely waited for arrival of Americans.* [14]

It should be noted that during the last few months of the war, when the German military began to use telephones rather than radio transmissions to communicate, the OSS missions in Germany collected valuable information. The British and American code breakers at Bletchley Park[15] were receiving increasingly fewer coded German dispatches sent by radio, and the value of information collected by OSS agents in Europe consequently rose.

Colonel G. Edward Buxton,[16] deputy director of the OSS (who later served as head of the Special Services Unit, or SSU), in his final report to the US Joint Chiefs of Staff praised the effort and the valuable information collected by the OSS agents sent into the Third Reich:

> *During the eight months preceding the unconditional surrender more than 100 OSS intelligence missions penetrated into Germany to obtain information on the enemy's situation and movements, on hidden factories and storage dumps, on the effectiveness of Allied bombings, on the treatment of Allied prisoners-of-war, and on the strength of Nazi control over the civilian population. Information from these missions reached Allied military headquarters promptly and in a steady stream throughout the rapid advances in March and April and into the last weeks of crumbling Nazi resistance.[17]*

AWARDS MADE BY THE US ARMY

After the dissolution of the OSS on October 1, 1945, President Harry S. Truman established the Special Services Unit (SSU). It was an organization created from the fusion of the much-reduced OSS departments of Secret Intelligence and Counter-Espionage—X2. Assistant Secretary of War John J. McCloy struggled to save these two parts of the OSS as a starting point toward the establishment of a new, peacetime intelligence service. On the same day the OSS was disbanded, President Truman created by Executive Order #9621 the SSU, which was to be part of the Department of War with General John Magruder[18] at its head.[19]

On January 22, 1946, the National Intelligence Authority was established, along with a small organization known as the Central Intelligence Group (CIG), whose budget and staff came from several departments or agencies connected with intelligence. Already at the beginning of April the entire staff and budget of the Strategic Services Unit was absorbed into the newly established group and now received a new name, the Office of Special Operations. In 1947, in accord with the 1947 National Security Act, the Central Intelligence Agency arose, which absorbed the CIG.[20]

On March 3, 1948, CIA director Admiral Roscoe Hillenkoetter[21] responded to a request by General William J. Donovan to supply a list, based on OSS personnel documents, of former OSS staff and foreigners connected with the OSS who had received awards and medals from the United States military. In his letter to Donovan, Admiral Hillenkoetter noted that the list was not 100 percent complete because not all citations had been received by the Citations Office in General Eisenhower's headquarters during the first few months following the cessation of hostilities, but that the list contained "all of the awards for which official notification was received." The list numbered 116 pages, and it included the following twenty-two names of Project Eagle members:[22]

Adrian, Leon	Silver Star
Barski, Edmund	Medal of Freedom
Bartoszek, Józef	Medal of Freedom
Bogdanowicz, Aleksander	Medal of Freedom
Celer, Józef	Medal of Freedom
Chojnicki, Wacław	Silver Star
Czarnecki, Wiktor	Medal of Freedom
Czogowski, Jan	Silver Star
de Gaston, René	Silver Star
Gajewski, Bolesław	Bronze Medal
Gawor, Józef	Silver Star
Gołąb, Zbigniew	Medal of Freedom
Grimmel, Ernest	Medal of Freedom
Jankowski, Józef	Medal of Freedom
Leszko-Sokolowski, Władysław	Medal of Freedom
Matuszowicz, Józef	Bronze Medal
Piotrowski, Władysław	Medal of Freedom
Prądzyński, Jan	Medal of Freedom
Rawski, Tadeusz	Medal of Freedom
Sobiechowski, Julian	Medal of Freedom
Synowiec, Fryderyk	Medal of Freedom
Turzecki Wladyslaw	Medal of Freedom

Interestingly, and notwithstanding his July 1945 assessment of the Poles above, London OSS SI director William Casey had to have approved the citations before they were signed and forwarded by OSS London Branch director Colonel J. Russell Forgan.

Following their service with the OSS, some members of Project Eagle received awards differing from those listed by OSS in their initial citations. For example, Sergeants Leon Adrian and Józef Gawor, according to their original citations, should have received the Distinguished Service Cross, but instead received the Silver Star. Julian Sobiechowski was to have received the Bronze Star but ultimately was awarded the Medal of Freedom. Nor do we know why nine members of Project Eagle whose citations were forwarded to ETO headquarters were not among the two

thousand OSS members listed by Admiral Hillenkoetter. This includes
Zygmunt Orłowicz, whose name was on a citation dated June 20, 1945,
for a Silver Star.[23] Ultimately, the Bronze Medal was awarded to Sergeant
Orłowicz, whose medals and a copy of his citation are in the possession of
and cherished by his sons Edward and Richard Tydda.

CITATIONS

In order to acquaint the reader with the content of American citations for
military awards, a few examples of citations as initially forwarded are provided below.

Martini Mission: Leon Adrian[24]

HQ. & HQ Det.
Office of Strategic Services
European Theater of Operations
U.S. Army
(Main)

APO 413
13 June 1945

*SUBJECT: Recommendation for Award of DISTINGUISHED SERVICE
CROSS*
*TO: Commanding General, European Theater of Operations, APO 887,
U.S. Army.*

1. *a. It is recommended that Leon Adrian, Senior Sergeant, Polish Army,
   detached for temporary duty with the Office of Strategic Services be
   awarded the Distinguished Service Cross.*
   *b. Senior Sergeant Leon Adrian was serving as a secret agent with the office
   of Strategic Services at the time of the performance of the service for which
   this award is recommended.*

   Marta Markowska (wife)
   ul. średnia, No. 6
   Starogard, Poland

   d. Entered Polish military service from England.
   e. Decorations previously awarded: United States
   none

    f. The entire service of Senior Sergeant Leon Adrian has been honorable since the rendition by him of the service upon which this recommendation is based.

    g. A similar recommendation for this individual has not been submitted.

2.   *The officer recommending this award has personal knowledge of the service upon which this recommendation is based.*

3. *a. Senior Sergeant Leon Adrian, while serving in close collaboration with the armed forces of the United States, distinguished himself by extraordinary heroism in connection with military operations against an armed enemy.*

    b. Detailed narrative of the service for which the award is recommended:

[A brief excerpt follows.]

    Senior Sergeant Adrian withstood unflinchingly the most inhuman and brutal treatment and grilling. First, he swallowed a special solution; and then, after he still refused to talk, they hit him in the jaw with the butt of a rifle, knocking out three teeth, and kicked him in the knee. The Gestapo guards had noticed him chewing something while in the train and when he did not vomit sufficiently, he was subjected to the pressure of two rubber rollers, one on his stomach and the other on his back, and which were squeezed together and rolled from the thigh up to his ribs to get everything out of his stomach. They found pieces of paper which he explained as being paper from a caramel he had eaten. He then was beaten with a rubber club.

    Senior Sergeant Adrian was successful in escaping from the Gestapo jail and on 15 April 1945, contacted the American troops. He gave valuable information about retreating troops to the nearest American G-2 and despite his weakened condition, Senior Sergeant Leon Adrian worked with CIC detachment for 14 days, rounding up Gestapo and SS men and uncovering storages of arms.

    c. The accomplishment of the service for which award is recommended extended from 18 March 1945 to 7 May 1945 and has been completed. The service was performed in the region of AUGSBURG-HALLE, Germany. Senior Sergeant Leon Adrian was injured during the time he served with the American forces.

4.   *Proposed citation: For the DISTINGUISHED SERVICE CROSS: Senior Sergeant Leon Adrian, Polish Army, in recognition of extraordinary heroism in connection with military operations against an armed enemy. As a member of a special mission he contributed greatly to its success by his high courage, initiative and endurance, proving himself deserving of the highest admiration and esteem of the armed forces.*

5.   *In order to support this recommendation, it has been necessary to divulge in the preceding paragraphs information classified as Secret. However, the*

proposed citation has been made sufficiently general to permit publication of it separately with the classification of restricted.

JAMES R. FORGAN
Colonel, GSC [General Staff Corps]
Commanding

Pink Lady Mission: Wacław Chojnicki[25]

Office of Strategic Services
European Theater of Operations
U.S. Army
(Main)

APO 413
20 June 1945

SUBJECT: *Recommendation for Award of Silver Star.*
TO: *Commanding General, European Theater of Operations, APO 887, U.S. Army.*

1. a. *It is recommended that Wacław Chojnicki, Sergeant, Polish Army, attached for temporary duty with the Office of Strategic Services, be awarded the Silver Star.*
   b. *Sergeant Wacław Chojnicki was serving as a secret agent with the Office of Strategic Services at the time of the performance of the service for which this award is recommended.*
   c. *Name and address of nearest relative:*
            Klara Kujawska (mather)
            ul. Warszawska No. 7
            Chojnice (Pomorze) Poland
   d. *Entered Polish military service from England.*
   e. *Decorations previously awarded: United States*
                 none.
   f. *The entire service of Sergeant Wacław Chojnicki has been honorable since the rendition by him of the service upon which this recommendation is based.*
   g. *A similar recommendation for this individual has not been submitted.*
2. *The officer recommending this award has personal knowledge of the service upon which this recommendation is based.*
3. a. *Sergeant Wacław Chojnicki, while serving in close collaboration with the Army of the United States, distinguished himself by extraordinary heroism in connection with military operations against an army enemy.*
   b. *Detailed narrative of the service for which this award is recommended:*

[A brief excerpt follows.]

> *Sergeant Chojnicki collected extremely detailed information concerning German units, and later turned this information over to the American G-2. He listed the 11th Panzer Division, giving the approximate strength, depleted armament and location of the arms and ammunition hidden prior to American occupation; 71st Nachrichten (Communications) Regiment, which dominated the entire territory south ERFURT and, when the Americans came, had planted several agents, all of whom were identified by Sergeant Chojnicki in front of the CIC officers; an underground airfield between NAUENDORF and BAD BERKA, passed unnoticed by American troops; heavy artillery emplacement at STERGEN WALD, southeast of ERFURT, a battalion of Hungarian SS troops and one regiment of Cossacks, both near BAD BERKA. By eavesdropping in police headquarters while being held for questioning, he was able to report telephone conversations between the Burgermeister of BAD BERKA and the Burgermeisters of all the cities coming within his jurisdiction, revealing the defense preparations, the proposed Volkssturm activities and subsequent action to be taken upon the arrival of American troops.*

> *Sergeant Chojnicki spent thirteen days in Germany, for ten of which he sustained himself on one twenty-four-hour ration, a few loaves of bread and beer, and suffered from exposure, fatigue and malnutrition. Sergeant Chojnicki was not wounded while serving with the American Armed forces.*

   c. *The accomplishment of the service for which the award is recommended extended from 30 March 1945 to 13 April 1945 and has been completed. The service was performed in the region of ERFURT, Germany.*

4. *Proposed citation: For the Silver Star:*

> *Wacław Chojnicki, Polish Army, in recognition of extraordinary heroism in connection with military operations against an armed enemy. As a member of a special mission, he risked his life constantly and contributed greatly to its success by his exceptional courage, initiative and determination. In all respect he proved himself deserving of the highest admiration and esteem of the armed forces.*

5. *In order to support this recommendation it has been necessary to divulge in the preceding paragraphs information classified as Secret. However, the proposed citation has been made sufficiently general to permit publication of its separately with the classification of restricted.*

James R. Forgan
Colonel, GSC
Commanding

Pink Lady Mission: Zygmunt Orłowicz[26]

HQ. & HQ Det.
Office of Strategic Services
European Theater of Operations
U.S. Army
(Main)

APO 413
20 June 1945

SUBJECT: *Recommendation for Award of Silver Star.*
TO: *Commanding General, European Theater of Operations, APO 887, U.S. Army.*

1. a. *It is recommended that Zygmunt Orłowicz, Sergeant, Polish Army, attached for temporary duty with the Office of Strategic Services, be awarded the Silver Star.*

   b. *Sergeant Zygmunt Orłowicz was serving as a secret agent with the Office of Strategic Services at the time of performance of the service for which this award is recommended.*

   c. *Name and address of nearest relative:*

   Wacław Drzewianowski, brother
   58 M.U. RAF Station, Newark
   Lincoln Rd., Notts, England

   d. *Entered Polish military service from England.*

   e. *Decorations previously awarded: United States*

   none.

   f. *The entire service of Sergeant Zygmunt Orłowicz has been honorable since the rendition by him of the service upon which this recommendation is based.*

   g. *A similar recommendation for this individual has not been submitted.*

2. *The officer recommending this award has personal knowledge of the service upon which this recommendation is based.*

3. a. *Sergeant Zygmunt Orłowicz, while serving in close collaboration with the Army of the United States, distinguished himself by extraordinary heroism in connection with military operations against an armed enemy.*

   b. *Detailed narrative of the service for which this award is recommended:*
   [A brief excerpt follows.]

   The information concerning German units which Sergeant Orłowicz collected and turned over to the American G-2 was extremely detailed.

He listed the 11th Panzer Division, giving the approximate strength, depleted armament and location of the arms and ammunition hidden prior to American occupation; the 71st Nachrichten (Communications) which dominated the entire territory south of ERFURT and, when the Americans came, had planted several agents, all of whom were identified by Sergeant Orłowicz in front of the CIC officers; an underground airfield between NAUENDORF and BAD BERKA, passed unnoticed by American troops; heavy artillery emplacement at STERGEN WALD, southeast of ERFURT, a battalion of Hungarian SS troops and one regiment of Cossacks, both near BAD BERKA. He also reported on telephone conversations the Burgenmeister of BAD BERKA and the Burgenmeisters of all the cities coming within his jurisdiction, revealing the defense preparations, the proposed Volkssturm activities and subsequent action to be taken upon the arrival of American troops. This last information Sergeant Orłowicz had obtained by coolly eavesdropping in police headquarters where he was held for questioning after being apprehended.

Sergeant Orłowicz spent thirteen days in Germany, for ten of which he sustained himself on one twenty-four-hour ration, a few loaves of bread and beer, and suffered from exposure, fatigue and malnutrition. Sergeant Orłowicz was not wounded while serving with the American Armed forces.

c. The accomplishment of the service for which the award is recommended extended from 30 March 1945 to 13 April 1945 and has been completed. The service was performed in region of ERFURT, Germany.

4. Proposed citation: For the SILVER STAR:

Sergeant Zygmunt Orłowicz, Polish Army, in recognition of extraordinary heroism in connection with military operations against an armed enemy. As a member of a special mission, he risked his life constantly and contributed greatly to its success by his exceptional courage, initiative and determination. In all respect he proved himself deserving of the highest admiration and esteem of the armed forces.

5. In order to support this recommendation it has been necessary to divulge in the preceding paragraphs information classified as Secret. However, the proposed citation has been made sufficiently general to permit publication of its separately with the classification of restricted.

James R. FORGAN
Colonel, GSC
Commanding

Alexander Mission: Józef Czogowski[27]

HQ. & HQ. DET.
Office of Strategic Service
European Theater of Operations
U.S. Army
(Main)

APO 413
13 June 1945

SUBJECT: *Recommendation for Award of SILVER STAR.*
TO: *Commanding General, European Theater of Operations, APO 887, U.S Army.*

1. a. *It is recommended that Józef Czogowski, Sergeant, Polish Army, attached for temporary duty with the Office of Strategic Services, be awarded the SILVER STAR.*

  b. *Sergeant Józef Czogowski was serving as a secret agent with the Office of Strategic Services at the time of the performance of the service for which this award is recommended.*

  c. *Name and address of nearest relative:*
        Jan Czogala (father)
        Stara Wieś Pow. Pszczyna
        Górny śląsk, Poland

  d. *Entered Polish military service from England.*

  e. *Decorations previously awarded: United States:*
        none.

  f. *The entire service of Sergeant Józef Czogowski has been honorable since the rendition by him of the service upon which this recommendation is based.*

  g. *A similar recommendation for this individual has not been submitted.*

2. *The officer recommending this award has personal knowledge of the service upon which this Recommendation is based.*

3. a. *Sergeant Józef Czogowski, while serving in close collaboration with the Army of the United States, distinguished himself by gallantry in action.*

  b. *Detailed narrative of the service for which award is recommended:*
[A brief excerpt follows.]

   As soon as British troops began to arrive in the neighborhood of OSNABRUCK, Sergeant Czogowski located the Intelligence officer and reported on the period of his operations, giving him the details of the city's defenses and the plan for retreat beyond OSNABRUCK. He then volunteered to guide the troops through this region and led an attack on the airdrome. He and his partner proceeded alone ahead of the troops to show them how the field could be taken with the lowest possible cost in

British lives and equipment. *Through his daring attack on the field and his careful observation in the OSNABRUCK area, Sergeant Czogowski made an important contribution to the British efforts in this area and successfully completed his mission.*

Sergeant Czogowski worked behind German lines for a period of fourteen days and was not wounded during this mission. The accomplishment of the service for which the award is recommended from 23 March 1945 to 7 April 1945 and has been completed.

4. *Proposed citation: For the SILVER STAR:*

   Sergeant Józef Czogowski, Polish Army, in recognition of his great courage and skill while on an exceptionally hazardous mission behind enemy lines. Through his rare resourcefulness and extraordinary tenacity of purpose, he was able to fully complete his assignment and to make a material contribution to the success of the Allied military operations.

5. *In order to support this recommendation it has been necessary to divulge in the preceding paragraphs information classified as Secret. However, the proposed citation has been made sufficiently general to permit publication of it separately with the classification of Restricted.*

James R. Forgan
Colonel, GSC
Commanding

Manhattan Mission: René de Gaston[28]

HQ. & HQ Det.
Office of Strategic Services
European Theater of Operations
U.S. Army
(Main)

APO 413
27 June 1945

SUBJECT: *Recommendation for Award of Silver Star.*
TO: *Commanding General, European Theater of Operations, APO 887, U.S. Army.*

1. a. *It is recommended that Rene de Gaston, Sergeant, Polish Army, attached for temporary duty with the Office of Strategic Services, be awarded the SILVER STAR.*

   b. *Sergeant Rene de Gaston was serving as a secret agent with the Office of Strategic Services at the time of performance of the service for which this award is recommended.*

c. *Name and address of nearest relative:*
   Maksymilian Barwikowski, father
   Marienburgelstr. 20
   Tczew, Pomorze, Poland.

d. *Entered Polish military service from England.*

e. *Decorations previously awarded: United States:*
   none.

f. *The entire service of Sergeant Rene de Gaston has been honorable since the rendition by him of the service upon which this recommendation is based.*

g. *A similar recommendation for this individual has not been submitted.*

2.   *The officer recommending this award has personal knowledge of the service upon which this recommendation is based.*

3. a. *Sergeant Rene de Gaston, while serving in close collaboration with the Army of the United States, distinguished himself by gallantry in action.*

   b. *Detailed narrative of the service for which this award is recommended:*
[A brief excerpt follows.]

On 13 April 1945 Sergeant de Gaston contacted the Americans at ZEITZ and turned over to G-2 the material he had obtained during the operations in CHEMNITZ. He then agreed to be assigned to the CIC for the purpose of interviewing prisoners and detecting Nazi leaders posing as sympathizers to the Allied cause. He was of great value to the CIC in uncovering political prisoners and exposing possible underground activities in American-held zones, and it was with great reluctance on the part of the CIC that he was released after three weeks to be returned to the Office of Strategic Services.

All of this time Sergeant de Gaston demonstrated exceptional courage and coolness in the face of great danger and carried his cover with such success that he avoided all suspicions. He demanded the best hotel rooms and requested and received large sums of money from the German Labor Front. Denied the protection of working with another agent, he succeeded in bringing the mission to a successful conclusion entirely on his own resources.

Sergeant de Gaston was not wounded while serving with the American Armed Forces.

4.   *Proposed citation: For the SILVER STAR:*

Sergeant Rene de Gaston, Polish Army, in recognition of unsurpassed bravery and skill in the conduct of military operations against an armed enemy. By his unselfish devotion to duty and his ingenuity in the face of great opposition, Sergeant de Gaston made a significant contribution to the success of the Allied military operations. His conduct was at all times deserving of the highest praise of the Armed forces.

5.   *In order to support this recommendation it has been necessary to divulge in the preceding paragraphs information classified as Secret. However, the*

proposed citation has been made sufficiently general to permit publication of its separately with the classification of restricted.

James R. FORGAN
Colonel, GSC
Commanding

Sidecar Mission: Józef Gawor[29]

HQ. & HQ Det.
Office of Strategic Services
European Theater of Operations
U.S. Army
(Main)

APO 413
13 June 1945

SUBJECT: *Recommendation for Award of Silver Star.*
TO: *Commanding General, European Theater of Operations, APO 887, U.S. Army.*

1. a. *It is recommended that Józef Gawor, Sergeant, Polish Army, attached for temporary duty with the Office of Strategic Services, be awarded the* SILVER STAR.

   b. *Sergeant Józef Gawor was serving as a secret agent with the Office of Strategic Services at the time of performance of the service for which this award is recommended.*

   c. *Name and address of nearest relative:*
   Brunon Bambynek, father
   ul. Dolna 18
   Nikiszowiec, pow. Katowice, Poland

   d. *Entered Polish military service from England.*

   e. *Decorations previously awarded: United States:*
   none.

   f. *The entire service of Sergeant Józef Gawor has been honorable since the rendition by him of the service upon which this recommendation is based.*

   g. *A similar recommendation for this individual has not been submitted.*

2. *The officer recommending this award has personal knowledge of the service upon which this recommendation is based.*

3. a. *Józef Gawor, while serving in close collaboration with the Army of the United States, distinguished himself by gallantry in action.*

   b. *Detailed narrative of the service for which this award is recommended:*
[A brief excerpt follows.]

Throughout the thirty-eight days of his stay in German-held territory he showed great ability in amassing a large volume of accurate and detailed military intelligence.

When the German army withdrew from the EIHINGEN area on 24 April 1945, Sergeant Gawor rounded up some of the Poles who had been working for him and set out to cut off the escape of a company of SS and SA men. When two of the SS men tried to get away, Gawor shot one and turned the other over to American soldiers who arrived soon afterward. He also led the American troops to the place where the Burgomaster had hidden arms and ammunition and assisted them in identifying a large number of German soldiers in civilian clothes. Sergeant Gawor then reported to G-2, turning over the intelligence he had obtained during his operation in German territory.

Sergeant Gawor was not wounded while serving with the American armed forces.

4. *Proposed citation: For the SILVER STAR:*

Sergeant Józef Gawor, Polish Army, for his extraordinary bravery and determination in the face of great hazards. As a member of a special mission, he contributed greatly to its success and distinguished himself by his courage, initiative and wholehearted devotion to duty. His gallantry and ingenuity behind enemy lines were in keeping with the finest traditions of the service.

5. *In order to support this recommendation it has been necessary to divulge in the preceding paragraphs information classified as Secret. However, the proposed citation has been made sufficiently general to permit publication of it separately with the classification of restricted.*

James R. FORGAN
Colonel, GSC
Commanding

The contents of these citations complement and support the positive evaluations cited earlier by Colonel Dasher and Major Dups. Many of the agents of Project Eagle collected and forwarded detailed intelligence to G-2 about German military units and their defensive positions. They are at odds with the cold assessment of William Casey of the agents as being generally unproductive made in July 1945, just a few weeks after the citations were sent to US Army Headquarters in June. The citations demonstrate that most of the Polish agents risked their lives to boldly fulfill their special missions. The citations show their determination in their struggle against the enemy and their bravery; their bios help inform why. Their intelligence helped the Allied forces capture important targets, like bridges and German airfields, with minimal losses in personnel or equipment. Some were unable to accomplish what they were sent to do: some landed many kilometers from their drop zones without their partners, one broke an ankle, two others did not survive the drop. However, the Americans in charge of Project Eagle felt that their charges deserved the respect of and recognition from the US Armed Forces.

We do not know whether the members of Project Eagle or agents of other nations working for the OSS were aware of Hitler's secret *Kommandobefehl* of October 18, 1942, that ordered the physical elimination of any Allied parachutists or saboteurs captured in Europe or Africa:

> *All enemy troops encountered by German troops during so-called commando operations in Europe or in Africa, even if they appear to be soldiers in uniform or demolition groups, armed or unarmed, are to be exterminated to the last man, either in combat or in pursuit. It matters not in the least whether they have landed for their operations by ships or planes or dropped by parachute. If such men appear to be about to surrender, no quarter shall be given them. . . . If individual members of such commandos, acting as agents, saboteurs, etc. fall into the hands of the Wehrmacht through different channels (for example, through the police in occupied territories) they are to be handed over without delay to the Sicherheitsdienst. It is formally forbidden to keep them, even temporarily, under military supervision (for example, in prisoner of war camps, etc.).*[30]

Whether they were aware of the order or not, the wartime experience of the agents, including those of Project Eagle, would have been sufficient for them to know what awaited them if caught and exposed, and it did not deter them. Nor did learning about the Yalta agreement and knowing that postwar Poland would come under another dictatorship, a Communist one, cause the Polish agents to withdraw from their missions and simply wait out the end of hostilities. Casey was right in sensing the demoralization that descended on his agents in February 1945. He was unable, however, to accept the fact that his strategic plan had been derailed by the speed on the ground of the Allied invasion of Germany and by the urgent need for tactical intelligence by the Allied forces poised to invade the Reich. Such is war.

As mentioned above, the OSS was no more as of October 1, 1945, and as a result of great administrative haste and chaos in liquidating the organization, personnel records concerning awards to individuals for their heroism and courage went missing. That is the case with the personnel records of Project Eagle, where there is no indication whether the citations were ultimately approved, and if so, whether the individual's award was the one cited; and secondly, whether the award was presented to the individual, by whom, and where. An example of the chaos surrounding awards for OSS members (and not only OSS members) is the case of Major Stephanie Czech Rader, an American of Polish heritage who served in Poland in 1946 for the SSU and who died at one hundred years of age in June 2016. Seventy years after her service, she received the Legion of Merit just before her interment at Arlington National Cemetery.[31]

AWARDS MADE BY THE POLISH ARMY

The Polish authorities in London were also aware of the bravery and efforts of the members of Project Eagle. Each of them was advanced in rank to sergeant,[32] and in September 1945 the president of the Polish Republic and the Minister of National Defense awarded the second highest military award, the Cross of Valor, to Leon Adrian, Wacław Chojnicki, Józef Gawor, and Zygmunt Orłowicz.[33] Zbigniew Strzeliński was awarded the Silver Cross of Merit with Swords, and twenty-three members of Project Eagle received the Bronze Cross of Merit with Swords.[34] A few months later, on February 6, 1946, the commandant of the School of Specialists drew up citations that were presented to the Polish authorities to authorize the award of the Cross of Valor and the Bronze Cross of Merit with Swords on behalf of Antoni Markotny and Aleksander Bogdanowicz, who perished during their missions.[35]

WHAT HAPPENED TO THE AGENTS OF PROJECT EAGLE?

With the end of hostilities in Europe, the members of Project Eagle were released from duty in the OSS. In the declassified records of the latter, there is no information as to their further activities. Records of their decorations and awards are spotty, and with the dissolution of the OSS, any official interest in them ceased. Polish Army documents record the postings of the men upon their return to duty in the Polish Army in the West. Senior Sergeant Adrian and Sergeants Chojnicki, Czapliński, Czogowski, Gawor, Matuszowicz, Orłowicz, Piotrowski, Prądzyński, Strzeliński, and Synowiec were sent to the First Corps Staff Company's Defense Intelligence Training Center. Sergeant de Gaston wound up posted to the Ministry of National Defense's Department of Defense Intelligence Administrative Unit. Sergeants Górski and Leszko-Sokołowski were attached to the Commander-in-Chief's Staff Administrative Unit. Sergeants Celer, Czarnecki, Nowicki,

Pająk, and Talerek were assigned to the Center for Occupation Work's Military Management Inspectorate. Sergeants Barski, Bartoszek, Gajewski, Gołąb, Grimmel, Sobiechowski, Turzecki, and Zagórski were sent to the Communication Battalion of the Commander-in-Chief's Staff. Sergeant Wolny was delegated to the Reserve Parachute Center.[36]

Even after the OSS was dissolved and the Special Services Unit was established, Colonel Dasher kept up his efforts to have the SSU enlist the services of his well-trained and experienced agents, and those efforts were not met with an unjaundiced eye. A report authored by Richard Helms, the then-head of the Central European Section of the SSU's umbrella organization, the Central Intelligence Group,[37] was sent to Lewis Crosby, the head of mission of the group in Germany. Helms referenced Colonel Dasher and his efforts to recruit the former members of Project Eagle into the SSU's work in Germany. The document refers to intelligence activities in Poland.

> *Your recent cables on Dasher, his recruitment of the Eagles in London, and the possibility of his employment with us were answered negatively by Colonel Quinn[38] who feels strongly the whole business involves an excellent opportunity for the British to penetrate us, or at least American intelligence. Certain it is that those Eagles are loyal first to Colonel Gano, and regardless of statements to the contrary, the definite impression prevails that Dunderdale controls those Poles and will continue to do so. . . .*
>
> *We keenly appreciate the difficulties of doing a job on Poland, but we would rather take it more slowly than to run the risk of getting enmeshed in the Dunderdale-Gano-Dasher net.[39]*

There is some evidence that representatives of US intelligence contacted individual Polish officers after the war. At the beginning of May 1946, Major Oliver Rockhill[40] approached Major Lucjan Jagodziński[41] with a proposal to organize an intelligence network aimed at gathering information concerning the situation in Poland. In a memo dated June 12, 1946, Major Mściwój Kokorniak,[42] a liaison officer in Linz, Austria, wrote to Colonel Wincenty Bąkiewicz,[43] intelligence chief of the Polish Army's Second Corps:

> *American OSS[44] approached me through Major Jagodzinski with a proposal for intelligence cooperation.*
>
> *The proposal suits me, but I reserved the right to clear this with you, Colonel, as my superior and the head of the Second Branch of the Second Corps, with the*

accompanying declaration that until now I have never carried out any intelligence tasks in Austria and that my duties consisted in caring for Polish refugees.

The OSS requests the following information:

Information from Poland and Russia of a political and military nature. What is happening behind the Curzon Line, what military units are stationed there; what emplacements, airfields and air power; what units are stationed in Poland; the fortification of Czerwony Bór, Ossowiec; units in the area of Kraków, Silesia, Pomerania, and Poznań. Supposedly the 3rd Guards Army is stationed south of Kraków.

[The Americans want to know] how large and where NKVD units are stationed; what preparations for the referendum are being readied by the Polish Workers' Party and the NKVD with the secret police, how many Russians there are in Żymierski's Army, etc.

All technical support and necessary resources are to be provided by the OSS. I did not go into financial matters, as I wanted first to check with you, Colonel.

The intelligence work plan. I set out a plan for six months, with the idea that for the first three months information would come from informants coming from our country, and later from agents who had been recruited, trained, and sent back through Czechoslovakia and Hungary to Poland and Russia. (Lately, 11 refugees from our country have arrived in Linz.) News from Poland would be gathered not only in Austria but also in Bavaria, where more people go than in Austria, amounting to some 1,000 monthly.

I would need an additional officer for the task, as my deputy and interrogator.

KOKORNIAK—major[45]

Unfortunately, we do not know whether agreement was reached and whether Major Kokorniak or other Poles were enlisted by American or British intelligence at that time.[46] When the OSS was dissolved at the end of September 1945 and the Special Services Unit was established to continue some of its activities, 5,713 people were employed in the OSS's larger bases abroad, including London, Paris, Rome, Vienna, Cairo, Chungking, Calcutta, New Delhi, and Rangoon, as well as in smaller units active in Germany, the Benelux countries, the Balkans, China, India, and Indochina.[47] In other words, more than 5,700 people worked for the SSU outside of the borders of the United States, of whom all but 2,700 were in active military service.

During the next few months, it became clear that the Soviet Union and its special services became the SSU's chief object of interest. The demobilization of the US armed forces at the end of hostilities and the personnel policy of the US War Department resulted in a radical reduction in SSU staffing. By March 1, 1946, the number of SSU personnel working overseas was about four hundred in twenty-four cities worldwide.[48] In such circumstances, it is not hard to imagine that the Americans would have sought help in intelligence gathering from among their tried-and-tested wartime allies, including the Poles. For his part, Colonel Dasher's efforts to integrate his Eagles into postwar American intelligence activities in Germany, Austria, and Poland continued.

Were any Polish intelligence agents recruited by the Allied intelligence services after the war, like Colonels Stanisław Gano and Wincenty Bąkiewicz? Commander Wilfred Dunderdale, arguably one of the British officers most closely associated with the Poles, was placed in charge of a dedicated Secret Intelligence Service (SIS) organization immediately after the war, concentrating on signals intelligence operations against the Soviet Union as controller special liaison. His unit collected intelligence from radio traffic intercepted by the Poles at their stations in Stanmore and Scotland, radio telegraph messages en clair, radio-telephone intercepts, and open sources, such as the Soviet press. Is it possible that Dunderdale would have overlooked the pool of trained Project Eagle radio-telegraphers that the SSU seemed determined to ignore?[49]

In the meantime, the Polish agents were faced, like all Polish soldiers in Western Europe, with the choice of whether to return to a Poland they would most likely find different from the one they had known before the war.

We know that the thirty men who survived their missions and returned to England from Germany were relieved of service with the OSS as of May 31, 1945. One may assume that at some point thereafter the former agents of Project Eagle, their comrades, and superiors turned in time to civilian pursuits in the United Kingdom, in other countries of the British Commonwealth, the United States, and possibly other countries. At least three of them settled in the United States.

Silver Star recipient Sergeant Zygmunt Barwikowski/René de Gaston of the Manhattan Mission sailed on the USNS *General R. M. Blatchford* from Bremerhaven, Germany, arriving at the Port of New York on December 22, 1950. Shortly thereafter he made his way to Cleveland, Ohio, where he applied for a Social Security number and got a job working for the Vlchek Tool Company, one of the largest automobile tool manufacturers in the United States, which ultimately merged with Ingersoll-Rand Incorporated. The Cleveland plant was closed in 1969. Eight years later, at age fifty-three, Sigmund Barwikowski, as he was known in the United States, who had been cited for "his unselfish devotion to duty and his ingenuity in the face of great opposition," died on December 11, 1977, and was buried in Potters Field, Highland Park Cemetery, Cuyahoga County, Ohio.[50]

Sigmund Barwikowski in postwar Cleveland, Ohio. (Photo Krzysztof Marek Barwikowski)

Sergeant Józef Herzyk/Józef Talarek of the Orange Blossom Mission sailed to the United States at some point following his demobilization from the Polish Army on November 16, 1946. He worked in manufacturing in New Haven, Connecticut, and worked his way up to the position of foreman in a plant operated by the Olin Corporation. He was appointed a member of New Haven's Civil Service Commission in 1985 and served until 1994. Joseph Herzyk died at age seventy-three on January 1, 1999, of heart failure and was buried in All Saints Cemetery in North Haven, Connecticut.[51]

Sergeant Tadeusz Hahn/Tadeusz Rawski of the Hot Punch Mission survived the mishap he suffered on landing near Passau, Germany, thanks in no small part to his teammate, Sergeant Zbigniew Strzeliński/Paprzycki, and the Singapore Sling Mission team that landed nearby and together helped Hahn to safety. A German doctor at the hospital in Osterhofen who could have turned the injured Hahn in to the authorities but did not do so also played a crucial role in the agent's survival. The broken ankle did not heal properly and he underwent surgery to fix the improperly healed break in a US military hospital after arriving in the UK, where he was also debriefed[52] and ultimately returned to duty in the Polish Army in summer 1945.

Hahn enrolled in the Polish Resettlement Corps and studied at the Battersea Polytechnic Institute in London during the academic year 1946–1947. On February 2, 1948, he married Jadviga (Harriett) J. Baginski of East Chicago, Indiana, in London and on March 22, 1948, he was demobilized from the Polish Resettlement Corps. Two months later the Hahns sailed from Southampton to New York City on the *Queen Mary*, arriving in New York on May 20, 1948. The couple lived in East Chicago and started a family. Thaddeus Hahn became a naturalized US citizen on December 17, 1951, and made a living working at various metal-working companies until the fall of 1955, when the Hahns and their two sons, Stephen and Raymond, moved to San Clemente in Southern California, and then relocated to Anaheim in Orange County in 1956, where Thaddeus lived until his death. A daughter, Diane, soon joined the family, and Thaddeus found employment with US Steel in Los Angeles, then Northrop Corporation (and its successor companies) in Anaheim and North American Aviation in Downey.

Hahn's professional background improved in 1964 when he earned a bachelor of science degree in engineering from California State University, Long Beach, in 1964. A year later, on March 17, 1965, he received a Letter of Appreciation from NASA for his work on the Apollo Space Program. Daughter Diane recalled her dad receiving a phone call from NASA in Houston, Texas, during the lunar landing in 1969, and a year later

Thaddeus Hahn married Jadviga (Harriett) J. Baginski of East Chicago in London on February 2, 1948. (Photo Ray, Stephen, and Diane Hahn)

Thaddeus Hahn's photo submitted for his US Certificate of Naturalization, issued on December 17, 1951. (Photo Ray, Stephen, and Diane Hahn)

he received an Apollo Achievement Award as a member of the Aeronautics and Space Team in commemoration of the Apollo 11 moon landing. Funding cuts in the US space program entailed a switch from his job at North American Rockwell to Litton Industries in Canoga Park, California, where he worked until returning to Rockwell International as a member of the Space Shuttle team in 1976. Thaddeus Hahn retired in 1989 and passed away on October 9, 2014, in Anaheim. He was predeceased by his wife and they are interred at the Holy Sepulcher Cemetery in Orange, California.[53]

NATIONAL AERONAUTICS AND SPACE ADMINISTRATION
MANNED SPACECRAFT CENTER
2101 WEBSTER-SEABROOK ROAD
HOUSTON, TEXAS 77058

IN REPLY REFER TO:

MARCH 17, 1965

T C HAHN
2229 E SYCAMORE ST
ANAHEIM CAL

AS ASTRONAUTS, WE FULLY APPRECIATE YOUR PLEDGE OF CONTINUED
DEDICATION AND SUPPORT IN YOUR WORK WITH THE APOLLO SPACECRAFT
PROGRAM.

IT IS THIS SENSE OF TEAMWORK AND THE DEDICATED EFFORTS OF EVERY
PERSON INVOLVED THAT IS OUR OWN ASSURANCE OF SUCCESS IN THE
EXPLORATION OF SPACE. AS MEMBERS OF THIS TEAM, WE GIVE YOU,
IN TURN, OUR PLEDGE TO DO OUR BEST IN THIS JOINT EFFORT.

TOGETHER, WITH PERSONAL DEDICATION IN APPLYING OUR SKILLS AND
KNOWLEDGE, WE WILL GET THE JOB DONE.

SINCERELY,

Apollo astronauts encourage Thaddeus Hahn in his work on behalf of the Apollo Space Program, March 17, 1965. (Photo Ray, Stephen, and Diane Hahn)

Space Division
North American Rockwell

W.B. Bergen
President

12214 Lakewood Boulevard
Downey, California 90241

July 20, 1970

MY FELLOW EMPLOYEES:

It is often my duty to convey to you the commitments and responsibilities that we must meet individually and as a division. In the critical years just passed, there have been many such occasions. At times, however, I've had the privilege of turning the coin – of handing out commendations. Such an opportunity is again presented, on this first anniversary of the first manned landing on the moon.

One year ago Neil Armstrong stepped upon the Sea of Tranquility, and into the pages of history. No other footprint has received more publicity . . . and few men more acclaim. Wherever Neil Armstrong has since set foot, he has graciously and generously shared that praise – acknowledging among others the contributions of the industry team that helped man to realize one of his reachable dreams.

There is no higher commendation, in my opinion, than that received from the customer, for he is the ultimate judge of our performance. However we define our motives and our goals, we succeed or fail by one fundamental measure: meeting his needs. And while you and I may know that we are fulfilling this responsibility, it is reassuring indeed to hear the words from the other quarter.

I'm happy to join the National Aeronautics and Space Administration in passing on a few of those words, in commemoration of the Apollo 11 lunar landing. Naturally, I'm very proud of the Space Division's role in that unforgettable achievement, and it gives me special pleasure to send you the enclosed pin and Apollo Achievement Award. The message on the latter is eloquent enough and requires no elaboration from me. So to the sentiment expressed there, I would like to add only one personal thought: *congratulations*.

W B Bergen
W.B. Bergen

NASA letter of thanks to Thaddeus Hahn celebrating the one-year anniversary of the Apollo lunar landing, July 30, 1970. (Photo Ray, Stephen, and Diane Hahn)

The National Aeronautics and Space Administration
presents the

Apollo Achievement Award

to

T.C. HAHN

In appreciation of dedicated service to the nation as a member of the team which has advanced the nation's capabilities in aeronautics and space and demonstrated them in many outstanding accomplishments culminating in Apollo 11's successful achievement of man's first landing on the moon, July 20, 1969.

Signed at Washington, D.C.

ADMINISTRATOR, NASA

At least six members of Project Eagle remained in Great Britain.

Sergeant Zygmunt Tydda/Zygmunt Orłowicz, the radio operator of the Pink Lady Mission, served with the Polish forces under British command until October 1947, when he joined the Polish Resettlement Corps from which he mustered out in October 1949. His British Ministry of Defense documents refer to his service tersely thus:

> *Served with the Polish Army from 27.8.39 and took part in the Campaign in Poland 1.9.39. He lived in the western part of Poland which was incorporated into Germany at the outbreak of World War II. Conscripted, served with the German Army from 8.2.43, to 30. 6, 44. Voluntarily joined the Polish Forces under British command in the United Kingdom, served there and on the continent, as above. He served on special mission behind enemy lines from 31.3.45 to 23.4.45.*[54]

Tydda settled in Middlesex, England; married Luisa Maria Rosa Bersani; and had two sons, Richard and Edward. He worked for an American electronics firm and died from complications following a stroke in 1979 at the age of sixty-one.

Zygmunt Tydda and Luisa Maria Rosa Bersani's marriage photo, March 28, 1948. (Photo Edward and Richard Tydda)

Zygmunt Tydda in the Polish Army in postwar England. (Photo Edward and Richard Tydda)

Sergeant Józef Bambynek/Józef Gawor was the observer of the Sidecar Mission. He embarked on his mission inauspiciously and needed a little coaxing to leave his B-24 in the air near the city of Ansbach,[55] but he behaved boldly on landing. For his actions, he was awarded the Silver Star, among other decorations. After leaving the OSS, he was seconded to the staff company of the First Polish Corps and in August 1945 assigned to the Reserve Parachutist and Assault Training Center. From October 1, 1946, until October 4, 1948, he served in the Polish Resettlement Corps. On May 19, 1947, he saved a drowning person in the Firth of Clyde off the Scottish coast and was cited by the Royal Humane Society for his action. Following demobilization in 1948, Bambynek remained in England and settled in Northwick Park, Gloucester, working in the construction industry and as a mechanic. On December 31, 1949, he married Ewa Jagielnicka, a Siberian survivor, and had two children, Teresa and John. Bambynek died of cancer at the age of seventy-three on December 17, 1993, and was interred at Gilroes Cemetery, Leicester.[56]

Józef Bambynek in the Polish Army in postwar England. (Photo Vanda Townsend)

Józef Bambynek and Ewa Jagielnicka at their wedding in postwar England. (Photo Vanda Townsend)

Józef Bambynek and some of his and his wife's wedding guests. (Photo Vanda Townsend)

Jan Czogała, right, in London. (Photo Janet and Stephen Smith)

Sergeant Jan Adam Tadeusz Czogała/Jan Czogowski decided to stay in Great Britain after meeting Ena Phillis Martin, with whose grandparents he lodged.[57] He married Ena on June 6, 1949, in Willesden, London. The family found him his first job, which was as a milkman, but he could not carry enough bottles as his fingers were too thick to fit into the top of the empty bottles. His second job was for the firm Mac Fisheries in their greengrocery department. He worked for them in London, and once he became a manager he was then moved to their shop in Bishop's Stortford, Hertfordshire, where his first daughter was born, and lastly to Welwyn Garden City, Hertfordshire, where a second daughter was born. After that he bought his first greengrocers shop in Knebworth, Hertfordshire.

In 1968 the family went to Brisbane, Queensland, Australia, where Czogała had another greengrocers shop, and in 1970 they all returned to London and then Ipswich, Suffolk, where he bought a newsagents that he ran until he retired. Ena died on January 2, 2004, and her husband followed on November 11, 2006.[58]

Sergeant Władysław Gatnar/Władysław Turzecki settled in London after the war. He married in 1956 and had two children, Roger and Linda. Gatnar trained to be a television engineer and worked as such until his retirement. In a letter dated November 14, 1946, he wrote his parents from

Władysław Gatnar, left, with his younger brother Alojzy in 1945 in London. (Photo Elżbieta and Piotr Gatnar)

Władysław Gatnar and family in Turza Śląska, Poland, 1968. (Photo Elżbieta and Piotr Gatnar)

Władysław Gatnar at work in postwar London. (Photo Andrea and Roger Gatnar)

Władysław Gatnar's retirement party. (Photo Andrea and Roger Gatnar)

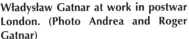

Portobello, Edinburgh, Scotland, reassuring them that his brother Alojzy and he were fine, that despite rumors to the contrary there was plenty of food to be had in Scotland, and that they should not worry about their boys in Great Britain. He thanked them for sending a copy of his birth certificate, and said that for the time being he was undergoing training that would last for a year, and that meant that he would not be coming home for Christmas holidays in 1946; in the meantime he sent his best wishes to his parents, his sister, and his brothers. It would be considerably longer before Władek, as he was known, would be reunited with his family in Turza Śląska in 1968. In the meantime his own family grew to include two children and three grandchildren. He died peacefully in his sleep in July 1986 and was buried at the City of London Cemetery and Crematorium.[59]

Wiktor/Viktor Szulik/Wiktor Czarnecki settled in Peterborough near Cambridge in England. He married twice and had children, but no further information is available on his life after the war. He died in 1995 and is interred in Peterborough.

Wilhelm Swoboda also settled in the United Kingdom.

Wiktor Szulik in Polish Army service in 1944. (Photo Rafał Niedziela)

Wilhelm Swoboda in Wehrmacht service sometime before June 1944. (Photo Rafał Niedziela)

One agent emigrated to Australia. Sergeant Wacław Kujawski/George Chojnicki was sixteen when Nazi Germany invaded Poland; his father was a postal worker who was murdered by the Germans in Chojnice during the first few days of the war. Following a stint as a forced laborer, Kujawski was conscripted into the Wehrmacht and sent to France, where he surrendered to the Americans and volunteered for service in Project Eagle. He left the Polish Army in England in November 1946 and served as a civilian investigation officer for the American occupation forces in Germany until 1948. In December of that year, he boarded the ship *Volendam* in Rotterdam and sailed to Melbourne, Australia, arriving on January 19, 1949. He found employment with the Postmaster General's office installing underground telecommunication lines from Melbourne to eastern Victoria in 1951–1952.

Kujawski was afraid that his family in Poland would suffer if the Communist authorities learned of his work with the OSS, so he changed his name to George Chojnicki. In 1951 he married Dorothy Petch, and they had three children: Susanne, John, and Margaret. John passed away in a car accident in 1980, and Margaret died suddenly from a brain aneurism around 1996. Chojnicki had learned the building trade from his father-in-law and was able to raise his family comfortably and happily, by

Wacław Kujawski before emigrating to postwar Australia. (Photo Shane Donnelly)

his grandson's account. He built his own house in the 1970s in Trafalgar, Gippsland, Victoria, where Susanne's family currently live.

As Stalinist rigors passed in Poland with the death of the Soviet dictator, Chojnicki's fear of the Polish Communists waned and he and his wife traveled to Poland in 1966 and 1980, and in 1986 he journeyed there on his own. George Chojnicki passed away at the age of seventy-nine in 2002 of complications from Parkinson's disease, and Dorothy passed away in 2012.[60]

Sergeant Chojnicki's trepidation at returning to Poland after the war was shared by about 60 percent of soldiers in the Polish forces in Western Europe who opted not to return to their homeland after the war ended. However, over 100,000 did, and the treatment they received by the Communist authorities in Poland was examined by Professor Ryszard Kaczmarek.[61] He found: "An unexpected problem for the [Communist] authorities at the end of December 1945–beginning of January 1946 was the matter of some 10,000 soldiers of the Polish Army in the West returning to Poland from Great Britain. The majority of them (70 percent) were Silesians who had been conscripted into the German Army and later deserted on the Western Front."[62]

They were detained for weeks, sometimes months, in so-called filtration camps where they were interrogated. One such repatriation point was a camp in Koźle[63] which received thirteen transports of 10,301 soldiers, 1,596 noncommissioned officers, and 32 officers from the Second Corps in Italy. As a result of interrogations and confidential information, it was determined that among the detainees, there were 9,571 former Wehrmacht soldiers and *Volksdeutsch* of the 1st, 2nd, and 3rd categories. They were separated from the remaining repatriates, and their interrogation reports were forwarded directly to Colonel Jan Rutkowski, the chief of the Polish Army's Main Directorate of Information.[64]

Taking into account the kind of activities the agents of Project Eagle had been trained for and their work with American intelligence during the last few months of the war, it would not be unreasonable to assume that in the event of their return to a now-Communist Poland, they would become the objects of surveillance of not only Polish military intelligence and counterintelligence, but also the Ministry of Security. I therefore visited the Institute of National Remembrance Archives in Warsaw, where I searched the materials of the Second Branch, later Second Board of the General Staff of the Polish People's Army, as well as the Ministry of Public Security (later, the Ministry of Internal Affairs), knowing that these institutions collected all kinds of information concerning soldiers, noncommissioned officers, and officers of the Polish Armed Forces in the West who opted to return to Poland.[65] Despite searching through numerous reports, personnel records, and spreadsheets, I found no information concerning Project Eagle or its members.

Notwithstanding the dearth of archival information, at least three agents did return to Poland.

Sergeant Edmund Zeitz/Edmund Barski was the radio operator for the Manhattan Mission. He seems to have had nearly as much trouble from Allied troops as from the Germans during his mission, mostly because he followed orders and refused to provide information on the OSS to conveying officers. If other Project Eagle members were content to remain outside of Poland after the war, Zeitz was not among them. He was undeterred by information reaching Great Britain about the treatment that returning soldiers experienced upon their return to Poland, and opted to go back himself in 1947. He disembarked from the transport ship in Gdańsk and was allowed to proceed to his hometown of Tuchola, where he married in 1949 the young lady who assisted Sergeant Zeitz's mother in corresponding with

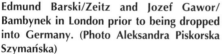

Edmund Barski/Zeitz and Jozef Gawor/ Bambynek in London prior to being dropped into Germany. (Photo Aleksandra Piskorska Szymańska)

Edmund Zeitz in Watford, England, in 1946. (Photo Aleksandra Piskorska Szymańska)

her son. In the 1950s he and his wife were "encouraged" to de-Germanize their name from Zeitz to Zeic, which apparently was the only form of repression that his family remembers him experiencing. He disclosed his service in the Wehrmacht to the authorities on numerous occasions, which his family explained were mere formalities. He married, had two daughters, and in the 1960s moved to the city of Toruń, where he advanced to supervisory roles in accounting. Edmund Zeic died at the age of seventy-nine on May 26, 2003.[66]

Zbigniew Paprzycki/Zbigniew Strzeliński returned to Poland at the beginning of April 1946[67] and landed at Gdynia. He and the rest of the former soldiers from the Polish Army in the West were herded from the docks to a camp, deprived of any valuables they may have brought with them, and interrogated. Many were taken by train to former German concentration camps where they were further interrogated. Sergeant Paprzycki was apparently one of the more fortunate cases and was allowed to proceed to Poznań. His widowed mother was an ethnic German who, like nearly

three million other Germans who found themselves on Polish territory following Stalin's redrawing of the Polish borders, fled or were forced west; in
her case to the part of Germany that was under occupation by the Western
Allies.

Paprzycki wanted to be an engineer and construct buildings. Engineers
were sorely needed in a country whose cities had suffered great destruction, so he went to an engineering school and got his degree. Among his
projects were the reconstruction of the German Kaiser's castle in Poznań
(now housing a part of Adam Mickiewicz University) and a power plant in
Gosławice near Konin. He advanced professionally as time went on, earned
a master's degree in engineering, and assumed supervisory roles in projects
beginning in the 1960s. Because of his wartime service in the Polish Army
in the West, he never was promoted to a directorial position, but was
awarded various medals for his work. He married his wife, Maria, in 1958
and started a family, which soon included two daughters. After the collapse
of Communism in Poland in 1989, Paprzycki and his family were surprised
by a knock on the door revealing two US consular officials who presented
him with the Medal of Freedom and an accompanying certificate to replace
the medal he had received in 1948 from the Americans and subsequently
lost during an abortive effort to escape to the West.[68] Zbigniew Paprzycki
died of complications from diabetes on May 31, 2019, in Poznań.[69]

Sergeant Gerard Haroński/Gerhard Nowicki returned to Poland
by ship via Szczecin in 1948. He had invited his wife, Małgorzata, and
five-year-old daughter to come to England, but his wife refused. Upon
leaving the ship, he and his fellow soldiers were interned, relieved of their
valuables, and placed in a camp where they were interrogated. Eventually, Haroński was allowed to go home to Ruda Śląska, where initially he
worked at a shoe store. He was harassed by men who, like him, had been
drafted into the Wehrmacht but who had not joined the Polish Army in
the West after surrender to or capture by the Western Allies, as Haroński
had. He and his family eventually moved to Łabędy, on the outskirts of
Gliwice, where he worked at a steel mill. Another daughter soon joined
the family. Interestingly, Haroński picked up English in England and spoke
fluent German and Silesian, while his Polish was not that proficient. His
elder daughter eventually emigrated to the Federal Republic of Germany in
the 1970s, while his younger daughter and her husband and daughter reside
in Gliwice. Gerard Haroński passed away in 1977 and is interred with his
wife in Gliwice.[70]

All members of Project Eagle were bound by their employment contracts never to disclose their wartime experiences in the OSS, and they

never did so publicly. Their children and grandchildren with whom I corresponded or spoke knew precious little of their father's or grandfather's work in the OSS late in the war, nor have I come across such information in the press. The OSS recruited Belgians, Danes, Germans, Scandinavians, and Czechoslovaks for other European operations, but as in the case of the Polish agents, their exploits went unknown to the wider public.

An exception are the German teams known as the TOOL missions. Recent revelations from East German archives show that the two members of the German Hammer Mission who were sent into Berlin in March 1945 had earlier provided the Soviets with top secret mission files and information on OSS sources and methods. Their wartime activities in Berlin earned them Silver Stars from the US military, which in the confusion following the termination of the OSS in September 1945 were never physically awarded. After the war, the former agents chose to return to their native town of Berlin, where they spent the remainder of their lives. Curiously, even after the 1991 disclosure of their association with a Soviet military intelligence (GRU) spy ring in England during their OSS training in 1944, the United States military authorities chose to posthumously award the Silver Stars to their families at a ceremony held at the US Embassy in Berlin on May 6, 2006.[71] The counterintelligence arm of OSS, known as X-2 and British MI-6, had clearly failed to identify one threat connected to the penetration of Nazi Germany in 1944 and for thirty years no one was the wiser.

Given the Cold War that was just developing, it is then serendipitous that the surviving agents of the TOOL missions were not engaged by US forces in Allied-occupied Germany immediately after the war. Nor were the agents of Project Eagle, but not for lack of trying on the part of Colonel Joseph Dasher. Many of them enlisted in the Polish Resettlement Corps, whose main task was to prepare demobilized soldiers of the Polish Armed Forces in the West for civilian life in Great Britain or beyond its borders.[72] Eventually, the Project Eagle members scattered around the world, leaving little information with which to trace them.

After a year of searching the internet and running ads in local Polish newspapers, I revised my original assumption that the nature of their activities and their training would dissuade the Polish agents from returning to Poland. Approximately 105,000 of 250,000 Poles did just that; despite the ramifications of the Tehran, Yalta, and Potsdam conferences the tragic news in the international press of repression, and a bloody struggle between the post–Home Army underground and the Communist authorities backed by the Soviets—despite everything. Nostalgia for their families, their homes, and for some an inability or refusal to accommodate themselves to a new life in Great Britain also played a part.[73] There were even those who chose to return to their homes that as a result of new borders were now in one of the Soviet Republics; their futures were perhaps the most precarious. Among those who chose to remain in Great Britain, a prevailing sentiment was that a third World War was bound to break out between the Soviet Bloc and their former wartime allies in the West. As time went on, a Cold War settled in like a wet blanket, and the agents of Project Eagle scattered in different directions, their missions largely forgotten, or, in the case of Kermit Roosevelt and authors who relied on his history of the OSS, intentionally downplayed.

In his 1979 account of the penetration of Nazi Germany, author Joseph Persico noted:

> In the beginning, it had seemed near suicidal to pit an intrepid handful against the institutionalized terror of the Third Reich. Years later, remembering their farewells to agents departing for Germany, OSS veterans would repeatedly voice a common refrain: "Of course, we never expected to see them again."[74]

The thirty surviving agents of Project Eagle did not become members of the postwar OSS society, did not attend its posh balls in Washington and New York, and were not part of the establishment that celebrated the OSS's achievements. They were unknown to the vast majority of the community that made up the Office of Strategic Services and later the CIA, their real identities never revealed, their whereabouts undetermined.

And during the Cold War, that was how the American intelligence community wanted it. Most, but not all, of the records of the OSS have been transferred to the National Archives and Records Administration in College Park, Maryland, where as one researcher put it, it would take several lifetimes to access and read the documents. As noted above, many employment records containing detailed information were destroyed by fire.

In a report dated June 16, 1945, to Polish Minister of National Defense General Marian Kukiel, Colonel Dasher summarized the goals and the execution of Project Eagle, and thanked the Polish Armed Forces for its cooperation. Dasher acknowledged that the quick Allied advance precluded the opportunity for the Polish agents to establish radio communications with their base, but that the men

> proved themselves courageous, well trained and capable for the work they undertook. As it turned out these Polish soldiers were able, nevertheless, after being overrun by the Allies to furnish the Armies with valuable items of intelligence

enabling these Armies to save men and equipment in their further drives, and
also to eliminate the maximum of Nazi elements from the occupied territories.
This alone justified the effort made by these Polish soldiers and is deserving of
the highest praise, considering the many difficulties and dangers these men had
to overcome.[75]

Colonel Dasher also informed General Kukiel that after analyzing the Polish soldiers' activities in Germany and paying them their salaries that the soldiers had returned to duty in the Polish Army as of May 31, 1945, with the exception of Sergeants Bogdanowicz, Markotny, Jankowski, and Jasiak, who had perished during their missions.[76] He also noted that Sergeant Rawski was in hospital recuperating from leg injuries.

Even if the chief organizer of Project Eagle was more than satisfied with his men's performance, did the actions of thirty-two men a few weeks before Hitler's suicide on April 30, 1945, and the subsequent capitulation of the Third Reich on May 8 in any way hasten the end of the conflict in Europe? Well-known author Douglas Waller summed up succinctly the activities of the OSS and indirectly the actions of the men of Project Eagle:

Did the OSS contribute to the war effort? His [Donovan's] operatives earned
more than two thousand medals for bravery and suffered relatively few casualties.
Was Donovan's organization key to winning the war? No. Did his shadow
organization shorten the conflict appreciably? Again, no. But that may be setting
the bar too high for his agency. Far more powerful forces were at work defeating
the Axis: Russian and American women in the 1920s who delivered more male
babies for the future fight than German, Italian, and Japanese mothers could
hope to produce. American industry and Roosevelt's mobilization of it for war,
vast oceans that made Axis attack of that industrial base impossible, the Mer-
chant Marine force, Army Quartermaster, and Navy Supply Corps that could
move more arms and machinery to the front than the Axis could. The atomic
bomb. The OSS agent played his part, just as the infantryman on the front
line in Europe, the sailor at sea in the Pacific, the sergeant in the motor pool
in Detroit, the riveter on the plane assembly line in Los Angeles. Donovan's
vision of covert warfare winning major battles on its own, making conventional
operations unnecessary, proved illusory. His heroic guerrilla raids were a bother
for Adolf Hitler, not a strategic threat. Shadow warfare was no match for brute
force. [. . .] Donovan and his men began their work as rank amateurs . . . . But
their mistakes and botched missions were no more or less than for other parts of
the American military . . . . And all the intelligence the OSS produced never
matched the value of the Ultra electronic intercepts in Europe [thanks to the
Polish code breakers who built copies of the Enigma machine before the
war] *and Magic in the Pacific.*[77]

What did the efforts of the men in Project Eagle do for Poland? Could they have influenced the ultimate disposition of the eastern provinces of prewar Poland that Stalin had annexed in 1940? No, nor is it likely that the Project Eagle team members even considered the prospect. The decision concerning Poland's eastern and western borders was taken at the Tehran Conference in Iran held from November 28 to December 1, 1943, between US President Franklin Delano Roosevelt, British Prime Minister Winston Churchill, and Soviet Premier Joseph Stalin. At that meeting Stalin pressed for a revision of Poland's eastern border with the Soviet Union to match the line set by British Foreign Secretary Lord Curzon in 1920, corresponding to what the USSR had incorporated three years earlier. Poland was to be compensated for the resulting loss of territory by moving the German–Polish border to the Oder and Neisse rivers. This decision was formally ratified at the Potsdam Conference of 1945. Whatever strategic or tactical information accrued from collecting intelligence behind German lines in the West would have no practical effect on a decision by the Big Three that was arrived at a year and a half earlier without the participation of Polish representatives.[78]

This book attempts to tell the story of a group of Polish volunteers who worked under the auspices of the Office of Strategic Services to bring the war against Hitler to an end as quickly as possible. In so doing we have learned the real identities of all but a few agents, and unearthed in some small part the postwar histories of thirteen of them. The officer responsible for the entire operation and for the citations for valor that were processed by General Eisenhower's General Staff, Colonel Joseph Dasher, evaluated the agents of Project Eagle thusly:

> *I can only say that the United States Forces were very fortunate indeed to have had the services of so fine and valiant a group of Polish soldiers. They absorbed the instruction given them in an exemplary manner and their deportment reflected credit on the good name of the Polish Army. They upheld the ancient and glorious traditions of the Polish Army.*[79]

The men of Project Eagle were collectively as "fine and valiant" a group as the OSS fielded during its short existence. They epitomized the partnership in arms that characterized the relationship between their country, Poland, and their ally and best chance for a fair deal after the war. That did not happen, for geopolitical reasons. Polish soldiers in Great Britain, including the men of Project Eagle who had been returned to duty with the Polish Army, did not participate in the Victory Parade in London on

June 8, 1945. The contribution of the fourth-largest Allied armed forces to
the war effort fell victim to Allied efforts to seek a postwar modus vivendi
with the Soviet Union. On June 29, 1945, France withdrew its recognition
of the legitimate Government of the Republic of Poland, and the United
States and Great Britain followed suit on July 5, 1945. The newly established Provisional Government of National Unity included former prime
minister Stanislaw Mikołajczyk[80] and his large Polish Peasant Party, who
were subject to overt and covert repression by the Communist-dominated
Democratic Bloc, which some scholars claim resulted in the deaths of some
30,000 people and the incarceration of many more, up to 72,000 in 1947
alone. The Democratic Bloc rigged the elections of January 19, 1947, and
won the vote with an ostensible 80.1 percent.[81] The illusory specter of free
elections that Roosevelt and Churchill had agreed to at the meeting of
the Big Three in Tehran between November 28 and December 1, 1943,
committed the nations of East Central Europe to nearly a half century of
non-sovereignty, political oppression, and a long-lasting but ill-fated effort
by Soviet puppets to liquidate all opposition.

Even as British Foreign Minister Ernest Bevin wrote to each Polish
soldier in March 1946 beseeching them to return home, both the American
SSU and the British SIS began to focus their attention on the Soviet Union.
The Central Intelligence Group/CIA and SIS ran spy operations in Poland
later in the 1940s and the 1950s, not terribly effectively as many agents
who were infiltrated were quickly caught and some "turned."[82] The largest
of these organizations was Freedom and Independence (WiN), which was
infiltrated and "captured" by a Polish/Soviet counterintelligence operation
in 1948. From spring 1948 through December 1952, when the Soviets
decided to end the operation, the CIA provided seventeen radio sets, over
$1 million, and several hundred kilograms of gold to their Soviet-controlled
"agents" in Poland. As early as 1954, the CIA received an internal Polish analysis of Operation Cezary, the Soviet/Polish effort "to neutralize
Western special services' activities by planting agents from Poland into
their operating centers abroad, to mis-lead and disorient them, and to lead
them into fruitless operations and blunders."[83] Cezary was successful from
the Soviet perspective, and the CIA still deems its relationship to WiN as
top secret.

Project Eagle remained a classified operation for the next four decades,
and to this day has remained officially unnoticed by the United States, by
the Republic of Poland, and by Poles in Poland and in the diaspora. While
General "Wild Bill" Donovan received various well-deserved accolades for
his part in the secret war against the Axis, including one at his alma mater,

Columbia University,[84] there are no monuments or plaques commemorating the men who volunteered to pursue Allied goals and risked their lives in penetrating the Third Reich at war's end. That is a pity but one that can be remedied.

Tightrope Walker, General William J. "Wild Bill" Donovan. (Photo John S. Micgiel)

Appendix 1

POLISH REPORTS FORWARDED BY THE SECOND BUREAU OF THE POLISH GENERAL STAFF TO US MILITARY INTELLIGENCE

Period	Number of Reports Supplied	Notes
October 1, 1941–June 30, 1942	610	Until September 16, 1942, 74% of the information, studies, and reports were supplied to OSS, 19% to G-2, 4% to the FBI, 2% to the Psychological Warfare Branch, and 1% to Naval Intelligence Service; 176 were on Germany, 80 France, 54 North America, 38 Russia, 29 Italy, and 74 other states.
July 1, 1942–June 30, 1943	6,041	Of which 3,195 were delivered via "Estezet."
July 1–December 30, 1943	9,761	Of which 3,002 reports for OSS, 2,302 for G-2, and 702 for NIS.
January 1–June 30, 1944	6,006	Of which 1,832 reports for OSS, 124 for G-2, and 1,106 for NIS.
July 1–December 31, 1944	6,062	Of which 88 items for OSS, 720 for G-2, and 61 for NIS.
January 1–February 15, 1945	869	
February 16–May 1945	unknown	
Total	**>29,349**	

Source: Jan Stanisław Ciechanowski, "North and South America," in *Intelligence Co-Operation*, 353.

Appendix 2

AGENT TEAMS SUCCESSFULLY DISPATCHED TO GERMANY, AUSTRIA, AND HOLLAND

Field detachments of the OSS recruited, among others, civilians living or temporarily residing near the front line to gather intelligence. As the front stabilized, volunteers known as "tourists" were inserted into enemy territory with the task of noting everything of importance during their return to American lines. The OSS detachment working with the US Ninth Army in northern Germany inserted between January and the end of April 1945 only seven agents. The US Third Army sent ten groups, but before their agents were able to return to the field detachments with their reports, they were overrun by Allied troops.

The US Seventh Army, the southernmost unit of the Twelfth Army Group, achieved the best results, mainly because it ignored the ban on recruiting agents from among German prisoners of war. Between December 1944 and May 1945 the Seventh Army sent forty-four or forty-five (it is unclear) tourist groups deep behind enemy lines. Unfortunately, thirty-six agents, or 40 percent of all the agents, either disappeared or were killed. The weakest results were noted by the US First Army, which sent only a single agent across enemy lines and then disbanded its field detachment. The best results of all agents in terms of the number and quality of intelligence reports was a female agent named "Marietta" who was a member of the Dutch group "Melanie."[1]

Below is a list of intelligence missions inserted variously into Germany, Austria, and Holland (note: the sources provide two different totals, 100 or 101):

Agent Teams Successfully Dispatched to Germany, Austria, and Holland by SI Branch, OSS European Theater of Operations & Field Detachments

1. "Downend"
2. "Tyl"
3. "Rubens"
4. "Hammer"
5. "Sidecar"
6. "Martini"
7. "Painter"
8. "Chisel"
9. "Daiquiri"
10. "Doctor"
11. "Alexander"
12. "Eggnog"
13. "Highball"
14. "Abnoki"
15. "Old Fashioned"
16. "Pink Lady"
17. "Zombie"
18. "Chauffeur"
19. "Cuba Libre"
20. "Pick Axe"
21. "Luxe I"
22. "Manhattan"
23. "Buzzsaw"
24. "Boyard"
25. "Sultane"
26. "Georgia"
27. "Virginia"
28. "Luxe II"
29. "Gauloise"
30. "Ruppert"
31. "Eclipse"
32. "Ragweed"
33. "Crocus"
34. "Hofer"
35. "Comet"
36. "Pitt"
37. "Troy"
38. "Mimi"
39. "Lulu"
40. "Coco"
41. "Dubuque"
42. "Joshua"
43. "Mickie"
44. "Anzio"
45. "Sally"
46. "Conte"
47. "Hamilton"
48. "Raleigh"
49. "Morris"
50. "Vacuum"
51. "Cleaner"
52. "Queen"

53. "Jack"
54. "Dubarry"
55. "Ace"
56. "Arrow"
57. "Isabel"
58. "Waldorf"
59. "Sherwood"
60. "Baer"
61. "Leone"
62. "Tobacco"
63. "Dolly"
64. "King"
65. "Seahorse"
66. "Marietta"
67. "Florida"
68. "Fat"
69. "Brahms"
70. "Alex"
71. "Godfrey"
72. "Katga"
73. "Mac"
74. "Fred"
75. "Godfrey"
76. "Raymond"
77. "Liberation"

78. "Student"
79. "Bowman"
80. "Serpent"
81. "Tiger"
82. "Kangaroo"
83. "Camel"
84. "Hound"
85. "Hare"
86. "Rabbit"
87. "Camel II"
88. "Cachalot"
89. "Zebra"
90. "Elephant"
91. "Hyena"
92. "Faro"
93. "Balto"
94. "Planters Punch"
95. "Orange Blossom"
96. "Mallet"
97. "Singapore Sling"
98. "Hot Punch"
99. "Tom Collins"
100. "Farmer"
101. "Melanie"

Source: OSS/London [microform]: Reel 7, Vol. 1: Introductory Survey of Establishment, Activities, and Plans of SI/ETO, p. 4.

Appendix 3

MISSIONS DISPATCHED BY OSS EUROPEAN THEATER OF OPERATIONS FROM LONDON INTO GERMANY AND AUSTRIA

1. "Downend"	18. "Daiquiri"
2. "Ruppert"	19. "Old Fashioned"
3. "Hammer"	20. "Highball"
4. "Pickaxe"	21. "Alexander"
5. "Faro"	22. "Pink Lady"
6. "Doctor"	23. "Planters Punch"
7. "Chauffeur"	24. "Cuba Libre"
8. "Painter"	25. "Orange Blossom"
9. "Farmer"	26. "Zombie"
10. "Balto"	27. "Singapore Sling"
11. "Boyard"	28. "Hot Punch"
12. "Sultane"	29. "Tom Collins"
13. "Gauloise"	30. "Virginia"
14. "Sidecar"	31. "Georgia"
15. "Martini"	32. "Luxe I"
16. "Manhattan"	33. "Luxe II"
17. "Eggnog"	

Source: Roosevelt, *War Report of the OSS*, vol. 2, 316.

Appendix 4

PROJECT EAGLE FLIGHTS

The sixteen Project Eagle groups were sent on their missions from three bases:

Harrington, via Douglas A-26 Invader,[1] on:

April 2	1 group
April 11	2 groups

Namur, via Douglas A-20 Havoc,[2] on:

March 21	1 group
March 23	3 groups
March 25	1 group
March 30	1 group
April 9	2 groups
April 10	1 group

Dijon, via Consolidated B-24 Liberator,[3] on:

March 1	1 group
March 8	2 groups
April 7	1 group

Source: OSS/London [microform]: Reel 8, Vol. 12: German Operations—1945, Book 3: The Desks and Their Missions; The Polish Desk, 289–90.

NOTES

PREFACE

1. William D. Leahy (1875–1959) was a US naval officer who held various responsible positions during World War II. *Encyclopedia Britannica Online*, s.v. "William Daniel Leahy," accessed May 2, 2022, https://www.britannica.com/biography/William-Daniel-Leahy.

2. William Joseph Casey (1913–1987) was born in Elmhurst, Queens, New York. A lawyer by profession, he was active in the OSS during World War II. He was chief of the OSS Secret Intelligence Branch in Europe, and between 1981 and 1987 director of the CIA. Encyclopedia Britannica Online, s.v. "William J. Casey," accessed May 2, 2022, https://www.britannica.com/biography/William-J-Casey.

3. OSS/London [microform]: *Special Operations Branch and Secret Intelligence Branch War Diaries* (Frederick, MD: University Publications of America, 1985). Henceforth OSS/London [microform].

4. Kermit Roosevelt Jr. (1916–2000), grandson of President Theodore Roosevelt, graduated from Harvard and worked as an intelligence officer in the OSS and CIA.

5. Ryszard Kaczmarek, *Polacy w Wehrmachcie* (Kraków: Wydawnictwo Literackie, 2010), 448.

6. "Joseph Dasher, Chief of Polish Section, United States Office of Strategic Services, Europe, Describes Secret School for Polish Soldiers," *Critical Past*, accessed October 19, 2018, http://www.criticalpast.com/video/65675072308_Project-Eagle_Office-of-Strategic-Services_Soldiers-of-Poland-in-Exile.

7. OSS/London [microform]: Reel 8, Vol. 12: German Operations—1945, Book: The Desks and Their Missions; The Polish Desk, 294–383.

8. NARA, RG 226, A1 224; RG 226, Entry 210; RG 226, Entry 210.

9. Waldemar Grabowski, *Zapomniani polscy spadochroniarze: Operacje 'Dunstable' i 'Eagle' w Niemczech*, Materiały: Dokumenty, Archiwalia, Studia, z. 16 (London: Instytut Polski i Muzeum im. gen. Sikorskiego, 2011), 111.

CHAPTER 1

1. Arkadiusz Machniak, "Polski wywiad i kontrwywiad wojskowy w latach 1918–1939 wobec Związku Sowieckiego. Charakterystyka działalnos´ci zawarta w dokumentach Głównego Zarządu Informacji Wojska Polskiego," *UR Journal of Humanities and Social Sciences*, Nr. 1(2) / 2017.

2. The Saxon Palace was destroyed during the war. It housed the Tomb of the Unknown Soldier in a colonnade connecting its two wings. The tomb survived the war, and in November 2018 Polish President Andrzej Duda announced that the palace would be rebuilt. The palace housed the Cypher Bureau's German Section, which cracked the German codes and built the Enigma there. The Cypher Bureau moved in 1937 to secluded, specially constructed premises on the southern outskirts of Warsaw in the Kabaty Forest, where in July 1939 the Polish Cypher Bureau delivered copies of Enigma and its technical manual to British and French colleagues.

3. Machniak, "Polski wywiad i kontrwywiad wojskowy," 4.

4. Regina Czarnecka, "Oddział II Sztabu Głównego (Generalnego) w Latach 1921–1939: Zarys Organizacyjny i Przegląd Zawartości Inwentarza," *Biuletyn Wojskowej Słuz´by Archiwalnej*, no. 28 (2006): 63–73.

5. Czarnecka, "Oddział II Sztabu Głównego (Generalnego)," 73–105.

6. Fort Legionów, originally built by the Russians between 1851 and 1853 as part of the ring of fortifications surrounding the Citadel and known as Fort Vladimir. At the time of this writing, it serves as a restaurant and entertainment venue.

7. Wilfred Dunderdale (1899–1990), RNVR, Commander, known as "Wilski" or "Dun" to the Poles and "Biffy" to the British, was the son of a British sea merchant in Odessa and educated in St. Petersburg. He joined SIS in 1921 and served in Istanbul, and in 1926 was sent to Paris, where he remained until the fall of France in 1940. He was responsible for the French and Polish Intelligence Services, and worked in London throughout the war in close collaboration with Polish II Bureau. After the war he ran SIS's SIGINT operations, in cooperation with the Poles, against Soviet targets as controller special liaison. After his retirement from SIS in 1959, he was appointed British consul-general in Chicago, and he died in New York in November 1990. See Eugenia Maresch, "SOE and Polish Aspirations," in *Intelligence Co-Operation between Poland and Great Britain during World War II*, vol. 1, *The Report of the Anglo-British Historical Committee*, ed. Tessa Stirling, Daria Nałecz, and Tadeusz Dubicki (Edgware, UK: Valentine Mitchell, 2005), ff 36, 213–14. See also Nigel West, *Historical Dictionary of British Intelligence* (Lanham, MD: Scarecrow Press, 2014), 188.

8. Gill Bennett, "Polish-British Intelligence Co-Operation," in *Intelligence Co-Operation*, vol. 1, 166.

9. *Intelligence Co-Operation between Poland and Great Britain during World War II*, vol. 2, *Documents*, ed. Jan Stanisław Ciechanowski (Warsaw: Naczelna Dyrekcja Archiwów Pan´stwowych, 2005), 409–11.

10. Keith Jeffrey, *The Secret History of MI6* (New York: Penguin Random House, 2011), 529.

11. "[1945, Londyn]. Sprawozdanie z pracy Wydziału Wywiadowczego Oddziału Informacyjno-Wywiadowczego Sztabu Naczelnego Wodza za 1944 r.," in *Intelligence Co-Operation*, vol. 2, 414.

12. *Intelligence Co-Operation*, vol. 2, 474–76.

13. Jan Stanislaw Ciechanowski, "Wywiad polski w Ameryce Północnej i Południowej w czasie II wojny światowej," *Zeszyty Historyczne* (Częstochowa), T. 12 (2013), 99–100.

14. *Intelligence Co-Operation*, vol. 2, 413–14.

15. Daria Nałęcz, "Existing Archival Sources," in *Intelligence Co-Operation*, vol. 1, 7.

16. Chief of the Military Intelligence Division, or G-2.

17. Andrzej Pepłoński and Andrzej Suchcitz, "Organization and Operations of the II Bureau of the Polish General Staff," in *Intelligence Co-Operation*, vol. 1, 90.

18. Jan Stanisław Ciechanowski, "North and South America," in *Intelligence Co-Operation*, vol. 1, 5.

19. Andrzej Pepłoński, "Współdziałanie polskiego wywiadu wojskowego z zachodnimi aliantami (1939–1945)," in *Polski Wywiad Wojskowy 1918–1945*, ed. Piotr Kołakowski and Andrzej Pepłoński (Toruń: Adam Marszalek, 2006), 506–7.

20. Władysław Kozaczuk, *W kręgu Enigmy* (Warsaw: Książka i Wiedza, 1979), 14.

21. Leon Mitkiewicz, *Z generałem Sikorskim na obczyźnie* (Paris: Instytut Literackie, 1968), 1.

22. Pepłoński, *Współdziałanie polskiego wywiadu wojskowego*, 510.

23. Pepłoński and Suchcitz, "Organization and Operations of the II Bureau," 101–2.

24. Andrzej Pepłoński and Jan Ciechanowski, "The Role of the II Bureau of the Union of Armed Struggle–Home Army (ZWZ-AK) Headquarters in the Intelligence Structures of the Polish Armed Forces in the West," in *Intelligence Co-Operation*, vol. 1, 110. For photographs of some of the leading officers in the Polish and British Intelligence Services, see *Intelligence Co-Operation*, vol. 1, photos pp. 168–69.

25. Pepłoński and Ciechanowski, "Role of the II Bureau," 114–15.

26. Elźbieta Zawacka (March 19, 1909–January 10, 2009), aka "Zo," was the only woman among the "Silent and Unseen" (*Cichociemni*) parachuted into occupied Poland by the VI Bureau in February 1943. In 1944 Zawacka fought in the Warsaw Uprising and after its collapse moved to Kraków, where she continued her underground activities. In 1945 she joined the anti-Communist organization Freedom and Independence (WiN), but quit soon afterwards and took up a teaching job. In 1951 she was arrested and tortured by the Security Service of the Ministry of Internal Affairs. She was sentenced to ten years in prison for treason and espionage, but her sentence was shortened and she was released in 1955. After

her release from prison, she earned a doctorate from Gdańsk University. She was a tenured professor at the Institute of Pedagogy at Mikołaj Kopernik University in Toruń, where she established the department of andragogy (adult education). She retired from teaching in 1978 after the secret police closed the department. She was an active member of the World Union of Home Army Soldiers and cooperated with Solidarność in the 1980s. Zo was awarded the Polish Virtuti Militari Cross and the Cross of Valor (five times). In 1995 she was awarded the Order of the White Eagle. Zawacka had the rank of major in 1944, and the Republic of Poland appointed her a lieutenant colonel in 1990, colonel in 1996, and brigadier general in 2006. See "Elżbieta Zawacka (1909–2009)," Institute of National Remembrance, https://ipn.gov.pl/pl/aktualnosci/konkursy-i-nagrody/nagroda-kustosz-pamieci/2002/24226,Elzbieta-Zawacka-19092009.html?search=588182857989. See also Katarzyna Minczykowska, *Cichociemna Generał Elżbieta Zawacka "Zo"* (Warsaw: Rytm, 2014).

27. Pepłoński and Ciechanowski, "Role of the II Bureau," 115–16.

28. Jan Librach (1904–1973) was the first secretary of the Polish Embassy in Paris between 1935 and 1939. When the war broke out, he served from October 1939 to June 1940 as a volunteer in the Polish Army in France. Thereafter until March 1944, he was chief of the Central Bureau of the Continental Action in London and an employee of the Polish Ministry of Foreign Affairs, where he served successively as chief of the British section, then chief of the Anglo-American section, and vice secretary general of the ministry. Between 1950 and 1954 he was minister plenipotentiary of the Ministry of Foreign Affairs of the Republic of Poland. After emigrating to the United States, he was employed by the Free Europe Committee and became director of the Polish Institute of Arts and Sciences in New York. See Joseph Piłsudski Institute of America, New York, Archival Fond Nr. 66, Jan Librach Papers.

29. Andrzej Pepłoński, "The Operation of the Intelligence Services of the Ministry of Internal Affairs (MSW) and of the Ministry of National Defense," in *Intelligence Co-Operation*, vol. 1, 118–19.

30. Sir John Rupert "Jock" Colville (January 28, 1915–November 19, 1987), CB, CVO, was a British civil servant. He is best known for his diaries, which provide an intimate view of 10 Downing Street during the wartime prime ministership of Winston Churchill. See *Oxford Dictionary of National Biography*, s.v. "Colville, Sir John Rupert (1915–1987)," by Philip Ziegler, September 23, 2004, https://www.oxforddnb.com/display/10.1093/ref:odnb/9780198614128.001.0001/odnb-9780198614128-e-39878.

31. Victor Frederick William Cavendish-Bentinck, Ninth Duke of Portland (1897–1990), was educated at Wellington College but did not pursue a university education, instead entering the diplomatic service in 1919. His diplomatic career was distinguished. In 1922 he took charge of administrative arrangements for the Lausanne Conference. He served in the British Embassy in Paris and also in the League of Nations Department in the Foreign Office. Other postings included Athens in

1932 and Santiago in 1933. The high point of the Ninth Duke's diplomatic career came in 1939 when he was appointed chairman of the British Joint Intelligence Committee. He managed to develop the body as a highly effective instrument of government and as a result became counselor to the Services Liaison Department of the Foreign Office in 1942. In 1945 the duke was given his final diplomatic posting on his appointment as ambassador to Poland. He held the position for two years. Victor succeeded to the title in 1980, on the death of his brother, the Eighth Duke. See "Biography of Victor Frederick William Cavendish-Bentinck," University of Nottingham, https://www.nottingham.ac.uk/manuscriptsandspecialcollections/ collectionsindepth/family/portland/biographies/biographyofvictorfrederickwilliam cavendish-bentinck,9thdukeofportland(1897-1990).aspx (accessed October 21, 2017). See also *Oxford Dictionary of National Biography*, s.v. "Bentinck, Victor Frederick William Cavendish-[Bill Bentinck], Ninth Duke of Portland (1897–1990)," by Bassano, September 23, 2004, https://www.oxforddnb.com/display/10.1093/ ref:odnb/9780198614128.001.0001/odnb-9780198614128-e-1004022.

32. Jan Stanisław Ciechanowski, "British Special Services," in *Intelligence Co-Operation*, vol. 1, 145–46.

33. Andrzej Pepłoński, "Co-operation between the II Bureau and SIS," in *Intelligence Co-Operation*, vol. 1, 189.

34. Estezet was established in August 1941 following the signing of a preliminary cooperative agreement between the Polish and American intelligence services. Estezet covered the United States, Canada, Brazil, Argentina, Chile, Paraguay, Uruguay, Peru, and Bolivia and had outposts in those countries. Their main tasks were to observe the military situation in North and South America, the state of Poles living there (Polonia) and developments in the community, and agitation by Communist agents and penetration by them of Polonia, with a special eye toward the Communists' attitude toward the United States and Canada and toward Polish matters. Estezet also concerned itself with the current state, development of, and attitude of Ukrainian associations and the analysis of the ethnic press (Polish, German, Ukrainian, Czech, Slovak, Lithuanian, and Jewish). See Joseph Piłsudski Institute of America, New York, Archival Fond Nr. 70, Samodzielna Placówka Wywiadowcza Estezet, http://archiwa.pilsudski.org/inwentarz.php?nonav=0&nra r=701&nrzesp=111.

35. Ciechanowski, "British Special Services," 190–91.

36. Pepłoński, "Współdziałanie polskiego wywiadu wojskowego," 515–16.

37. Pepłoński and Suchcitz, "Organization and Operations of the II Bureau," 86.

38. Pepłoński and Suchcitz, "Organization and Operations of the II Bureau," 100.

39. Pepłoński, "Współdziałanie polskiego wywiadu wojskowego," 525.

40. William Casey, *The Secret War against Hitler* (Washington, DC: Regnery Gateway, 1988), 44.

41. Stanisław Włodzimierz Paweł Gano (1895–1968), Certified Lieutenant Colonel/Colonel of Infantry, was a career officer with much experience in intelligence gathering. Beginning September 6, 1939, he was chief of Evacuation and Transport of Special Equipment of the General Staff. He escaped to Romania and from an internment camp in Călimăneşti to France in early October 1939. From mid-November 1940 to December 1942, he was chief of the Second Intelligence Department and deputy chief of the Intelligence Information Department of the Staff of the Commander-in-Chief. From December 1941 to January 1946, he was chief of the Intelligence Information Department of the Staff of the Commander-in-Chief. He was promoted to colonel in January 1943; from January 1946 until 1948, he was acting deputy Chief of Staff for General Affairs. He remained in emigration after the war, serving as an expert in intelligence matters dealing with Central Europe in Marshall B. J. Montgomery's staff, and worked in Paris and Morocco as an administrator in the L. Śliwiński mining company. He was promoted to brigadier general in January 1964 and died in Casablanca in July 1968, where he was buried. *Intelligence Co-Operation*, vol. 2, 190–91.

42. *Intelligence Co-Operation*, vol. 2, 178.

43. See OSS/London [microform]: Reel 7, Vol. 1: Introductory Survey of Establishment, Activities, and Plans of SI/ETO, 30.

44. Michael Warner, "COI Came First," in *The Office of Strategic Services: America's First Intelligence Agency* (Washington, DC: Public Affairs, Central Intelligence Agency, 2000), https://permanent.fdlp.gov/websites/www.cia.gov/library/publications/intelligence-history/oss/art02.htm.

45. Warner, "COI Came First," section on William J. Donovan.

46. For his outstanding service, Major Słowikowski was awarded the Legion of Merit by the Americans and the Order of the British Empire by the British. Later promoted to brigadier general, Rygor documented, in a very modest way, his and his organization's service in North Africa in *W tajnej służbie* (London: Mizyg Press, 1977). For an excellent appraisal of the complicated relationships that existed and flourished among the Allies in North Africa, see Hal Vaughan, *FDR's 12 Apostles: The Spies Who Paved the Way for the Invasion of North Africa* (Guilford, CT: Lyons Press, 2006). See also the illuminating article on, among other things, taking credit by Allies where little credit was due, by John Herman, "Rygor's Franco-Polish Network and Operation Torch," *Journal of Contemporary History* 22, no. 4 (October 1987): 681–706.

47. See David A. Walker, "OSS and Operation Torch," *Journal of Contemporary History* 22 (1987): 667–79.

48. Colonel Eddy's bio can be found here: C. A. Prettiman, "The Many Lives of William Alfred Eddy," *Princeton University Library Chronicle* 53, no. 2 (Winter 1992): 200–216.

49. Kermit Roosevelt, *War Report of the OSS (Office of Strategic Services)*, vol. 1 (New York: Walker, 1976), x.

50. John Herman, "Rygor's Franco-Polish Network and Operation Torch," *Journal of Contemporary History* 22, no. 4 (October 1987): 695.

51. Ciechanowski, "Wywiad polski," 106.

52. *Oxford Dictionary of National Biography*, s.v. "Brittain, Sir Herbert (1894–1961)," by Alan Booth, September 23, 2004, https://www.oxforddnb.com/display/10.1093/ref:odnb/9780198614128.001.0001/odnb-9780198614128-e-66844.

53. The Poles sought an increase from 6,220 pounds to 11,000 pounds. *Intelligence Co-Operation*, vol. 2, 477–78.

54. Douglas George MacArthur (1880–1964) was an American five-star general and field marshal of the Philippine Army. He was named commander of the United States Army Forces in the Far East in 1941, and in 1942 became supreme commander of the Southwest Pacific Area. He was awarded the Congressional Medal of Honor at the end of the war and was one of only five army officers to attain the rank of general of the army during and after the war. *Encyclopedia Britannica Online*, s.v. "Douglas MacArthur," by James D. Clayton, accessed April 1, 2022, https://www.britannica.com/biography/Douglas-MacArthur.

55. Chester William Nimitz (1885–1966) was a fleet admiral of the United States Navy. He played a major role in the naval history of World War II as commander in chief of the US Pacific Fleet and the Pacific Ocean Areas, commanding Allied air, land, and sea forces during World War II. *Encyclopedia Britannica Online*, s.v. "Chester W. Nimitz," accessed February 20, 2022, https://www.britannica.com/biography/Chester-W-Nimitz.

56. This is no doubt partially due to the fact that by early 1942, the US Navy had made considerable progress in decrypting Japanese naval messages. The US Army also made progress on the Japanese Army's codes in 1943, including codes used by supply ships, resulting in heavy losses to their shipping. *Encyclopedia Britannica Online*, s.v. "Ultra," by B. J. Copeland, accessed April 4, 2019, https://www.britannica.com/topic/Ultra-Allied-intelligence-project.

57. William Phillips (1878–1968) was born in Beverly, Massachusetts, and finished law at Harvard. He was US Ambassador to Belgium, Canada, and Italy and in July 1942 was named chief of the OSS branch in London. After the war, he practiced law and wrote his memoirs. See Phillips, William, 1878–1968 (Interviewee), Link, Wendell (Interviewer), Reminiscences of William Phillips, 1951, Columbia Center for Oral History, Columbia University, especially 130–40.

58. Gustav B. Guenther (1896–1944) worked in the Military Intelligence Department of the War Department in Washington, DC, before the war and was responsible for Eastern Europe. When the United States entered the war, Guenther was posted to Cairo and then in 1942 to London, where he briefly served as the chief of OSS Special Operations. In 1944 he returned to England and in June of that year was killed during a V1 raid in London. See Jan Gore, *Send More Shrouds: The V1 Attack on the Guards' Chapel, 1944* (Barnsley, Yorkshire: Pen & Sword Military, 2017), 113–14.

59. Richard P. Heppner (1909–1958), colonel, worked for William Donovan's law firm before the war and was OSS chief in China during the war. He served as Deputy Assistant of Defense for International Security Affairs in the Eisenhower administration. See "Postwar Period: End of the OSS and Return to the Park Service," National Park Service, last updated August 14, 2017, https://www.nps .gov/articles/postwar-period-end-of-the-oss-and-return-to-the-park-service.htm.

60. Ellery C. Huntington (1893–1987), colonel, was commanding officer of OSS units in the 5th Army in Italy in 1943, and later liaison officer between OSS units and Tito's Partisans in Yugoslavia. His main task was informing the United States about the guerrilla fight against the German and Italian occupation troops and arranging for parachute drops of supplies and nightly air evacuation of the wounded. After the war, Colonel Huntington returned to New York, where he headed the Equity Corporation of New York. See *New York Times*, Ellery Huntington Jr. obituary, July 6, 1987, https://www.nytimes.com/1987/07/06/obituaries/ellery-huntington-jr.html.

61. Whitney Hart Shepardson (1890–1966), colonel, finished law at Harvard. During the interwar years he worked for the Department of State and was the director of the Woodrow Wilson Foundation. When the United States entered the war, Colonel Shepardson worked at the US Embassy in London and became the first director of OSS's Secret Intelligence branch in London, and in 1943 became the head of OSS SI in Washington. Between 1953 and 1956 he was the president of the National Committee for a Free Europe. For a brief bio, see "The Whitney H. Shepardson Fellowship," Council on Foreign Relations, https://www.cfr.org/ whitney-h-shepardson-fellowship (accessed May 3, 2022).

62. William Percy Maddox (1901–1972), colonel, Harvard graduate. Between 1925 and 1942, Dr. Maddox was a professor of political science at several US universities. Between 1942 and 1944, he was the head of OSS Secret Intelligence. After the war, Maddox began a long career in various positions at the Department of State. Between 1967 and 1969, he served as president of the Pratt Institute in New York. See https://www.nytimes.com/1972/09/29/archives/william-maddox-career-diplomat-lxhead-of- foreign-service-institute.html.

63. Peter Kross, *The Encyclopedia of World War II Spies* (Fort Lee, NJ: Barracade Books, 2001), 233–35.

64. In December 1944, the OSS numbered some 13,000 members, of whom 5,500 were based in the United States and 7,500 abroad. These statistics are cited in Roosevelt, *War Report of the OSS*, vol. 1, 116. This is a declassified version of a manuscript completed in 1947.

65. Michael Warner, "What Was OSS?" in *The Office of Strategic Services: America's First Intelligence Agency* (Washington, DC: Public Affairs, Central Intelligence Agency, 2000), https://www.cia.gov/static/7851e16f9e100b6f9cc4ef002028ce2f/ Office-of-Strategic-Services.pdf. That would be some $178 billion in 2023 dollars.

66. Roosevelt, *War Report of the OSS*, vol. 1.

67. The legacy of OSS Operational Groups today are the Operational Detachments Alpha (ODA) of today's Special Forces. See the US Army's dedicated website at https://www.soc.mil/OSS/operational-groups.html (accessed October 25, 2017).

68. Sir Peter Allix Wilkinson (1914–2000), KCMG, DSO, OBE, was a British intelligence officer and diplomat. He served in SOE during the war and afterwards became a diplomat and served as coordinator of intelligence in the Prime Minister's Office. In 1966–1967 he was Great Britain's ambassador to Vietnam. Listen to the British Imperial War Museum's Oral History 1993 interview and view Wilkinson's bio at https://www.iwm.org.uk/collections/item/object/80013010 (accessed May 30, 2022).

69. Stacy Barcroft Lloyd (1908–1994) joined the US Army in December 1942 and served with the OSS in England, North Africa, and Italy, where he commanded field units. He also served on General William Donovan's staff. He finished his service as a lieutenant colonel in July 1945 and received, among other honors, the Legion of Merit and Croix de Guerre. See "Stacy Lloyd," Little Sis, https://littlesis.org/person/98364-Stacy_Lloyd (accessed March 16, 2018).

70. OSS/London [microform]: Reel 3, Vol. 3, Book 13: Western Europe, Poles in France, 125.

71. Kermit Roosevelt, *War Report of the OSS (Office of Strategic Services)*, vol. 2, *The Overseas Targets* (New York: Walker, 1976), 4–5.

72. This had begun quietly a year earlier when the Polish intelligence network in North Africa turned over its results directly to the Americans before Operation Torch.

73. Roosevelt, *War Report of the OSS*, vol. 2, 208. Project "Proust" was intended to create a pool of reserve agents who would become active after the invasion. Fifty agents with various tasks were dropped into France in June 1944. See Roosevelt, *War Report of the OSS*, vol. 2, 213–15.

74. Plan SUSSEX involved dropping agents behind German lines in occupied northern France to collect intelligence for the American 1st Army Group. One hundred twenty French agents were trained in England in schools jointly operated by OSS SI and SOE. The first two-man groups were dropped into France in June 1944 and gathered information judged to be very helpful by G-S SHAEF. A 500-page description of SUSSEX can be found in OSS/London [microform]: Reel 7, Vol. 3: Sussex Operation.

75. Stewart G. Menzies (1890–1968) was deputy director of MI6 (SIS) and director of SIS between 1939 and 1952. He retired as a major general. See *Oxford Dictionary of National Biography*, s.v. "Menzies, Sir Stewart Graham," revised by A. O. Blishen, September 23, 2004, https://www.oxforddnb.com/view/10.1093/ref:odnb/9780198614128.001.0001/odnb-9780198614128-e-34988.

76. Jeffrey, *Secret History of MI6*, 501.

77. Roosevelt, *War Report of the OSS*, vol. 2, 305.

78. Roosevelt, *War Report of the OSS*, vol. 2, 305. Patrick O'Donnell, *Operatives, Spies, and Saboteurs: The Unknown Story of the Men and Women of World War II's OSS* (New York: Free Press, 2004), 255.

79. OSS/London [microform]: Reel 7, Vol. 1: Introductory Survey of Establishment, Activities, and Plans of SI/ETO, 28–29.

80. OSS/London [microform]: Reel 7, Vol. 1: Introductory Survey of Establishment, Activities, and Plans of SI/ETO, 40.

81. OSS/London [microform]: Reel 7, Vol. 1: Introductory Survey of Establishment, Activities, and Plans of SI/ETO, vol. 2, 161–62.

82. Joseph Dasher (1903–1991) was born Józef Daszewski in Łódz, then in the Russian Empire. During World War I he and his family were evacuated deep into Russia. In 1921 he emigrated to the United States, and between 1926 and 1936 worked in the Polish consulate in Pittsburgh. In December 1941 he enlisted in the US Army with the rank of lieutenant. Thanks to his command of languages, he was seconded to military intelligence and in early 1944 completed a two-month OSS intelligence course in Washington, following which he was sent to London as chief of the Polish Section in OSS SI. Major Dasher was responsible for the organization, training, administration, and running of Project Eagle, and served as liaison officer between OSS SI London and the Polish Armed Forces in the West. After the war, he served at the Pentagon in Washington as head of the History Section of the Joint Chiefs of Staff. He died in 1991 and was interred at Arlington National Cemetery. The author is indebted to information provided by email on March 20, 2018, by Colonel Dasher's son and daughter-in-law, Mark and Kim Dasher, and Ancestry .com (see Colonel Joseph Dasher).

83. For an excellent analysis of the situation in Germany at war's end, see Ian Kershaw, *The End: The Defiance and Destruction of Hitler's Germany, 1944–1945* (New York: Penguin, 2011). The terror campaign has been documented ably in Wolfram Wette, Ricarda Bremer, and Detlef Vogel, eds., *Das letzte Halbe Jahr: Stimmungsberichte der Wehrmachtpropaganda 1944/45* (Essen: Klartext Verlag, 2001).

84. The *Volkssturm* was a national militia formed by the Nazi Party late in the war and staffed by conscripting males between the ages of sixteen and sixty who were not already serving in some military unit. See Earl R. Beck, *Under the Bombs: The German Home Front 1942–1945* (Lexington: University Press of Kentucky, 1986), 161–62.

CHAPTER 2

1. The history of the Independent Grenadiers Company of the Polish Armed Forces has been published by Piotr Witkowski, *Polskie jednostki powietrzno-desantowe na Zachodzie* (Warsaw: Bellona, 2009), 275–346. Of particular interest is the Polish version of the abortive Bardsea Operation.

2. Ryszard Kaczmarek, *Polacy w Wehrmachcie* (Kraków: Wydawnictwo Literackie, 2010).

3. Kaczmarek, *Polacy w Wehrmachcie*, 2.

4. Engineers and construction experts of the Todt Organization oversaw forced laborers working on projects that the Third Reich deemed vital during World War II, collaborating closely with the SS throughout Nazi-occupied Europe and in the heart of the Reich. Fritz Todt's paramilitary organization, which was led by his successor, Albert Speer, for the last three years of the war, played a far greater part in the deaths of slave laborers than previously believed. See Charles Dick, *Hitler's Slave Drivers: The Role of the Organisation Todt as Overseers of Force Labour under Nazism* (Birkbeck University of London: ProQuest Dissertations Publishing, 2019).

5. Kaczmarek, *Polacy w Wehrmachcie*, 16–21.

6. Excerpts from the bios were part of the citations forwarded by the OSS for military awards. These were unclassified in 2008 and are housed at NARA, College Park, Maryland.

7. Private First Class Józef Pająk, member of the Alexander Mission, NARA, RG 226, Entry 210, Box 5, Folder 29.

8. In his wartime memoir titled *Bez ostatniego rozdziału: Wspomnienia z lat 1939–1946* (Lublin: Test, 1992), General Władysław Anders writes that during his talks in Algeria with British General Henry Maitland Wilson, Supreme Allied Commander in the Mediterranean Theater, he tried to convince Maitland to accept the premise that Poles who had previously served in the Wehrmacht should be accepted into service as Polish soldiers by, among others, the Second Polish Corps. Anders explained that the Polish Army in the West had no way to raise enlistments in occupied Poland and that this was the only way that the Polish Army in the West could increase its numbers. Wilson was at first skeptical but after several conversations agreed to the scheme.

9. Kaczmarek, *Polacy w Wehrmachcie*, 27.

10. Kaczmarek, *Polacy w Wehrmachcie*, 27–28.

11. SUSSEX was meant to furnish intelligence in the field for American forces in France by the use of undercover agents in enemy-occupied territory in northern France beginning two months before D-Day. See Roosevelt, *War Report of the OSS*, vol. 2, 208–13.

12. Colonel John H. F. Haskell (1904–1987) was a West Point graduate, Class of 1925, and vice-president of the New York Stock Exchange in 1939. He rejoined the army in October 1940 and served on the War Department General Staff at the Pentagon, where he was detached for duty in the OSS and served in the Middle East, Italy, Russia, London, and France during its liberation. See "John H. Haskll 1925," West Point Association of Graduates, https://alumni.westpointaog.org/memorial-article?id=a04b52dc-5762-416a-836c-282bd7d5b603 (accessed March 14, 2018).

13. Nelson D. Lankford, *The Last American Aristocrat: The Biography of David K. E. Bruce, 1898–1977* (Boston: Little, Brown, 1996).

14. Marian Włodzimierz Kukiel (1885–1975), Brigadier/Major General, earned his doctorate at the Philosophy Department of Jan Kazimierz University in Lwow. From his youth he participated in revolutionary and independence activities. In 1914 he was active in organizing the Polish Legions in Lwow and Krakow. He fought as a regimental commander in the Polish-Bolshevik War, following which he became chief of the Historical Section, later the Historical Bureau of the General Staff. After the May 28, 1926, coup d'etat he retired from service. In September 1939 he volunteered for military service and fought near Lvov. After the September debacle, he emigrated to France and after its fall to England. He became commander of the First Polish Corps in Scotland and from 1942 to 1949 was Minister of National Defense. He remained in the United Kingdom after the war and was very active in émigré academic affairs. See *Intelligence Co-Operation*, vol. 1, 505.

15. Kazimierz Sosnkowski (1885–1969), Lieutenant General, was active in the Polish independence movement and was a close associate and deputy of Joseph Pilsudski. He held various high-ranking military and political positions throughout the interwar period. He served as commander of the Southern Front during the September Campaign, and evacuated to Hungary and later to Paris in October 1939. He served in a variety of positions simultaneously from November 1939 until August 1941, resigning from all of them except as the president's successor in protest over the signing of the Sikorski-Maisky Agreement. From September 1943 to September 1944, the Supreme Commander dismissed him at the request of the British and expelled him from the Polish Army following his criticism of the Western Allies for failing to provide assistance to the Warsaw Uprising. He was dismissed by President Wladyslaw Raczkiewicz as his successor in August 1944. He emigrated to Canada at the end of 1944, where he was active in efforts to unify Polish émigrés until his death. *Intelligence Co-Operation*, vol. 2, 263.

16. Eric Edward Mockler-Ferryman (1896–1978) was a British brigadier general and general staff officer. From March 1943 to 1945 he served as chief of SOE Directorate for Operations in Western Europe and until 1944 for the liaison with COSSAC (the Chief of Staff to the Allied Supreme Commander). In 1945–1946 he was a member of the Allied Control Commission in Hungary; he retired in 1947. *Intelligence Co-Operation*, vol. 2, 219.

17. Thomas Jeffries Betts (1894–1977) was born in Baltimore, Maryland. He graduated from the University of Virginia in 1916 and was commissioned into the Coast Artillery Corps the following year. In 1918 he served the AEF in the 49th Artillery. From 1929 to 1933 he served the military intelligence division and returned again from 1938 to 1943. He rose to brigadier general in 1943 and went on to serve as deputy assistant chief of staff for intelligence at SHAEF between 1943 and 1945. At the 1946 Bikini atomic tests, he was the chief intelligence officer. He was honored with the Distinguished Service Medal, the Bronze Star, and the Purple Heart. He retired in 1953. See "Betts, Thomas J. (Thomas Jeffries)," National Archives Catalog, https://catalog.archives.gov/id/10610494 (accessed March 16, 2018).

18. OSS/London [microform]: Reel 8, Vol. 7: Miscellaneous Operations with Allied Services, 4–8.

19. Casey, *Secret War against Hitler*, 142.

20. Ouges-Longvic airbase number 102. US designation Y-9. My thanks to Ronald Knoth for identifying the airfield.

21. Janusz Rowiński (1899–1994) was active in the Polish scouts and a soldier in Pilsudski's First Legionary Brigade. In 1937, as a major, he took charge of the Third Battalion of 5th Regiment of the Highlander Rifles and led them during the September 1939 campaign. He made his way through Hungary to France and finished a course for battalion commanders and staff officers. He then commanded the 2nd Battalion of the 8th Infantry Division. Following France's fall, he was evacuated to England, where he commanded the 4th Battalion of the Parachute Brigade between 1941 and 1943, and then until war's end headed the Infantry Training Center in Scotland. The author thanks the Pilsudski Institute in London for the information on Colonel Rowiński.

22. Ronald Hazell (1902–?), captain, later lieutenant colonel, was employed by United Baltic Corporation as a shipping agent in Gdynia from 1929 to 1939. He joined the Military Mission to Poland as a captain in 1939, was sent on a mission to Romania, and joined SOE in charge of the Polish Minorities Section, 1941–1944. He was British vice consul in Gdynia from 1947 to 1953, where he assisted in Stanislaw Mikołajczyk's escape from Poland in October 1947. See *Intelligence Co-Operation*, vol. 1, 154, and Andrea Mason, *British Policy Towards Poland* (London: Palgrave MacMillan, 2018), 173.

23. OSS/London [microform]: Reel 8, Vol. 7: Miscellaneous Operations with Allied Services, 8–41.

24. NARA, RG 226, Entry 115, Container 46, Folder 606.

25. Special Training School 25a—Garramor, South Morar, Inverness-shire.

26. Tadeusz Szumowski (1899–1971), major/certified lieutenant colonel (equivalent to the US acronym GSC, General Staff College), was an officer of the II Bureau from 1935, Polish attaché in Stockholm, and chief of the Saigon intelligence cell there. He was chief of the Western Section of the Intelligence Department of the II Bureau from March to August 1939, and was transferred to Bern, Switzerland, to lead the Polish intelligence unit there in September 1939. He next served in the Foreign Office as head of the Personnel and General Departments. From February 1940 until war's end, he served as secretary, then counselor, in the Polish Embassy in London and simultaneously as head of the Special Affairs Department of the Ministry of National Defense until 1944, and military attaché to the Czechoslovak government from October 1940 to July 1945. He was jailed by the Communist authorities upon his return to Poland. Jan Bury, "From the Archives: Polish Interwar MFA's Cipher Compromised?" *Cryptologia* 31, no. 3 (July 2007): 268–77.

27. OSS/London [microform]: Reel 8, Vol. 7: Miscellaneous Operations with Allied Services, 41–47.

28. NARA, RG 226, Entry 210, Box 249, Folder 7.

29. NARA, RG 226, Entry 115, Box 42, Final Report Project Eagle.

30. Roosevelt, *War Report of the OSS*, vol. 2, 309. For an account of their experiences, see Jonathan S. Gould, *German Anti-Nazi Espionage in the Second World War: The OSS and the Men of the TOOL Missions* (London and New York: Routledge, 2019).

31. NARA, RG 226, Entry 210, Box 5.

32. NARA, RG 226, Entry 210, location 250 64/21/1, Box 5.

33. NARA, RG 226, Entry 115, Box 42, Final Report on Project Eagle.

34. This was the idea of William Casey, who had advanced to direct SI London on December 1, 1944. See the letter from Lieutenant Colonel Joseph Dasher to Allen Dulles, NARA, RG 226, Entry 115, Container 47, Folder 608.

35. NARA, RG 226, Entry 115, Container 47, Folder 608.

36. NARA, RG 226, Entry 115, Container 47, Folder 608.

37. NARA, RG 226, Entry 115, Container 47, Folder 609.

38. NARA, RG 226, Entry 115, Container 47, Folder 609.

39. NARA, RG 226, Entry 115, Container 47, Folder 609.

40. James Russell Forgan (1900–1974) was a businessman and investment banker who directed the OSS in the European Theater of Operations. Colonel Forgan was highly decorated. He later chaired two committees whose work led to the establishment of the CIA in 1947. See "J. Russell Forgan Dead at 73; Banker was Official of O.S.S.," *New York Times*, February 1, 1974, https://www.nytimes .com/1974/02/01/archives/j-russell-forgan-dead-at-73-banker-was-official-of-oss-won-many.html.

41. NARA, RG 226, Entry 115, Container 47, Folder 608.

42. Jerzy Antoni Łunkiewicz (1892–1956), certified colonel, served in the artillery service of the Tsarist Army until captured at the Battle of Kaniów and held prisoner from May 11 to November 11, 1918. He joined the Polish Army as a captain on November 14, 1918, advancing to colonel on January 1, 1936. In September 1939 he evacuated through Romania to France, where he worked at the Ministry of National Defense and later the General Staff. In fall 1942 he became adjutant in charge of the Minister's Office, where he remained until war's end. A biography was published in 1973 in volume 18 of the *Polish Biographical Dictionary*, https://www.ipsb.nina.gov.pl/a/biografia/jerzy-antoni-lunkiewicz (accessed September 24, 2018).

43. NARA, RG 226, Entry 115, Container 47, Folder 609.

44. Colonel Dasher reported to SI Branch on February 27, 1945, that training would conclude the next day, February 28, and that operational implementation of Project Eagle would start March 1, 1945. NARA, RG 226, Entry 210, Box 5.

45. NARA, Entry 115, Container 47, Folder 609.

46. NARA, Entry 115, Container 47, Folder 609.

47. NARA, Entry 115, Container 47, Folder 609.

48. NARA, Entry 115, Container 47, Folder 609.

49. NARA, Entry 115, Container 47, Folder 608.

50. Roosevelt, *War Report of the OSS*, vol. 2, 16.

51. OSS/London [microform]: Reel 7, Vol. 1: Introductory Survey of Establishment, Activities, and Plans of SI/ETO, 4–8.

52. See Joseph E. Persico, *Piercing the Reich: The Penetration of Nazi Germany by American Secret Service Agents during World War II* (New York: Barnes and Noble Books, 2000), 2.

53. See Gould, *German Anti-Nazi Espionage*.

54. Roosevelt, *War Report of the OSS*, vol. 2, 291–97, 305–14.

55. OSS/London [microform]: Reel 8, Vol. 12: German Operations—1945, Book 1, 21–22.

56. SSTR-1, Strategic Services Transmitter Receiver–Number 1, was a "suitcase radio" used during World War II by the OSS. See https://militaryradio.com/spyradio/sstr1.html (accessed December 15, 2017) and https://www.youtube.com/watch?v=L2qENm9XNCk&list=PLDMeFyCMi9z1otMv1KoHE-dDbFwE-qOsjk (accessed February 12, 2018).

57. Kross, *Encyclopedia of World War II Spies*, 127–29.

58. Roosevelt, *War Report of the OSS*, vol. 2, 306–7.

59. OSS/London [microform]: Reel 5, Vol. 6: January, February, March 1944—Air Operations, Aircraft, 41, 45.

60. OSS/London [microform]: Reel 6, Vol. 1, Book 2: Miscellaneous cont., Agent Leaves for Field, 10.

61. Lieutenant A. R. Waters was administrative officer of the Polish Section SI London.

62. Lieutenant Leonard Łysz was an instructor at the School of Specialists. See "Łysz, Leonard," Bohaterowie 1939, http://www.bohaterowie1939.pl/polegly,lysz,leonard,11035.html (accessed May 9, 2019), and Ian Valentine, *Station 43: Audley End House and Polish SOE Section* (Stroud: History Press, 2006).

63. An incomplete summary of operations listing half of the Project Eagle drops shows that Eggnog Mission had at least four incomplete drop attempts, Daiquiri four, and Singapore Sling one; it does not include the seven failed attempts that the Manhattan team endured. See "Summary of Operations Carried Out on Operation Carpetbagger During WW2," Carpetbagger Aviation Museum, Harrington, https://harringtonmuseum.org.uk/wp-content/uploads/2018/05/Carpetbagger-Mission-Reports-Summary.pdf (accessed February 9, 2020).

64. Ensign Edmund Hadrian was an officer of the School of Specialists. Polish Institute and Sikorski Museum [henceforth PISM], "Sprawozdanie z działalności Szkoły Specjalistów," A .XII 85/14, k. 42–56, in Grabowski, *Zapomniani polscy spadochroniarze*, 58–59.

65. NARA, RG 226, Entry 115, Container 46, Box 47, Folder 605.

66. CAO: chief administrative officer.

67. PISM, "Sprawozdanie z działalności Szkoły Specjalistów," 59.

68. Beck, *Under the Bombs*, 8.

69. Derek Stephen Zumbro, "Battle for the Ruhr: The German Army's Final Defeat in the West" (PhD diss., Louisiana State University and Agricultural and Mechanical College, 2006), 595; Kershaw, *The End*, 379.

70. Kershaw, *The End*, 137.

71. Zumbro, "Battle for the Ruhr," 68.

72. Beck, *Under the Bombs*, 30.

73. Beck, *Under the Bombs*, 191.

74. Kershaw, *The End*, 3.

75. From Paprzycki's correspondence of October 10, 1998, with "Tedy," his Hot Punch teammate Tadeusz Rawski.

76. Kershaw, *The End*, 234.

77. Kershaw, *The End*, 224.

78. See Wette, Bremer, and Vogel, *Das letzte halbe Jahr*, 176n122.

79. Zumbro, "Battle for the Ruhr," 252–53.

80. Beck, *Under the Bombs*, 187.

81. Kershaw, *The End*, 259–60.

82. Kershaw, *The End*, 261.

83. PISM, "Zestawienie schematyczne akcji bojowej absolwentów Szkoły Specjalistów," A XII 85/14, k. 41, as cited in Grabowski, *Zapomniani polscy spadachronionarzy*, 84.

CHAPTER 3

1. NARA, RG 226, Entry 115, Container 47, Box 610; NARA, RG 226, Entry 210, Location 250 64/21/1, Box 5.

2. OSS/London [microform]: Reel 8, Vol. 12: German Operations—1945, Book: The Desks and Their Missions; The Polish Desk, 294–300.

3. NARA, RG 226, Entry 210, Box 5, Folder 29; NARA, RG 226, Entry 210, Location 250 64/21/1, Box 5.

4. OSS/London [microform]: Reel 8, Vol. 12: German Operations—1945, Book: The Desks and Their Missions; The Polish Desk, 300–308.

5. Probably Lieutenant Colonel Robert W. Clark, commanding the First Battalion of the 414th Infantry Regiment. See "Saale River Offensive: The Seizure of Halle," 104th Infantry Division, National Timberwolf Pubs Association, http://www.104infdiv.org/saale.htm (accessed May 12, 2019).

6. NARA, RG 226, Entry 210, Box 15, Folder 7; NARA, RG 226, Entry 210, Location 250 64/21/1, Box 5.

7. OSS/London [microform]: Reel 8, Vol. 12: German Operations—1945, Book: The Desks and Their Missions; The Polish Desk, 308–16.

8. NARA, RG 226, Entry201, Box 15, Folder 4; NARA, RG 226, Entry 210, Location 250 64/21/1, Box 5.

9. OSS/London [microform]: Reel 8, Vol. 12: German Operations—1945, Book: The Desks and Their Missions; The Polish Desk, 17–24.

10. NARA, RG 226, Entry A1 224, Box 860; NARA, RG 226, Entry 210, Location 250 64/21/1, Box 5.

11. OSS/London [microform]: Reel 8, Vol. 12: German Operations—1945, Book: The Desks and Their Missions; The Polish Desk, 324–30.

12. NARA, RG 226, Entry 210, Box 5, Folder 29; NARA, RG 226, Entry 210, Location 250 64/21/1, Box 5.

13. OSS/London [microform]: Reel 8, Vol.12: German Operations—1945, Book: The Desks and Their Missions; The Polish Desk, 331–35.

14. Sergeant Banaszkiewicz/Bogdanowicz used the pseudonym Jonas Januskis and was later listed as missing presumed dead. A search performed by the German Federal Archives found no evidence of his interment in Germany. Letter from the Bundesarchiv in Berlin to the author, September 16, 2021.

15. NARA, RG 226, Entry 210, Box 5, Folder 29; NARA, RG 226, Entry 210, Location 250 64/21/1, Box 5; Grabowski, *Zapomniani polscy spadochroniarze*, 4.

16. OSS/London [microform]: Reel 8, Vol. 12: German Operations—1945, Book: The Desks and Their Missions; The Polish Desk, 335–36.

17. Most likely the IG Farbenindustrie A.G.'s third large plant for synthetic rubber and liquid fuels at Monowice/Monowitz.

18. NARA, RG 226, Entry 210, Box 5, Folder 29; NARA, RG 226, Entry 210, Location 250 64/21/1, Box 5.

19. OSS/London [microform]: Reel 8, Vol. 12: German Operations—1945, Book: The Desks and Their Missions; The Polish Desk, 336–42.

20. NARA, RG 226, Entry 210, Box 5, Folder 29; NARA, RG 226, Entry 210, Location 250 64/21/1, Box 5.

21. OSS/London [microform]: Reel 8, Vol. 12: German Operations—1945, Book: The Desks and Their Missions; The Polish Desk, 342–51.

22. NARA, RG 226, Entry 210, Box 5, Folder 29; NARA, RG 226, Entry 210, Location 250 64/21/1, Box 5.

23. OSS/London [microform]: Reel 8, Vol. 12: German Operations—1945, Book: The Desks and Their Missions; The Polish Desk, 351–54.

24. NARA, RG 226, Entry 210, Box 5, Folder 29; NARA, RG 226, Entry 210, Location 250 64/21/1, Box 5.

25. OSS/London [microform]: Reel 8, Vol. 12: German Operations—1945, Book: The Desks and Their Missions; The Polish Desk, 354–60.

26. NARA, RG 226, Entry 210, Box 5, Folder 29; NARA, RG 226, Entry 210, Location 250 64/21/1, Box 5.

27. OSS/London [microform]: Reel 8, Vol. 12: German Operations—1945, Book: The Desks and Their Missions; The Polish Desk, 360–65.

28. NARA, RG 226, Entry 210, Box 5, Folder 29; NARA, RG 226, Entry 210, Location 250 64/21/1, Box 5.

29. OSS/London [microform]: Reel 8, Vol. 12: German Operations—1945, Book: The Desks and Their Missions; The Polish Desk, 365–70.

30. NARA, RG 226, Entry 210, Box 5, Folder 29; NARA, RG 226, Entry 210, Location 250 64/21/1, Box 5.

31. OSS/London [microform]: Reel 8, Vol. 12: German Operations—1945, Book: The Desks and Their Mission; The Polish Desk, 370–74.

32. Please note the typist's mistake found in the photo on page 140 regarding the name of Rawski's father.

33. NARA, RG 226, Entry 210, Box 5, Folder 29; NARA, RG 226, Entry 210, Location 250 64/21/1, Box 5.

34. OSS/London [microform]: Reel 8, Vol. 12: German Operations—1945, Book: The Desks and Their Missions; The Polish Desk, 374–77.

35. NARA, RG 226, Entry 210, Box 5, Folder 29; NARA, RG 226, Entry 210, Location 250 64/21/1, Box 5.

36. OSS/London [microform]: Reel 8, Vol. 12: German Operations—1945, Book: The Desks and Their Missions; The Polish Desk, 377–78.

CHAPTER 4

1. NARA, RG 226, Entry 115, Box 42.

2. Casey, *Secret War against Hitler*, "Chief SI, ETO, Final Report on SI Operations into Germany, 24 July 1945," 289–90.

3. Casey, *Secret War against Hitler*, 290–91.

4. Roosevelt, *War Report of the OSS*, vol. 2, 308.

5. See, for example, O'Donnell, *Operatives, Spies, and Saboteurs*, 251.

6. See the mission reports in chapter 3.

7. Roosevelt, *War Report of the OSS*, vol. 2, 307.

8. William Casey, *The Hidden Struggle for Europe*, draft manuscript, 1976, p. 28, William J. Casey Papers, Box 26, Folder 9, Hoover Institution Archives, in Seth G. Jones, *A Covert Action: Reagan, the CIA, and the Cold War Struggle in Poland* (New York and London: W. W. Norton, 2018), 57.

9. Casey, *Secret War against Hitler*, 44.

10. General Stanisław Maczek (1892–1994) was a Polish tank commander in World War II, whose division was instrumental in the Allied liberation of France, closing the Falaise pocket, resulting in the destruction of fourteen German Wehrmacht and SS divisions. Maczek had been the commander of Poland's only major armored formation during the September 1939 campaign, and later commanded a Polish armored formation in France in 1940. He was the commander of the famous 1st Polish Armored Division and later of the I Polish Army Corps under Allied Command in 1942–1945. Maczek's division continued to spearhead the Allied drive across the battlefields of northern France, Belgium, the Netherlands, and finally Germany. Thanks to an outflanking maneuver, Breda in the Netherlands was

liberated after a hard fight but without incurring losses in the town's population. A petition on behalf of 40,000 inhabitants of Breda resulted in Maczek being made an honorary Dutch citizen after the war. The division's finest hour came when its forces accepted the surrender of the German naval base of Wilhelmshaven, taking captive the entire garrison, together with some 200 vessels of Hitler's *Kriegsmarine*. See Evan McGilvray, *Man of Steel and Honour: General Stanisław Maczek, Soldier of Poland, Commander of the 1st Polish Armoured Division in North-West Europe, 1944–45* (Solihull, West Midlands, UK: Helion & Company, 2012).

11. Stanisław Maczek, *Od podwody do czołga: wspomnienia wojenne 1918–1945* (London: Orbis, 1984), 217.

12. NARA, RG 226, Entry 115, Box 42, Final Report on Project Eagle.

13. NARA, RG 226, Entry 115, Box 42, Final Report on Project Eagle.

14. NARA, RG 226, Entry 115, Box 42.

15. Bletchley Park is an estate located eighty kilometers northwest of London. During World War II it housed Great Britain's code breakers and cipher experts. See David Kenyon, *Bletchley Park and D-Day* (New Haven, CT: Yale University Press, 2019).

16. Gonzalo Edward "Ned" Buxton Jr. (1880–1949) was a Harvard Law School graduate and colonel in the American Expeditionary Force during World War I. He was appointed OSS First Assistant Director in June 1942 by General Donovan. Buxton was a key person in developing the OSS's tactics and operational decisions. After World War II, he received the US Medal of Merit and made a Commander of the Order of the British Empire Order, and from the Polish government in London was awarded the Order of Polonia Restituta. See "Rhode Island Hall of Fame Honorees: Six Legal Luminaries," *Rhode Island Bar Journal* 63, no. 6 (May/June 2015): 30.

17. Gould, *German Anti-Nazi Espionage*, 101–2.

18. Brigadier General John Magruder (1887–1958), a career military who was commissioned in 1910, served in the OSS as Deputy Director for Intelligence. He played a formative role in the creation of the civilian Central Intelligence Agency (CIA) in 1947, which absorbed the SSU. See John Ranelagh, *The Agency: The Rise and Decline of the CIA* (London: Weidenfeld and Nicolson, 1986), 101.

19. Perhaps the most detailed description of General Donovan's efforts to establish and lead the postwar successor to the OSS and his struggles with the Washington bureaucracy is to be found in the excellent biography by Douglas Waller, *Wild Bill Donovan: The Spymaster Who Created the OSS and Modern American Espionage* (New York: Simon and Schuster, 2011).

20. See Center for the Study of Intelligence, ed., *The Creation of the Intelligence Community: Founding Documents* (Washington, DC: CIA, 2012).

21. Peter Kihss, "Adm. Roscoe H. Hillenkoetter, 85, First Director of the C.I.A., Dies," *New York Times*, June 21, 1982, https://www.nytimes.com/1982/06/21/obituaries/adm-roscoe-h-hillenkoetter-85-first-director-of-the-cia-dies.html.

22. "Decorations Awarded to OSS Personnel," OSS Reborn, accessed October 1, 2018, http://www.ossreborn.com/files/ossmedals.pdf.

23. NARA, RG 226, A1 226, Box 576.

24. NARA, RG 226, A1 224, Box 4.

25. NARA, RG 226, Entry A1 224, Box 122.

26. NARA, RG 226, Entry A1 224, Box 576.

27. NARA, RG 226, Entry A1 224, Box 162.

28. NARA, RG 226, Entry A1 224, Box 162.

29. NARA, RG 226, Entry 224, Box 265.

30. Cornell University Law Library, Donovan Nuremberg Trial Collection, cited in Albert Lulushi, *Donovan's Devils: OSS Commandos behind Enemy Lines—Europe, World War II* (New York: Arcade, 2016), 57–58.

31. Adam Bernstein, "Stephanie Rader, Undercover Spy in Postwar Europe, Dies at 100," *Washington Post*, January 21, 2016.

32. The Polish Minister of Defense advanced all members of Project Eagle to the rank of sergeant on the day of their parachute drop into Germany, and Sergeant Adrian to the rank of senior sergeant. See PISM, "Sprawozdanie z działalności Szkoły Specjalistów," A.XII 85/14, k. 42–56, as cited in Grabowski, *Zapomniani polscy spadochroniarze*, 59.

33. IPMS, "Zarządzenie Prezydenta Rzeczypospolitej z dnia 19 września 1945 roku o nadaniu Krzyża Walecznych," A. XII 85/14, p. 1.

34. IPMS, "Zarządzenie Prezydenta Rzeczypospolitej," A. XII 85/19, p. 3.

35. IPMS, "Notatka," A. XII 85/96.

36. PISM, A.XII.85/14, k. 42–56, Sztab NW i MSWojsk/MON, Biuro Ministerstwa Obrony Narodowej, Sprawozdanie z działalności Szkoły Specjalistów, załącznik nr 10, 20/VI/45.

37. On April 2, 1946, the Strategic Services Unit was transferred to the Central Intelligence Group as the Office of Special Operations.

38. Colonel William W. Quinn (1907–2000) became head of the SSU at the end of 1945, and in July 1946 was named Head of Operations of the Central Intelligence Group. J. Y. Smith, "Gen. William Quinn, Intelligence Leader, Decorated Officer Dies," *Washington Post*, September 12, 2000, https://www.washingtonpost.com/archive/local/2000/09/12/gen-william-quinn-intelligence-leader-decorated-officer-dies/f42ec17a-6aa2-4e9d-a81f-0070cfd4bd85.

39. NARA, RG 226, Entry 210, Box 167.

40. Most likely Oliver Schneditz, aka Oliver W. Rockhill (1917–1984). See "Widerstand: Exilösterreicher in amerikanischer Uniform," *Die Presse*, February 19, 2016, https://diepresse.com/home/zeitgeschichte/4929624/Widerstand_Exiloester-reicher-in-amerikanischer-uniform.

41. Lucjan Jagodziński (1894–1968), captain/major of artillery, served in the German Army during World War I. From 1919 he was in the Polish Army and served as an intelligence officer specializing in German affairs in the "West' Section of the Intelligence Department of the Second Branch of the General Staff. In Octo-

ber 1936 he was chief of the intelligence unit "Müller" operating out of the Polish Consulate in Essen, and from December 1936 after the unit was moved to Düsseldorf (now known as Outpost "Madras") he operated under cover of a trade officer under contract. At the end of 1939 he became head of the intelligence outpost in Brussels, and later taught in the Intelligence Officers' School; from spring 1943 he was deputy chief of unit "Afr." in Algiers. He stayed in emigration in Great Britain after the war, where he died. *Intelligence Co-Operation*, vol. 2, 46.

42. Mściwój Kokorniak (1907), captain of infantry, was an intelligence officer active in Germany before the war; with the start of the war he transferred to Polish intelligence in Copenhagen, and from February 1942 to Branch "Pln"/"SKN" in Stockholm. He completed intelligence officer training in March 1942 and from June 1942 until 1943 served in the intelligence branch "P" in Lisbon, then in Branch "Afr." In 1944 he was expected to be sent to Branch "Italy" but left the intelligence service as the result of misunderstandings with other intelligence officers. Toward war's end he posted as liaison officer of the Second Corps in Linz. *Intelligence Co-Operation*, vol. 2, 144.

43. Wincenty (Adam Emil) Bąkiewicz (1897–1974), major/lieutenant colonel/ certified colonel of infantry, was born in Gieraszowice near Sandomierz. From 1917 he was in the Russian Army, from July 1918 in the Polish Army's Officer Training School in Ufa, Siberia, and next in the Kościuszko First Siberian Rifle Regiment in Siberia. He fought and was wounded in 1920 in the Polish-Bolshevik War. He served in the Polish Army, among other assignments in the Infantry Department of the Ministry of Military Affairs; from March 1936 to January 1939 chief of the Independent "Russia" Section of the Studies Department of the Second Branch of the General Staff; and from September 1939 until September 1939 chief of the Second Branch of Army "Prussia." Between 1939 and 1941 he was jailed by the Soviets and tortured, severely affecting his health. He was promoted to lieutenant colonel in December 1941; in 1941–1942 he was deputy chief, later chief, of the Second Branch of the Polish Army in the USSR. From October 1941 he was head of the "Sandomierz" intelligence subsection of Polish intelligence in Buzuluk near Kujbyshev, the headquarters of the Polish Army in the USSR, and consequently viewed as suspicious and undesirable. From 1942 to 1943 he was head of the Second Branch of the Polish Army in the East and from 1943 to 1945 of the Polish Second Corps. From November 1944 he was commander of the Second Brigade of the Carpathian Rifles and promoted to colonel in January 1945. He remained in London after the war, where he died in 1974. He was awarded the Virtuti Militari cross and the Order of the British Empire. *Intelligence Co-Operation*, vol. 2, 562.

44. Major Kokorniak probably used the acronym OSS from habit; the OSS was dissolved on October 1, 1945, and some of its intelligence and counterintelligence functions were transferred to the War Department's newly formed Special Services Unit.

45. Polish Underground Movement Trust in London, Collection 18/244, Wincenty Bąkiewicz, *Informatorzy i osoby podejrzane, 1945–1946*.

46. Cooperation between SIS, the CIA, and the underground Freedom and Independence (Wolność i Niezawisłość, or WiN) began later.

47. "Memorandum from the Director of the Strategic Services Unit, Department of War (Magruder) to the Assistant Secretary of War (McCloy)," dated October 9, 1945, in *Foreign Relations of the United States, 1945–1950: Emergence of the Intelligence Establishment*, eds. C. Thomas Thorne Jr., David S. Patterson, and Glenn W. LaFantasie (Washington, DC: Government Printing Office, 1976), https://history.state.gov/historicaldocuments/frus1945-50Intel/d96.

48. Michael Warner and Kevin C. Rufher, "Moving Up to the Big Leagues: The Founding of the Office of Special Operations," *Studies in Intelligence* 44, no. 2 (2000): 2.

49. For more on Dunderdale's postwar activity as special liaison, see West, *Historical Dictionary of British Intelligence*, 558–59.

50. See "Vlchek Tool Company," *The Encyclopedia of Cleveland History*, ed. David D. Van Tassel and John J. Grabowski (Bloomington: Indiana University Press in association with Case Western Reserve University and the Western Reserve Historical Society), 19.

51. Information provided by the Polish Army Veterans Association in New York City. See also the letter from the Mayor of New Haven to Joseph Herzyk dated January 28, 1994, in the Mayor John D. Stefano Papers, SouthernDigital, the Hilton C. Buley Library at Southern Connecticut State University, https://digital-lib.southernct.edu/islandora/object/470002%3ADeStefano (accessed August 2, 2021).

52. US Army Hospital 4211, Brookmans Park, Hertfordshire, England. See IPMS, "Sprawozdanie z działalnos´ci Szkoły Specjalistów," A .XII 85/14, k. 26–40, Dokument 2, in Grabowski, *Zapomniani polscy spadochroniarzami*, 83.

53. Thaddeus Hahn traveled to Poland to visit family in 1966. My thanks to his children, Stephen, Raymond, and Diane, for the information on their father and the many documents I received from them.

54. Letter from the British Ministry of Defense to Mrs. Luisa Tydda dated February 22, 1979, concerning Staff Sergeant Zygmunt Tydda's service record. I am indebted to Edward and Richard Tydda for information on their father

55. See Lieutenant Raczkiewicz's report in chapter 3.

56. Rafał Niedziela, "Powstanie i działalność Szkoły Specjalistów MON oraz akcje bojowe je jabsolwentów na terenie Niemiec w 1945 r," in *Studia z Dziejów Polskich Sil Zbrojnych (1939–1947)* (Rzeszów-Warsaw: Instytut Pamięci Narodowej, 2019), 301–27. The author wishes to thank Jozef Bambynek's granddaughter, Vanda Townsend, for information included in email correspondence between February 23, 2020, and March 23, 2020.

57. Czogała is sometimes referred to in OSS documents as Józef Czogala.

58. My sincere appreciation goes to Janet and Stephen Smith, daughter and son-in-law of Sergeant Czogała.

59. I am grateful to Piotr and Elżbieta Gatnar, Władysław Gatnar's nephew and his wife, and Andrea and Roger Gatnar, daughter-in-law and son, for their contribution to this volume.

60. I am indebted to Shane Donelly, George Chojnicki's grandson, and Wojciech Lamczyk, grand-nephew of Chojnicki, for the information included herein.

61. Kaczmarek, *Polacy w Wehrmachcie*, 373–84.

62. Kaczmarek, *Polacy w Wehrmachcie*, 378.

63. Most likely in one of the former German subcamps of the Blechhammer concentration camp in Cosel, now part of Kędzierzyn-Koźle. Blechhammer was the second-largest subcamp of Auschwitz-Birkenau. Franciszek Piper, "Blechhammer," in *The United States Holocaust Memorial Museum Encyclopedia of Camps and Ghettos, 1933–1945*, vol. 1, ed. Geoffrey P. Megargee (Bloomington: Indiana University Press, 2009), 227–28.

64. Institute of National Remembrance, Warsaw [henceforth IPN], Collection BU 286/1459, II Referat Oddziału O.W. "Śląsk."

65. IPN BU 0021/4, t. 1; IPN BU 0021/197; IPN BU 0021/197/1; IPN BU 0021/197/5; IPN BU 168/3; IPN BU 2602/85; IPN BU 2602/46; IPN BU 2602/82; IPN BU 2602/1444; IPN BU 2602/1149; IPN BU 2602/1452; IPN BU 2602/1475; IPN BU 2602/1459.

66. The author is indebted Aleksandra Piskorska-Szymańska for the information on her grandfather's return to Poland and his experiences there. Email correspondence with Aleksandra Piskorska-Szymańska, February 12–17, 2020.

67. The date is from Paprzycki's correspondence with "Tedy" of October 10, 1998.

68. This detail is from Paprzycki's correspondence with "Tedy" of October 10, 1998.

69. I was able to locate Zbigniew Paprzycki's family in Poznań thanks to Zbigniew Redlich and extend my gratitude to him and to Sergeant Paprzycki's wife, Maria Paprzycka, and to his daughter and son-in-law, Małgorzata and Witold Jachowski.

70. I extend my thanks to Zbigniew Redlich for locating Andrzej Koniczek, Gerard Haroński's grandson-in-law, who was kind enough to provide me with details about his postwar life.

71. See Gould, *German Anti-Nazi Espionage*, chap. 1, "The HAMMER Mission and the GRU," 1–49.

72. The Polish Resettlement Corps was formed by the British government in 1946 as a holding unit for members of the Polish Armed Forces who had been serving with the British Armed Forces and did not wish to return to a Communist Poland after the end of the Second World War. It was designed to ease their transition from military to civilian life and to keep them under military control until they were fully adjusted to British life. It was mainly run by the British Army. The corps was disbanded after fulfilling its purpose in 1949. See Wiesław Rogalski, *The*

Polish Resettlement Corps 1946–1949: Britain's Polish Forces (Warwick, UK: Helion & Company, 2019).

73. For an excellent analysis of the complex reasons for remaining abroad or returning to Poland, see Mark Ostrowski, *To Return to Poland or Not to Return: The Dilemma Facing the Polish Armed Forces at the End of the Second World War* (London: University of London, 1996).

74. Persico, *Piercing the Reich*, 334.

75. NARA, RG 226, Entry 115, Box 47, Folder 18.

76. Jankowski and Jasiak turned up in July with rather colorful and differing explanations of what happened to them after parachuting into Germany.

77. Waller, *Wild Bill Donovan*, 388–89.

78. Office of the Historian, "The Tehran Conference, 1943," Milestones 1937–1945, US Department of State, 2016, accessed October 17, 2023, https://history .state.gov/milestones/1937-1945/tehran-conf. For Polish efforts to secure Poland's prewar eastern border, see Richard C. Lukas, *The Strange Allies: The United States and Poland, 1941–1945* (Knoxville: University of Tennessee Press, 1978).

79. Excerpt from a report dated June 16, 1945, by Colonel Joseph Dasher, Chief of the Polish Desk of OSS London, to General Marian Kukiel, Acting Minister of National Defense of the Republic of Poland, NARA, RG 226, Entry 115, Box 47, Folder 18.

80. Stanislaw Mikołajczyk was a member of the interwar Polish Peasant Party, through whose ranks he rose to lead the party during World War II. He was designated prime minister of the Polish government following General Wladyslaw Sikorski's death in a plane crash at Gibraltar on July 19, 1943, at a time when the Polish government was becoming increasingly internationally isolated. A realist, Mikołajczyk succumbed to his own analysis of Poland's situation and Churchill's steady pressure on him to strike a deal with Stalin, which was deemed unacceptable by the majority of Poland's political leadership in the wake of the Katyn Massacre. He resigned his position in November 1944 and agreed to join the Provisional Government of National Unity in Warsaw, thereby becoming a political pariah among his colleagues in London. He was replaced by his deputy, Socialist Tomasz Arciszewski. See Andrzej Paczkowski, *Stanisław Mikołajczyk, czyli, Klęska realisty: zarys biografii politycznej* (Warsaw: Wydawnictwa Szkolne i Pedagogiczne, 1994).

81. See John S. Micgiel, "'Bandits' and 'Reactionaries': The Suppression of the Opposition in Poland, 1944–1947," in *The Establishment of Communist Regimes in Eastern Europe, 1944–1949: A Reevaluation*, ed. Norman Naimark and Leonid Gibianskii (Boulder, CO: Westview Press, 1996), 93–110.

82. For an English-language analysis of the Soviet endgame with postwar British and US intelligence services in Poland, see T. H. Bagley, *Spy Wars: Moles, Mysteries, and Deadly Games* (New Haven, CT: Yale University Press, 2007), 120–29. For an extensive and well-documented analysis of how the Soviet managers of Operation Cezary were able to ensnare even the most experienced Polish military

operatives, see Krzysztof A. Tochman, *Skok po niepodległość: Pułkownik Adam Bory-czka (1913–1988)* (Warsaw: Instytut Pamięci Narodowej, 2016).

83. Bagley, *Spy Wars*, 126.

84. *Tightrope Walker* by Kees Werkade, presented by friends and colleagues to Columbia University in honor of William J. "Wild Bill" Donovan on May 24 ,1979. The sculpture is placed appropriately in front of the campus-level entrance to the School of Law, from which Donovan graduated in 1907.

APPENDIX 2

1. See Roosevelt, *War Report of the OSS*, vol. 2, 291–97; John Mancini, "OSS in Germany," *Warfare History* 11, no. 6 (September 2012), https://warfarehistorynet-work.com/article/oss-in-germany.

APPENDIX 4

1. The A-26 Invader was an American two-engine light bomber produced by the Douglas Aircraft Company during World War II that began to fly in Europe in November 1944.

2. The Douglas A-20 Havoc was an American light bomber used by the OSS during World War II that began to be flown over Western Europe in July 1942.

3. The Consolidated B-24 Liberator was an American heavy bomber used by the OSS from August 1943.

BIBLIOGRAPHY

ARCHIVES

Archive of the Institute of National Remembrance, Warsaw:
  Anders Army IV Department of the Staff of the Commander in Chief's Staff and
  Agents of the II Department of the General Staff; Codename "Targowica"
  VI Department of the Commander in Chief's Staff in London
  Report of the Polish Military Mission in the Camps in the Allied Zones
  Collective lists of soldiers of the Polish Amy in the West in Great Britain
  Repatriation questionnaires
  List of soldiers in the Polish repatriation camps
  Record sheets and service records of service in the Polish Army in the West

Bundesarchiv, Berlin:
  Department of Personal Information on the First and Second World War

Columbia University Library, New York:
  OSS/London [microform]: *Special Operations Branch and Secret Intelligence Branch
    War Diaries*, Frederick, MD: University Publications of America, 1985

The Statue of Liberty—Ellis Island Foundation, Inc. (https://heritage.statueof
  liberty.org):
  Passenger Lists

Joseph Piłsudski Institute of America, Brooklyn:
  Archival Fond Nr. 66, Jan Librach Papers, 1933–1973
  Archival Fond Nr. 70, Samodzielna Placówka Wywiadowcza Estezet

National Archives and Records Administration (NARA), College Park, Maryland:
  Strategic Services Unit, RG 226, Entry 16 and microfilm M153A and following
  History Office, RG 226, Entry 99
  OSS Records, Record Group (RG) 226, Entry 115
  OSS withdrawn files, RG 226, Entry 210
  Personnel Files, Record Group (RG) 226, Entry 224
  Photographic Collection, RG 226—FPL, Box 1

Polish Institute and Sikorski Museum, London:
  A.XII 85/14
  A.XII 85/19

Polish Underground Movement Study Trust, London:
  Collection 138/244, Wincenty Bąkiewicz

BOOKS

Anders, Władysław. *Bez ostatniego rozdziału: Wspomnienia z lat 1939–1946*. Lublin: Wydawnictwo Test, 1992.

Bagley, T. H. *Spy Wars: Moles, Mysteries, and Deadly Games*. New Haven, CT: Yale University Press, 2007.

Beck, Earl R. *Under the Bombs: The German Home Front, 1942–1945*. Lexington: University Press of Kentucky, 1986.

Bułhak, Władysław, ed. *Wywiad i kontrwywiad Armii Krajowej*. Warsaw: Instytut Pamięci Narodowej, 2008.

Casey, William. *The Secret War against Hitler*. Washington, DC: Regnery Gateway, 1988.

Center for the Study of Intelligence, ed. *Creation of the Intelligence Community: Founding Documents*. Washington, DC: CIA, 2012.

Ceraficki, Joachim. *Wasserpolacken: Relacja Polaka w służbie Wehrmachtu*. Warsaw: Ośrodek Karta, 2014.

Chambers, John Whiteclay II. *OSS Training in the National Parks and Service Abroad in World War II*. Washington, DC: US National Park Service, 2008.

Dick, Charles. *Hitler's Slave Drivers: The Role of the Organisation Todt as Overseers of Force Labour Under Nazism*. Birkbeck University of London: ProQuest Dissertations Publishing, 2019.

Dubicki, Tadeusz, ed. *Wywiad i kontrwywiad wojskowy II RP: Studia i materiały z działalności Oddziału II SG WP*. Vols. 1–7. Łomianki: LTW, 2010–2017.

Gore, Jan. *Send More Shrouds: The V1 Attack on the Guards' Chapel, 1944*. Barnsley, Yorkshire: Pen and Sword Books, 2017.

Gould, Jonathan S. *German Anti-Nazi Espionage in the Second World War: The OSS and the Men of the TOOL Missions*. London and New York: Routledge, 2019.

Grabowski, Waldemar. *Zapomniani polscy spadochroniarze: Operacje 'Dunstable' i 'Eagle' w Niemczech.* Materiały: Dokumenty, Archiwalia, Studia, z. 16. London: Instytut Polski i Muzeum im. gen. Sikorskiego, 2011.

Intelligence Co-Operation between Poland and Great Britain during World War II. Vol. 1, *The Report of the Anglo-British Historical Committee.* Edited by Tessa Stirling, Daria Nałecz, and Tadeusz Dubicki. Edgware, UK: Valentine Mitchell, 2005.

Intelligence Co-Operation between Poland Great Britain during World War II. Vol. 2, *Documents.* Selected and edited by Jan Stanisław Ciechanowski. Warsaw: Naczelna Dyrekcja Archiwów Państwowych, 2005.

Jeffrey, Keith. *The Secret History of MI6.* New York: Penguin Random House, 2011.

Jones, Seth G. *A Covert Action: Reagan, the CIA, and the Cold War Struggle in Poland.* New York and London: W. W. Norton, 2018.

Kaczmarek, Ryszard. *Polacy w Wehrmachcie.* Kraków: Wydawnictwo Literackie, 2010.

Kenyon, David. *Bletchley Park and D-Day.* New Haven, CT: Yale University Press, 2019.

Kershaw, Ian. *The End: The Defiance and Destruction of Hitler's Germany, 1944–1945.* New York: Penguin, 2011.

Kołakowski, Piotr, and Andrzej Pepłoński, eds. *Polski Wywiad Wojskowy 1918–1945.* Toruń: Wydawnictwo Adam Marszalek, 2006.

Kozaczuk, Władysław. *W kręgu Enigmy.* Warsaw: Książka i Wiedza, 1979.

Kross, Peter. *The Encyclopedia of World War II Spies.* Fort Lee, NJ: Barricade Books, 2001.

Lankford, Nelson D. *The Last American Aristocrat: The Biography of David K. E. Bruce, 1898–1977.* Boston: Little, Brown, 1996.

Liptak, Eugene. *Office of Strategic Services, 1942–1945.* Botley, Oxford: CQB Publications, 2009.

Lukas, Richard C. *The Strange Allies: The United States and Poland, 1941–1945.* Knoxville: University of Tennessee Press, 1978.

Lulushi, Albert. *Donovan's Devils: OSS Commandos behind Enemy Lines—Europe, World War II.* New York: Arcade, 2016.

Maczek, Stanisław. *Od podwody do czołga: Wspomnienia wojenne 1918–1945.* London: Orbis Books, 1984.

Mason, Andrea. *British Policy Towards Poland.* London: Palgrave MacMillan, 2018.

McGilvray, Evan. *Man of Steel and Honour: General Stanisław Maczek, Soldier of Poland, Commander of the 1st Polish Armoured Division in North-West Europe, 1944–45.* Solihull, West Midlands, UK: Helion & Company, 2012.

Micgiel, John S. *"Project Eagle": Polscy wywiadowcy w raportach i dokumentach wojennych amerykańskiego Biura Służb Strategicznych.* Kraków: Universitas, 2019.

Minczykowska, Katarzyna. *Cichociemna Generał Elżbieta Zawacka "Zo."* Warsaw: Rytm, 2014.

Mitkiewicz, Leon. *Z generałem Sikorskim na obczyźnie*. Paris: Instytut Literackie, 1968.

O'Donnell, Patrick K. *Operatives, Spies, and Saboteurs: The Unknown Story of the Men and Women of World War II's OSS*. New York: Free Press, 2004.

Ostrowski, Mark. *To Return to Poland or Not to Return: The Dilemma Facing the Polish Armed Forces at the End of the Second World War*. London: University of London, 1996.

Paczkowski, Andrzej. *Stanisław Mikołajczyk, czyli, Klęska realisty: zarys biografii politycznej*. Warsaw: Wydawnictwa Szkolne i Pedagogiczne, 1994.

Persico, Joseph E. *Piercing the Reich: The Penetration of Nazi Germany by American Secret Agents During World War II*. New York: Barnes and Noble Books, 1979.

Poksiński, Jerzy. *"TUN": Tatar—Utnik—Nowicki*. Warsaw: Wydawnictwo Bellona, 1992.

Purnell, Sonia. *A Woman of No Importance*. New York: Penguin Publishing Group, 2020.

Ranelagh, John. *The Agency: The Rise and Decline of the CIA*. London: Weidenfeld and Nicolson, 1986.

Rogalski, Wiesław. *The Polish Resettlement Corps 1946–1949: Britain's Polish Forces*. Warwick, UK: Helion & Company, 2019.

Roosevelt, Kermit. *War Report of the OSS (Office of Strategic Services)*. Vol. 1. New York: Walker, 1976.

———. *War Report of the OSS (Office of Strategic Services)*. Vol. 2, *The Overseas Targets*. New York: Walker, 1976.

Schnabel, James F. *History of the Joint Chiefs of Staff: The Joint Chiefs of Staff and National Policy 1945–1947*. Washington, DC: Office of Joint History, Office of the Chairman of the Chiefs of Staff, 1996.

Słowikowski, Mieczysław Z. *W tajnej służbie*. London: Mizyg, 1977.

Tochman, Krzysztof A. *Skok po niepodległość: Pułkownik Adam Boryczka (1913–1988)*. Warsaw: Instytut Pamięci Narodowej, 2016.

Valentine, Ian. *Station 43: Audley End House and SOE's Polish Section*. Stroud, UK: History Press, 2013.

Vaughan, Hal. *FDR's 12 Apostles: The Spies Who Paved the Way for the Invasion of North Africa*. Guilford, CT: Lyons Press, 2006.

Waller, Douglas, C. *Disciples: The World War II Missions of the CIA Directors Who Fought for Wild Bill Donovan*. New York: Simon & Schuster, 2015.

———. *Wild Bill Donovan: The Spymaster Who Created the OSS and Modern American Espionage*. New York: Free Press, 2011.

West, Nigel. *Historical Dictionary of British Intelligence*. Lanham, MD: Scarecrow Press, 2014.

Wette, Wolfram, Ricarda Bremer, and Detlef Vogel, eds. *Das letzte Halbe Jahr: Stimmungsberichte der Wehrmachtpropaganda 1944/45*. Essen: Klartext Verlag, 2001.

Witkowski, Piotr. *Polskie jednostki powietrzno-desantowe na Zachodzie*. Warsaw: Wydawnictwo Bellona, 2009.

ARTICLES, PAPERS, AND INTERNET SOURCES

"Awards of the Silver Star." Home of Heroes, accessed February 18, 2018. http://www.homeofheroes.com/silverstar.

Bernstein, Adam. "Stephanie Rader, Undercover Spy in Postwar Europe, Dies at 100." *Washington Post*, January 21, 2016.

"Betts, Thomas J. (Thomas Jeffries)." National Archives Catalog, accessed March 16, 2018. https://catalog.archives.gov/id/10610494.

"Biography of Victor Frederick William Cavendish-Bentinck." University of Nottingham, accessed October 21, 2017. https://www.nottingham.ac.uk/manuscriptsandspecialcollections/collectionsindepth/family/portland/biographies/biographyofvictorfrederickwilliamcavendish-bentinck,9thdukeofportland(1897-1990).aspx.

Bury, Jan. "From the Archives: Polish Interwar MFA's Cipher Compromised?" *Cryptologia* 31, no. 3 (July 2007): 268–77.

"Być ślązakiem." *Biuletyn Instytutu Pamięci Narodowej*, nr 6–7 (2004): 41–42.

Ciechanowski, Jan Stanisław. "Wywiad polski w Ameryce Polnocnej i Poludniowej w czasie II wojny światowej." *Zeszyty Historyczne*, t. 12 (2013).

Czarnecka, Regina. "Oddział II Sztabu Głównego (Generalnego) w Latach 1921–1939: Zarys Organizacyjny i Przegląd Zawartości Inwentarza." *Biuletyn Wojskowej Służby Archiwalnej*, no. 28 (2006): 63–73.

"Dasher, Joseph." AP Archives, YouTube, posted January 7, 2019. https://www.youtube.com/watch?v=vXVtMqrnKoA.

"Decorations Awarded to OSS Personnel." OSS Reborn, accessed October 1, 2018. http://www.ossreborn.com/files/ossmedals.pdf.

"Elżbieta Zawacka (1909–2009)." Institute of National Remembrance, accessed October 15, 2023. https://ipn.gov.pl/pl/aktualnosci/konkursy-i-nagrody/nagroda-kustosz-pamieci/2002/24226,Elzbieta-Zawacka-19092009.html?search=588182857989.

"Helms, Richard." Central Intelligence Agency, Center for the Study of Intelligence, accessed September 28, 2017. https://www.cia.gov/library/center-for-the-study-of-intelligence/csi-publications/csi-studies/studies/vol46no4/article06.html.

Herman, John. "Rygor's Franco-Polish Network and Operation Torch." *Journal of Contemporary History* 22, no. 4 (October 1987): 681–706.

Huntington, Ellery C., obituary. *New York Times*, July 6, 1987. https://www.nytimes.com/1987/07/06/obituaries/ellery-huntington-jr.html.

"J. Russell Forgan Dead at 73; Banker Was Official of O.S.S." *New York Times,* February 1, 1974. https://www.nytimes.com/1974/02/01/archives/j-russell-forgan-dead-at-73-banker-was-official-of-oss-won-many.html.

"John H. Haskell 1925." West Point Association of Graduates, accessed March 14, 2018. https://alumni.westpointaog.org/memorial-article?id=a04b52dc-5762-416a-836c-282bd7d5b603.

"Joseph Dasher, Chief of Polish Section, United States Office of Strategic Services, Europe, Describes Secret School for Polish Soldiers." Critical Past, accessed October 19, 2018. http://www.criticalpast.com/video/65675072308_Project -Eagle_Office-of-Strategic-Services_Soldiers-of-Poland-in-Exile.

Kihss, Peter. "Adm. Roscoe H. Hillenkoetter, 85, First Director of the C.I.A., Dies." *New York Times,* February 1, 1974. https://www.nytimes.com/ 1982/06/21/obituaries/adm-roscoe-h-hillenkoetter-85-first-director-of-the -cia-dies.html.

"Kukiel, Marian—historyk wojskowości." HistoriON, accessed March 14, 2018. http://historion.pl/marian-kukiel-historyk-wojskowości.

"Lloyd, Stacy." Little Sis, accessed March 16, 2018. https://littlesis.org/person/ 98364-Stacy_Lloyd.

"Łunkiewicz, Jerzy Antoni (1892–1956)." Polish Biographical Dictionary, accessed September 24, 2018. http://www.ipsb.nina.gov.pl/a/biografia/jerzy-antoni -lunkiewicz.

"Łysz, Leonard." Bohaterowie 1939, accessed May 8, 2019. http://www.bohat erowie1939.pl/polegly,lysz,leonard,11035.html.

Machniak, Arkadiusz. "Polski wywiad i kontrwywiad wojskowy w latach 1918– 1939 wobec Związku Sowieckiego. Charakterystyka działalności zawarta w dokumentach Głównego Zarządu Informacji Wojska Polskiego." *UR Journal of Humanities and Social Sciences,* Nr. 1(2) / 2017.

"Maddox, William Percy." In *Marquis Who Was Who in America 1607–1984.* New Providence, NJ: Marquis Who's Who, 2009.

Marcinkiewicz, Anna. "Akta dotyczące żołnierzy PSZ na Zachodzie w zasobie Archiwalnym Instytutu Pamięci Narodowej w Warszawie." *Przegląd Archiwalny Instytutu Pamięci Narodowej,* 2009, t. 2, 133-158.

"Memorandum from the Director of the Strategic Services Unit, Department of War (Magruder) to the Assistant Secretary of War (McCloy)," dated October 9, 1945. In *Foreign Relations of the United States, 1945–1950: Emergence of the Intelligence Establishment,* edited by C. Thomas Thorne Jr., David S. Patterson, and Glenn W. LaFantasie. Washington, DC: Government Printing Office, 1996. https://history.state.gov/historicaldocuments/frus1945-50Intel/d96.

"Menzies, Stewart Graham." Special Forces Roll of Honour, accessed October 23, 2017. http://www.specialforcesroh.com/archive/index.php/t-31478.

Micgiel, John S. "'Bandits' and 'Reactionaries': The Suppression of the Opposition in Poland, 1944–1947." In *The Establishment of Communist Regimes in Eastern Europe, 1944–1949: A Reevaluation,* edited by Norman Naimark and Leonid Gibianskii, 93–110. Boulder, CO: Westview Press, 1996.

"Mockler-Ferryman, Col. Eric Edward." Archives Hub, accessed March 16, 2018. https://archiveshub.jisc.ac.uk/search/archives/472a8323-2ebd-3852-9f9f -b6b0e15ec5f4.

Niedziela, Rafał. "Powstanie i działalność Szkoły Specjalistów MON oraz akcje bojowe jej absolwentów na terenie Niemiec w 1945 r." In *Studia z Dziejów*

Polskich Sil Zbrojnych (1939–1947), 301–27. Rzeszów-Warsaw: Instytut Pamięci Narodowej, 2019.

Office of the Historian. "The Tehran Conference, 1943." *Milestones 1937–1945*, US Department of State, accessed October 17, 2023. https://history.state.gov/milestones/1937-1945/tehran-conf.

"OSS Operational Groups." Office of Strategic Services, accessed October 25, 2017. https://www.soc.mil/OSS/operational-groups.html.

Phillips, William, 1878–1968 (Interviewee), Link, Wendell (Interviewer). Reminiscences of William Phillips, 1951. Columbia Center for Oral History, Columbia University, New York.

Piper, Franciszek. "Blechhammer." In *The United States Holocaust Memorial Museum Encyclopedia of Camps and Ghettos, 1933–1945*, vol. 1, edited by Geoffrey P. Megargee. Bloomington: Indiana University Press, 2009.

"Postwar Period: End of the OSS and Return to the Park Service." National Park Service, last modified August 14, 2017. https://www.nps.gov/articles/postwar-period-end-of-the-oss-and-return-to-the-park-service.htm.

Prettiman, C. A. "The Many Lives of William Alfred Eddy." *Princeton University Library Chronicle* 53, no. 2 (Winter 1992): 200–16.

"Rhode Island Hall of Fame Honorees: Six Legal Luminaries." *Rhode Island Bar Journal* 63, no. 6 (May/June 2015): 25–30.

Różanski, Piotr. "Dywersanci z armii Berlinga." Ale Historia, June 16, 2014. http://wyborcza.pl/alehistoria/1,121681,16149749,Dywersanci_z_armii_Berlinga.html.

"Saale River Offensive: The Seizure of Halle." 104th Infantry Division, National Timberwolf Pups Association, accessed May 12, 2019. http://www.104infdiv.org/saale.htm.

Smith, J. Y. "Gen. William Quinn, Intelligence Leader, Decorated Officer Dies." *Washington Post*, September 12, 2000. https://www.washingtonpost.com/archive/local/2000/09/12/gen-william-quinn-intelligence-leader-decorated-officer-dies/f42ec17a-6aa2-4e9d-a81f-0070cfd4bd85.

"Sosnkowski, Kazimierz." Encyklopedia PWN, accessed March 14, 2018. https://encyklopedia.pwn.pl/haslo/Sosnkowski-Kazimierz;3977804.html.

"SSTR-1 'Suitcase Radio.'" Military Radio, accessed December 15, 2017. http://militaryradio.com/spyradio/sstr.html.

"SSTR-1 'Suitcase Radio.'" YouTube, accessed February 12, 2018. https://www.youtube.com/watch?v=L2qENm9XNCk&list=PLDMeFyCMi9z1otMv1KoHE-dDbFwEqOsjk.

Stefano, John D. "Letter from the Mayor of New Haven to Joseph Herzyk dated January 28, 1994." Mayor John D. Stefano Papers, SouthernDigital, Hilton C. Buley Library at Southern Connecticut State University. https://digital-lib.southernct.edu/islandora/object/470002%3ADeStefano.

"Summary of Operations Carried Out on Operation Carpetbagger During WW2." Carpetbagger Aviation Museum, Harrington, accessed February 9, 2020.

https://harringtonmuseum.org.uk/wp-content/uploads/2018/05/Carpetbagger
-Mission-Reports-Summary.pdf.

"Vlchek Tool Company." In *The Encyclopedia of Cleveland History*, edited by David D. Van Tassel and John J. Grabowski. Bloomington: Indiana University Press in association with Case Western Reserve University and the Western Reserve Historical Society, 1996.

Walker, David A. "OSS and Operation Torch." *Journal of Contemporary History* 22 (1987): 667–79.

Warner, Michael. "COI Came First." In *The Office of Strategic Services: America's First Intelligence Agency*. Washington, DC: Public Affairs, Central Intelligence Agency, 2000. https://permanent.fdlp.gov/websites/www.cia.gov/library/pub
lications/intelligence-history/oss/art02.htm.

Warner, Michael, and K. C. Ruffner. "Moving Up to the Big Leagues: The Founding of the Office of Special Operations (U)." *Studies in Intelligence* 44, no. 2 (2000). https://nsarchive2.gwu.edu/NSAEBB/NSAEBB493/docs/intell
_ebb_016.PDF.

"The Whitney H. Shepardson Fellowship." Council on Foreign Relations, accessed May 3, 2022. https://www.cfr.org/whitney-h-shepardson-fellowship.

"Widerstand: Exilösterreicher in amerikanischer Uniform." *Die Presse*, February 19, 2016. https://diepresse.com/home/zeitgeschichte/4929624/Widerstand
_Exiloesterreicher-inamerikanischer-Uniform.

"Wilkinson, Peter Allix (Oral History)." Imperial War Museum, accessed June 8, 2022. https://www.iwm.org.uk/collections/item/object/80013010.

"William Maddox, Career Diplomat." *New York Times*, September 29, 1972. https://www.nytimes.com/1972/09/29/archives/william-maddox-career-diplo
mat-lxhead-of-foreign-service-institute.html.

"WWII OSS Clandestine Radio." U.S. Militaria Forum, accessed May 8, 2019. http://www.usmilitariaforum.com/forums/index.php?/topic/3024-wwii-oss
-clandestine-radio.

Zumbro, Stephen. "Battle for the Ruhr: The German Army's Final Defeat in the West." PhD diss., Louisiana State University and Agricultural and Mechanical College, 2006.

CORRESPONDENCE

Correspondence between the author and Sergeant Józef Bambynek's granddaughter, Vanda Townsend, March–October 2020.

Correspondence between the author and Sergeant Zygmunt Barwikowski's cousin Krzysztof Marek Barwikowski, April 2020–April 2023.

Correspondence between the author and Colonel Joseph Dasher's son and daughter-in-law, Mark and Kim Dasher, February–April 2018.

Correspondence between the author and Shane Donelly, grandson, and Wojciech Lamczyk, grand-nephew, of Sergeant Wacław Kujawski, April–October 2020.

Correspondence between the author and Sergeant Władysław Gatnar's son and daughter-in-law Roger and Andrea Gatnar, and nephew and niece-in-law Piotr and Elżbieta Gatnar, December 2020–May 2023.

Correspondence and a telephone interview between the author and Sergeant Tadeusz Hahn's children Diane, Raymond, and Stephen, April 2021–May 2023.

Correspondence and a telephone interview between the author and Andrzej Koniczek, grandson-in-law of Sergeant Gerard Haroński, October–November 2020.

Correspondence between the author and Rafał Niedziela, October 2020–May 2023.

Correspondence and a personal interview between the author and Mrs. Maria Paprzycka and Małgorzata and Witold Jachowski, wife, daughter, and son-in-law of Sergeant Zbigniew Paprzycki, July–October 2020.

Correspondence and personal interviews with Zbigniew Redlich, October 2019–May 2023.

Correspondence between the author and Sergeant Zygmunt Tydda's son, Edward Tydda, November 2018–February 2019.

Correspondence between the author and Sergeant Edmund Zeic's granddaughter, Aleksandra Piskorska-Szymańska, February–October 2020.

INDEX

References to photographs or lists are italicized.

Gliwice, 190
Goettingen, 54, 71
Gołąb, Zbigniew, *88, 157*
Górski, Leon, *see* Jan Prochowski
Gosławice, 190
Gould, Jonathan, xi, 220n30, 221n53,
    225n17, 229n73, 234
Grimmel, Ernest, *see* Musiol, Ernest
Gruden, 122
Grudziądz, 87–88, 117
Guenther, Gustav B., , 18, 213n58
Gunzburg, 78, 153

Hadrian, Edmund, 41, 55–56, 221n64
Hahn, Fryderyk, 141
Hahn, Maria, 141
Hahn, Tadeusz, xi, 60, 64, *140*, 141,
    157, 175–179. 193, 222n75
Halle, 63, 65, 76–77, 152, 154, 159,
    222n9
Hanau, 54, 60, 95
Hardheim, 90–91
Harońska, Małgorzata, 67
Haroński, Gerard, xi, 41, 67–68, 170.
    190, 229n72, 241
Harrington, 55, 120, 123, 129, 144,
    150, 205, 221n63, 239–240
Haskell, John H.F., 32, 217n12, 237
Hazell, Ronald, 35, 219n22
Hażlach, 143
Helms, Richard, 171, 237
Heppner, Richard, 118, 214n59
Herman Göring Works, 123, 144
Herzyk, Józef, 126, *128*, 175, 228n51,
    239
Herzyk, Stefanie, 128
Hillenkoetter, Roscoe H., 156, 158,
    225nn21–22, 238
Hohenfels, 72
Homburg, 99
Huntington, Ellery C., 18, 214n60,
    237

J-E radio, 54
Jagodziński, Lucjan, 171, 226n41
Jakubiak, Jan, 41
Jankowice Rybnickie, 101
Jankowski, Józef, see Parlich, Józef
Jarosz, Fryderyk, 143, *157*, 170
Jarosz, Zygfryd, 143
Jasiak, Józef, *see* Kowalski, Józef
Jettingen, 75, 78–79
Joint Chiefs of Staff, 9, 14, 16, 21,
    156, 216n82, 236
Joint Intelligence Committee, 11, 211

Kaczmarek, Ryszard, ix, 29, 187,
    207n5, 217nn, 2–3, 5, 9–10,
    229nn63, 64, 235
Kappius, Jupp, 52
Kapustka, Stanley, *44*
Karwina, 126
Kassel, 54, 81, 104, 123, 136
Katowice, 67, 93, 101, 122, 124, 144,
    167
Katyn massacre, 10, 13, 230n82
Kielce, 28
Kocur, Adela, 126
Kocur, Władysław,126, *127, 157*, 170
Kokorniak, Mściwój, 171–172,
    227nn42, 44
Kommandobefehl, 169
Konarzyny, 138
Konin, 190
Koperski, Roman Władysław, 41
Kościańska, Amanda, 88
Kościerzyna, 72
Kawalec, Raymond, 41
Kowalska, Helena, 98
Kowalski, Józef, 122
Kowalski, Zygfryd, *98, 157,* 171
Kraków, 4, 28, 172, 207n5, 209n26,
    218n14
Kreisau Circle, 57
Królówka, 136
Kroner, Hayes A., 7